Scapegoat!

Scapegoat!

Famous Courts Martial

John Harris

This title first published in Great Britain 1988 by
SEVERN HOUSE PUBLISHERS LTD of
40–42 William IV Street, London WC2N 4DF.

First published in the U.S.A. 1989 by
SEVERN HOUSE PUBLISHERS INC, New York

Copyright © John Harris 1988

British Library Cataloguing in Publication Data
Harris, John
Scapegoat!: famous courts martial.
1. Court-martial
I. Title
342.3′143
ISBN 0–7278–2103–2
ISBN 0–7278–2138–5 Pbk

Distributed in the U.S.A. by
Mercedes Distribution Center, Inc
62 Imlay Street, Brooklyn, New York 11231

Printed and bound in Great Britain
at the University Printing House, Oxford

Contents

Author's Note

There is a good story – apocryphal perhaps – of a man who, having disappeared from an Irish regiment in the British Army in 1941, unexpectedly turned up at the regimental depot in Northern Ireland in 1944, anxious to give himself up. He was not, he said, a deserter; having, while on leave in Dublin, unwisely talked in a pub about his skill with weapons, he had been kidnapped by the IRA and forced to give lessons to their members. If he had failed to do so, he said, his mother would have been murdered. He had been forced to co-operate for three years, kept at first under guard and then later allowed to walk about freely. Devoted to his mother, he had continued to give lessons until she had been killed in a traffic accident, at which time he had felt able to return to the army. He was court martialled as a deserter, but inevitably, there were no witnesses. His story was accepted and he was acquitted, the court even offering its sympathies on his mother's death. He became a minor hero.

There were repercussions, however. At the following week's pay parade, he claimed that the pay he had been given was wrong. By its verdict, the court martial had agreed that his absence had been involuntary and he was owed not one week's pay, but pay for three years and seven months. His claim was indisputable and three weeks later he was paid in full, whereupon he promptly deserted again, bought a small farm in Southern Ireland, and called on his mother – far from dead – to keep house for him.

All courts martial, of course, do not have such a happy ending, because they are convened for the purposes of trying offences against military, naval or air force discipline, or for administering martial law. I was never involved in court martial proceedings during the six years I was in uniform but I twice acted as guard to an accused man – once, whilst attached to the South African Air Force, to an enormous backvelder who appeared to be accused of everything under the sun. He was big enough to pick me up, complete with weapon, and bolt with the lot, but he bore no malice, and after doing a six months' stint in the glasshouse, he bumped into me in Cape Town one evening and proceeded to get me gloriously drunk in celebration of being set free.

On a later occasion, I was part of what I had always thought a long-abandoned and barbaric ceremony – the hollow square – to witness the removal of a guilty man's buttons and badges. The criminal, an old shellback from windjammer days, had been charged with being drunk in charge of a guard and somehow he continued to get drunk, even while in a prison cell. (It was finally discovered that a shipmate was busy placing half-bottles of Cape brandy in the cistern of the lavatory to which he was escorted from time to time.) When the removal of the buttons and badges took place, the officer in charge was foolish enough not to have checked that his knife was sharp and the guilty man actually offered his own to enable the job to be done efficiently.

Finally, I was once myself threatened with a court martial on a charge of mutiny. It occurred at a flying boat base in the swamps of Sierra Leone during the period when German U-boats were making a ship's graveyard of the seas off Freetown – at the time the only watering place on the west coast of Africa for allied convoys for the Middle East. Food was short and we were often hungry, and the cooks weren't showing a lot of imagination, or a lot of energy.

I was NCO in charge of a large number of mooring buoys for boats and aircraft, and took full advantage of having to work with the tide never to go on parade, strolling instead to the water's edge when it suited me best. One day I arrived to find nobody about. All the fitters and riggers who would normally have been swarming over the Sunderlands and Catalinas in the hangar, all the boat crews who should have been working around the slip, seemed to have vanished. A solitary NCO was trying, not very successfully, to push an enormous cradle containing a 60-foot launch. Unknown to me, a protest was taking place. It wasn't an attempt to overthrow authority and certainly not a mutiny, merely an attempt to stir someone into providing more and better food.

Doubtless because, being a writer, it was suspected I also had the gift of the gab, several men appeared from nowhere to slap a plate of half-consumed food in my hands and demand that I lead a deputation to the commanding officer to object. Having endured far worse fare in the Merchant Navy, I personally wasn't complaining and could think of nothing better than to see my section officer, an old friend from when he had been a sergeant, who, in his turn, could only suggest that I went, as requested, to see the Group Captain. Five more men, most newly out from England and all far more angry than I was, tagged on and I unwisely headed for headquarters, where we were met by the station warrant officer, a young man new to the job. Had we been sent for? No, we hadn't. Why were we there? It was a complaint.

'Any number more than five,' he yelled, 'constitutes a mutiny!'

We couldn't argue because we didn't know. I still don't.

'It's a court martial charge!' he went on. 'And in case you aren't aware of it, it could mean the glasshouse for a long time. For you –' this was me '– perhaps even death.'

Probably he was suffering from too much swamp – something that happened occasionally – but, while we stood in line, an RAF policeman was summoned to guard us, our names were taken and I began to have visions of the glasshouse and six months 'hard'. Fortunately, the Group

Captain showed more sense than the Station Warrant Officer and the affair was sorted out amicably.

Although all this has little to do with the following court martial cases, it does indicate how easily it is to find oneself on the wrong side of military law. And, having been charged with mutiny – even though the charge was never administered – at least I know what it feels like to be threatened with dire proceedings on a major offence.

Preface

A court martial might be said to be roughly equivalent to a civilian assize court or high court. There is no military equivalent of a magistrates' court because the sort of military offence that might be considered of equal severity with those tried in a magistrates' court is normally handled by the commanding officer in his own orderly room, into which an offender is marched briskly, wearing no cap, dealt with and marched out again. More serious offences are dealt with by a court martial, consisting of several officers sitting in judgement, roughly like a set of civilian judges.

Courts martial nowadays are divided into three classes – district courts martial, general courts martial, and field general courts martial. A district court martial is convened by a general officer and must be composed of at least three officers who have served at least two years. A general court martial is the only court with authority to try an officer, or to pass a death sentence or a sentence involving penal servitude. It must consist of at least five officers. A field general court martial is convened in war time, when it is impossible to convene an ordinary general court martial, but all ordinary procedures must still be maintained as far as possible.

The First World War changed attitudes to the infliction of military punishment. Despite their uniforms, British soldiers between 1914 and 1918 remained citizens and they continued to retain the privileges and obligations of other British subjects, except that certain military crimes and

1

misdemeanours were punishable by a process of military discipline. In fact, they had additional obligations but no compensating privileges, because the British military code was exacting and by the letter of the law far more severe than that of the French or German armies. British commanders were equally subject to the law, however, and had no summary authority to execute spies or mutineers as French generals did, or execute hostages as German generals did. The process of British military law was slow and formal and strictly prescribed by King's Regulations.

Most crimes were dealt with by commanding officers and the colonel had formidable powers. Field punishment Number One, a humiliating penalty, could, however, be either brutal or, with the degrading features much reduced, according to the temperament of the sergeant-major in charge. In those days, the custom of making an example of an offender was still regarded as normal enough and, while the Germans shot hostages to create an effect on civilians, the British occasionally shot a soldier to stiffen his comrades. Field punishment could mean being handcuffed to a wagon wheel or even spreadeagled against a grating with wrists and ankles made fast. This might seem brutal today, but it has to be remembered that between 1914 and 1918 there were still people about who could remember public hangings and soldiers and sailors being flogged until their backs were bloody.

At a field general court martial, which was the most common type of court martial in France between 1914 and 1918, the rules of evidence are strictly enforced, and there are handbooks to make plain that there *are* rules. King's Regulations, 1940, in fact contains 169 paragraphs dealing with how to conduct a court martial. In one official booklet on the subject, these procedures are actually described as 'stage directions'.

Occasionally word came down from the 'High Altar' that morale needed a sharp jolt, that a few severe sentences might have a good effect, and that it was expedient that some man who had deserted his post under fire should die to encourage the others. However, the military executions which so fascinate modern writers were few compared with the normal daily death toll. There was a daily drain in France of hundreds killed or wounded, and the 3080 death sentences that were pronounced during the First World War seem trivial by comparison. And of these 3080, only 346 were actually carried out. All the same, this meant that about once a week throughout the war a notice was read out on parade that some soldier had been shot for desertion or cowardice. However, nine times as many men were sentenced but reprieved, death sentences often being commuted to imprisonment. But, since this meant safety, after 1915 men were sometimes sent back to their units to try again.

When carried out, executions took place quietly but in front of a witnessing party from the victim's unit, and after a period when telegrams informed parents or wives of the brutal truth, the death sentence was recorded simply as a casualty on active service.

Soon after World War I the death penalty was abolished in certain cases. The practice of branding and flogging had long since been abandoned and now so was the tying of offenders to the wheels of guns. After the war, improvements were made in procedure and in the qualifications needed for officers constituting a court. Regimental courts martial were abolished, a change justified by the diminution of crime in the army, and the services of accused men was retained in the field by the Army Suspension of Sentences Act.

During World War II many thousands of soldiers didn't even await the test of battle before taking flight. Thousands were discharged on medical grounds and many were put to useful work in industry. Many might have made good soldiers but it is more than likely that most of them had no heart, no stomach, for the fight. By then also, following a lead set by the RFC and then the RAF in World War I, the army had become aware of battle fatigue and Lord

3

Moran made it clear that no man had a limitless amount of courage.

Then in October 1946, as a sequel to the quashing of the sentences on 243 paratroopers for mutiny against their living conditions in Malaya, Parliament demanded that soldiers should have the right of appeal to high court judges and this was introduced in 1951.

The RAF has its own code of law, largely based on military law. In the navy, until the time of George III, discipline was regulated only at the discretion of a ship's commanding officer, something which meant that in many cases the law depended too much on the temperament of the officer involved and was badly administered. Under the Naval Discipline Act of 1881, however, the court had to consist of from five to nine officers of certain fixed rank and the court had to be held on board one of HM ships of war, with at least two ships together at the time. These changes meant that a captain's whims became open to view and reduced the chances of wrong judgements. Court martial laws have continued to be improved and it can now be said that, in the British forces, a man has the right to a trial as fair as he would receive as a civilian.

Armed services in other countries have followed much the same pattern, though there are variations, according to the country and the temperament and natural inclinations of the men involved. In Mexico between 1911 and 1920, General Zapata liked to court martial officers who changed sides, but didn't hesitate to torture without trial captured enemy officers. General Villa liked to say of officers who had offended him, 'Let me have him. I'll give him a fair trial and then have him shot.' But the war in Mexico was a civil war and the ranks of Villa and Zapata might have been disputed by more regular generals.

The cases considered in this book go back a long way and cover a variety of charges. They are all unusual for one reason or another and, studying them, it is hard to avoid the belief that a large number of the accused were made scapegoats for the incompetence or guilt of others. Anyone who has served for any length of time in any of the forces, must have come across more than one case of unfairness.

As a volunteer in the first week or two of service in 1939, I was placed in the cookhouse and immediately found myself involved in a racket run by the cookhouse staff. I made a point of hurriedly finding myself another job in the coal dump, but there found myself involved in an even bigger racket involving men of higher rank. From then on, throughout the war, I came across one case after another of someone being accused of an offence, while a more senior individual got away with virtually the same thing. There is, in fact, a delicious story of a senior officer in Germany after the war who, while protesting his anger at looting, was knocked senseless by a piano he was taking home, which fell off a lorry he was escorting in his car.

The cases which follow show clear evidence of an accused being charged because an example had to be made, because a scapegoat was needed, because the accused had had the courage to speak out against things that were wrong, because someone had failed to do his job properly, or simply because he was swept away by circumstances when national passions were running high.

John Byng

In England, the court martial goes back to the time of the Civil War. Prior to 1640 ordinances were issued by the King for the trial of men accused of offences against discipline or to enforce martial law. Justice was administered under the old court of chivalry, of which the Earl Marshal was the president. However, the military laws adopted by commanders in the long and bitter Thirty Years War on the Continent of Europe, in which more than one English soldier who later became a commander in England took part, had their effect on English military law, and courts martial were instituted in England during the reign of Charles I, though they were not sanctioned by Parliament until the Mutiny Act of 1689 was passed.

Following the removal of James II from the throne, something only made possible by the disloyalty of certain of his regiments under John Churchill, later Duke of Marlborough, it was considered that, to keep a standing army in time of peace, certain provisions should be made. The first of these was to sanction the army's existence for the first time in England; another was the provision for the punishment of mutiny and desertion with death, and the empowering of the Crown to commission courts martial to deal with these offences in times of peace. From 1689 Parliament passed the Mutiny Act annually until 1881 when it was finally superseded and merged in the Army Act of that year, an act which is also annually renewed. The Jacobite Rebellion of 1715 made it necessary to increase the stringency of the Crown's disciplinary powers and, accordingly, the Mutiny Act of 1715 authorised the Crown to formulate Articles of war to regulate generally the forces in the United Kingdom in time of peace. Prior to that year, the Crown could only issue such articles in times of war or rebellion. Their guidelines were strictly laid down and could not be disputed, and the one thing that was made clear in them was that a protest in the army by a number of men was in fact not just a protest, but a mutiny. No matter what the protesters thought, the army could take only one view.

From that date, courts martial administered the discipline laid down in the articles of war. Inevitably, this meant a great many courts martial and a Kent soldier in 1845 wrote that in Chatham, 'we generally had one court martial a week and for the first three or four months three or four.' The crimes were usually drunkenness and absence without leave, things nowadays handled quickly and easily by a commanding officer alone. The Crimean War showed up not only what was wrong with the military command but also what was wrong with military law and in 1879 the Army Discipline and Regulation Act was passed, superseded two years later by the Army Act of 1881.

Up to the latter quarter of the nineteenth century, military prisoners were allowed to have legal advice but their lawyers were not allowed to speak on their behalf. This was a practice that was a remnant of the old usage by which, in all courts, prisoners in criminal cases were denied the assistance of counsel; meaning, in fact, that an accused had to conduct his own case, but if he were wealthy enough he could be prompted by a lawyer sitting alongside him. Opposite him would be the Prosecutor, an army officer, also prompted by a lawyer.

The court martial can be a two-edged weapon. It can condemn a man but it can also clear a man's name, and a serving soldier can demand a court martial with this in mind. He doesn't always get it, however. After the charge of the Light Brigade at Balaclava in 1854, Lord Lucan, the Commander of the Cavalry Division, was accused of losing the brigade and was eventually sent home. He twice demanded a court martial to clear himself of the accusation, but was twice refused, doubtless because, well known as an intelligent and articulate if ill-tempered man, it was thought he would have too much to say about the mismanagement of the campaign and the supplies provided by the government.

There were other ways of approaching a court martial. In 1905, a Russian fleet, which had sailed half-way round the world to fight, suffered a cataclysmic defeat at the hands of the emergent Japanese. Though made the scapegoat for the defeat because of his high rank, the admiral in command, Zinovi Petrovitch Rozhestvensky, was not accused, but his second-in-command and staff and the captains of ironclads which had surrendered, were. Indignant at the treatment he and his men were receiving when the real reason for the disaster was inefficiency at the top, Rozhestvensky insisted first on appearing at the court martial as a witness, and finally on joining the accused. His loyalty didn't help much. While he was acquitted, the others were sentenced to death and, though the Czar interceded, they all served long terms of imprisonment.

Over the years there have been courts martial for a variety of reasons. One, that of Colonel Thomas Crawley, of the 6th Inniskilling Dragoons, was for cruelty. Another, the famous Royal Oak court martial in 1928, arose from a farcical dispute aboard the battleship during a ship's dance in Malta when the admiral of the First Battle Squadron called the bandmaster a 'bugger'. The incident led to others and resulted in the captain of the ship, his executive officer – and the admiral – being dismissed by the Commander-in-Chief, Mediterranean, Sir Roger Keyes. The way the affair was handled, however, was considered to be the reason why Keyes never became First Sea Lord, as he had firmly expected. Noted for his courage, he was also known to intellectuals in the navy as 'a fighting blockhead', and the comment was heard, 'Thank God for the Royal Oak affair. Keyes as First Lord would have been a disaster.'

In some cases, the details of the courts martial are the least important of the facts concerning them and that a court martial was held at all was sometimes an event. Despite the convoluted truths of some cases, the evidence was sometimes so sparse as to be virtually non-existent. In others, a wealth of evidence was given to cover up what were, in fact, incidents of staggering triviality.

There was often unfairness. All too often officers got away with things a ranker would not have got away with. In World War I, an officer incapable of standing up to the strain of trenches was often quietly sent home sick, whereas a ranker often found himself on a charge. During the great battles, Military Policemen remained behind as troops went over the top to watch for shirkers and there were instances of men being filled with rum, often with their officer's acquiescence, and dragged forward by their friends to take their chance rather than have them picked up by the hated Redcaps and charged with failing in their duty.

The generals in these battles, however, had little knowledge of life in the front line. They were never seen by their soldiers and were consequently hated more than the Germans. Marlborough, old and ill, tramped the trenches in all weathers. Wellington also gave confidence, as did Montgomery; and Slim so had the support of his men that, after one of his talks, when a sergeant said, 'When the time comes, sir, we'll all be behind you,' he was able to reply amid laughter, 'Don't you believe it, Sergeant ... You'll be a long way in front.' That sort of rapport never existed between senior officer and fighting soldier between 1914 and 1918.

While courts martial, on the whole, are conducted with scrupulous fairness, there have certainly been cases when they have been used with spite, bigotry or meanness of spirit, and more than one man has been found guilty on a twist of words or a manipulation of evidence to hide the inefficiency of someone of higher rank, or the indifference of a man in an office safely away from danger.

Despite the honesty of most men and their anxiety to behave well, the services are full of ordinary people who have all the faults of ordinary people. Some attain power which they are loth to abandon and sometimes they have been guilty of a willingness to let someone less important suffer for their mistakes. But this is human nature and, no matter how carefully the rules are laid down, no matter how hard people try, it will always remain so.

One of the earliest courts martial of any consequence showed how clearly the system could be abused. The trial and execution of the Hon John Byng during the Seven Years War has been called 'one of the most cold-blooded and cynical acts of judicial murder in the whole of British history'. Byng was the only British Admiral ever to be shot as a result of his shortcomings, and there is little doubt that he was made the scapegoat for the inadequacies of the Admiralty and sacrificed to save the reputations of more powerful people in government. Although a brave man, Byng was never noted for his dash and the Government seized on this as a means of hiding their own lethargy, stupidity and neglect.

The son of Admiral Sir George Byng, later Lord Torrington, a Commander-in-Chief, Mediterranean, and First Lord of the Admiralty, John Byng's interests were furthered by his father's influence and he received rapid promotion that he did not altogether merit. He entered the navy in 1718, became Rear Admiral in 1745, Vice Admiral in 1747 and Admiral in 1755. In 1756, a plump pompous man used to privilege, he sailed from England with his ships to relieve a garrison besieged at Fort St Philip in the British base of Minorca.

Fort St Philip was known to have been badly neglected and was commanded by an 82-year-old general, but when the threat became clear, the Government of the day, headed by the Duke of Newcastle, was more concerned with the threat of a French invasion of England and for weeks they did nothing. In the end Byng was sent far too late, with a squadron of undermanned ships, that were considered to be 'the very worst of the fleet', and without clear instructions, hospital ships, fire ships, store ships or tenders. He fought an ineffectual naval battle off Minorca on 19 May 1756, not helped by captains who, in their turn, were impeded by a current set of Admiralty rules called 'Fighting Instructions', which governed the tactics to be used by British captains and admirals in battle.

In the days of slow-moving ships, when flag signals were often obscured by smoke, there had to be some sort of method so that an admiral could keep control of his ships, but the out-of-date 'Fighting Instructions' tied an admiral down to a few specific manoeuvres. The line of battle was sacrosanct, so that if a ship's gunfire drove a crippled opponent out of the fight, she was prevented from following to finish her off. The result was that if a battle became too brisk, an enemy knew he had only to drift out of line to survive.

But the instructions were rigid and captains knew well that any man who deviated from them did so at his peril. After the abortive Battle of Toulon in 1745 when, thanks to the 'Instructions', only a few of the twenty-eight British ships got into action, a whole series of courts martial were held. Several lieutenants were tried for giving their captains bad advice, and their courts martial were followed by those of eleven captains and, finally, of two of the three admirals involved. The lieutenants were acquitted but several captains were cashiered, while others were put on half pay. But it was the courts martial of the admirals which produced the most remarkable verdicts. By them, the man who had got to grips with the enemy, but broke the line of battle to do so, was dismissed from the navy, while the man who had endangered the fleet, but had not broken the line, was acquitted. Byng had been a member of that court and had played a consider-able part in influencing the verdicts that were returned, not

11

realising he was going a long way towards subsequently condemning himself to death.

Byng, of course, knew the 'Instructions' well and was even seen reading them as his ships approached the French squadron. Despite the fact that the French ships had heavier broadsides, the British ships did not refuse battle and four of the French ships were soon drifting to leeward out of the line. Yet, such was the rigidity of the 'Fighting Instructions', not one of the British ships broke the line in pursuit. Then, in the confusion of smoke, thanks to the stupidity of two of his captains concerned with observing the 'Fighting Instructions', whose manoeuvrings had thrown the line into disorder, Byng was obliged to stop his own ship dead to avoid a collision, and then to order the whole squadron to brace-to (or come to a stop by backing its sails). Though the situation soon resolved itself, Byng's order was to result in him being accused of cowardice, as it was made to appear that it was given because of a reluctance to close with the enemy.

The French now stood to the north-west, refusing further action and apparently making off, and the British sailors cheered what appeared to be a victory. As they busied themelves with repairs, Byng called a council of war at which it was decided that the squadron, with several of its ships badly damaged – as well as being undermanned from the beginning by 500 men and now short of another 600 through death or injury – could not raise the siege of Fort St Philip. The council was well aware that Byng had, in addition, to consider the safety of Gibraltar, for which he had been given responsibility but which, like Fort St Philip, had been allowed by the Admiralty to lapse into decay.

It was decided to head for Gibraltar and there Byng was reinforced by five more ships. He could have returned to guard Minorca but he delayed doing so, and in the meantime an excerpt from the enemy admiral's report on the battle, contained in a letter to the Spanish envoy in London from his opposite number in Paris, fell into the hands of the

British Government who, well aware that Byng had been sent to the Mediterranean too late and with an inadequate squadron, were dreading the first news.

The French Admiral had quite naturally made sure of presenting the best picture of himself but, in doing so, had suggested that Byng had backed away from the fight and that none of his ships had borne French fire for any length of time. In fact, Byng had behaved with a lot of sense and ability, but the fire-eating King, George II, was furious. George, who had fought at Dettingen, had a mania for wanting to be thought brave and he had a very short fuse. He was livid that Fort St Philip had not been saved and demanded that heads should roll. Its nerves on edge with the fear of invasion, the worried Government, under the wretched Newcastle, realised that the Frenchman's report presented them with a scapegoat and they decided to recall Byng in disgrace.

Admiral Hawke was sent out at once to relieve him but by this time nobody expected Minorca to be saved. While Byng was on his way home, to save their faces, the Government published his despatch, heavily censored so that every word that might be favourable to Byng was cut, along with anything that might be construed as criticism of the Government. In addition, a virulent piece of gossip, composed almost entirely of lies, was inserted in several newspapers. This suggested that, although Byng had sought the Mediterranean Command, he had shown reluctance to head there until pushed by the Admiralty. In fact, he had not received his orders until the last moment. It also suggested that he had not sought out the French fleet but had been sought out by them and that, after the battle, had fled to Gibraltar for safety.

As it was also the day of hack pamphleteers, the Government was quick to hire them to turn the mobs against the Admiral so that there were riots in various towns, and in London he was hanged and burned in effigy, while agitators were paid to yell for his death with:

'Swing! Swing!
Great Admiral Byng!'

News of the surrender of Fort St Philip arrived in the middle of June but, with Byng already about to become the scapegoat, the Government was unworried and, on his arrival, with the ground well prepared, he was arrested and his court martial was arranged.

There seems little doubt that the court was rigged by Admiral Lord Anson, the First Lord of the Admiralty, who was as guilty as anyone over the loss of Fort St Philip. The judges were supposed to be the senior officers of ships within the command of the Flag Officer, Portsmouth, where the trial was held, but of the four admirals and nine captains who sat in judgement on Byng, three of the admirals were known to be Anson's favourites and they were ordered to Portsmouth and told to hoist their flags just before the trial. Since they were senior to all other officers in the command, they had to be chosen for the trial. Captain the Hon Augustus Hervey, Byng's friend, who risked his career to save him, called it 'This most *infamous* court,' and said its members were selected by Anson for no other reason than to find Byng guilty. This seems to be confirmed by the fact that the three men hauled down their flags and left Portsmouth immediately after the trial.

The charges, covered by the 12th Article of War which described cowardice, negligence and disaffection, were that Byng had 'kept back' and not done his utmost against the French fleet or to relieve Fort St Philip. If he were to be proved guilty of cowardice and of 'not doing his utmost', the prosecution had to show there was no valid reason for his ship stopping when she did or for Byng ordering the rest of the ships in the squadron to stop. But witnesses lied, officers made sure they saved their own skins, and letters which might have been useful to Byng were suppressed – 'Sink them,' Anson ordered. Evidence in Byng's favour was kept out of court or twisted, and a fake log book was produced.

14

During the trial, Voltaire, the great French writer, sent a note to Byng, enclosing a copy of a letter from the Duc de Richelieu, the French commander in the Mediterranean. Richelieu thought that Byng had done everything that could be expected, that the measures he took were admirable and that there never was 'a more flagrant injustice' than that which was being attempted against him. This letter reached London on the last day of the trial but it passed through the hands of several politicians and only seems to have reached Byng almost a week later, after the trial was over. In any case, written by an enemy, it was never likely to affect the decisions of the British judges.

Byng was found guilty and sentenced to death, not for treachery or cowardice but for misconduct, an offence which up to then had never been thought to deserve the capital punishment. Perhaps the admirals expected their verdict to be commuted but they had been warned that the King would be furious if Byng were acquitted. Pitt pleaded with the King for the admiral but was 'cut very short'. Lord Temple managed to be so rude to the monarch on the subject that he was never forgiven. Dr Johnson used his pen to try to save him. Even the French Admiral in command spoke of his bravery. 'All that I saw and know of him could only add to his glory,' he said. It didn't help.

Byng didn't complain, asking only that he could defend his honour. He asked to be shot on the quarterdeck, not where common malefactors were executed and, not wishing to die with the reputation of a coward, was prepared to open his shirt to the bullets to show he was not afraid of them.

He was shot on the quarterdeck of his own ship, *Monarch*, at Spithead on 14 March 1757, behaving with great courage and dignity throughout. He refused to be blindfolded until he was told that the Marines in the firing squad, the foremost of whom would be so close that the muzzles of their muskets would be only two feet from his chest, would be unable to do their duty with his eyes on them. Byng himself gave the order to fire.

He was buried at Southill, Bedfordshire, and his monument bore the words:

'To the perpetual disgrace of public justice
The Honble John Byng, Esqr
Admiral of the Fleet
Fell a martyr to political persecution
March 14th in the year 1757, when
Bravery and loyalty
Were insufficient securities for the
Life and honour
Of a naval officer.'

A man who could always see two sides to every question, Byng had undoubtedly been hesitant and had made an error of judgement in not returning to Minorca when reinforced. But he died a scapegoat for the Government and the Admiralty who had neglected the British bases and, despite the dangers, had made no effort to send Byng to the relief of Fort St Philip for nearly three months and then only with an inadequate squadron. Whatever his faults, Byng did not deserve his fate, and Voltaire summed it up when he said that in England '. . . it is thought well to kill an admiral from time to time to encourage the others.'

Whether or not Byng's trial, which was reported as fully in France as in England, proved to governments that they had in their hands an instrument that could at times be used to their great advantage, it was certainly not the last court martial designed to destroy a single individual to save the reputations or offices of others.

John André

Treason is a dangerous game to play or even encourage at any time, but particularly in wartime when passions are aroused. Though not the scapegoat for politicians or for his superiors, John André was in a way as much a scapegoat as any – but, in his case, for the crime of a guiltier man who belonged to an enemy country.

But for the detestation this man's treason roused in the breasts of his fellow countrymen. André might have escaped, but the fact that his co-conspirator escaped, leaving André to be tried, was enough to seal André's fate. By a piquant chance, not only André, an English soldier, but Benedict Arnold, the man who brought about his downfall, had, at different times, fallen under the spell of the same woman, and without doubt she was a moving spirit in the plot that destroyed them both.

Even André's court martial – it was called a court of enquiry but it fulfilled the functions of a court martial – was unusual in that it left him in a position where the men who tried him accepted that he was guilty of the charges against him but, impressed by his bearing and his honour, would happily have freed him in return for the real guilty party. By that time, however, that individual was safely out of danger, and André's end was assured.

The situation arose towards the end of the American War of Independence. Tremendous patriotic passions were aroused by what the American Colonists considered British obduracy and what the British considered colonial rebelliousness, and it was hard for either side to see the other's point of view. Spying was far from unusual and spies were operating everywhere, the situation aggravated by the fact that both sides looked alike, spoke the same language, behaved in the same manner, had the same background, and all too often dressed alike.

There had been differences between Britain and her American colonies for a long time but, so long as there was a threat from France, there was no crisis. With the end of the Seven Years War and the defeat of the French, however, there was no longer any reason for the Colonists to show restraint. Even so, only a few extremists thought of breaking the ties with England so that, had the British Government pursued a policy of conciliation, they might well have averted serious trouble, because there was still plenty of goodwill. But the Government made several stupid and arrogant moves, and associations called 'The Sons of Liberty' sprang up to protest, with 'No taxation without representation' as their slogan.

Acts unpopular with the Colonists were repealed in an effort to reduce tension, but there remained hostility, and the throwing of snowballs at British soldiers in Boston led to five Americans being shot in what became known as the Boston Massacre. Even now the situation might have been saved but a newly imposed duty resulted in $75,000 worth of tea being flung into the harbour at Boston.

There was now little hope of a compromise and the British Government determined to make an example of the Colonists. A Continental Congress, arranged by the Colonists, met at Philadelphia and the British replied in 1775 by landing a British Force to take possession of a store of arms held by the Colonists at Concord. The plan leaked out and one of the Colonists, Paul Revere, rode furiously ahead of the troops to warn his compatriots. When the British soldiers reached Lexington they were met by the Colonists and the exchange of shots began the war.

Two months later the Battle of Bunker Hill revealed the incompetence of British leadership. Congress had chosen George Washington, an aristocratic Virginian, to command its forces. He had served in the war against the French and had experienced the arrogance and incompetence of British officers. Though he was not a military genius, he possessed the qualities of leadership, based on faith in the justice of his cause and, forced to pursue a harassing policy because his troops were inferior in numbers and discipline, he showed skill in keeping his men together after a withdrawal following the loss of New York.

While during the long years of the war the British leaders were all professionals, the American leaders were businessmen, planters and farmers who had been the leaders in civil life and, since they lost favour if they were no good at the job, in the end those who were left were natural leaders. Among them was Benedict Arnold, the son of a Connecticut cooper who had married the widow of a shipowner. Trying to expand his business, the father had over-extended himself and tried to cheat his creditors, and the family fortune had been swept away by failure. His son, Benedict, born in 1741, high-spirited, powerfully built and with a reputation for courage, had been apprenticed to the trade of apothecary but had been released to fight in the war against the French.

After the war, living with the wealthy family to whose trade he was apprenticed, he began to enjoy luxury, and learned the business so well that when his apprenticeship ended, he was given £500 to establish himself as an apothecary and went to London to buy goods to stock his store. He enjoyed elegant London life but, when he returned to Connecticut to open his new store, his style of life put him in a debtors' jail within two years. He managed to get on his feet again, selling drugs, books and other goods, but shop-keeping was not to his taste and he became a shipowner.

Though Arnold now began to make money, curiously he never won the respect of his neighbours, and when the war against England broke out, he was happy to march off to

19

fight. He distinguished himself in the Battles of Ticonderoga and Quebec and reached the rank of Major-General to become one of Washington's most trusted officers. He was strong and brave but there was an odd streak of bitterness in him, a moody envy when other men were promoted ahead of him, that made him feel he was being 'put upon'.

As the fighting progressed the secret services began to play a key role. There had always been spies and agents but now, probably for the first time, helped by the sentiment of those loyal to the Crown, known as Tories or Loyalists, espionage became more and more important. The commanders on both sides relied on spies and in both armies the man in charge of Intelligence was the Adjutant-General, a member of the General's staff.

The Adjutant-General on the staff of the British General commanding in New York, was John André, an Englishman descended from a family of French Huguenots who had migrated from Nîmes, in Southern France, and reached England via Genoa and Geneva. Born in 1751, handsome, unmarried, skilled in mathematics, writing, drawing and the flute, he had other gifts – among them a great natural charm. His father was an importer and André had entered the family business, but he was a romantic with dreams of glory, and in 1771 he quit the business and purchased a commission in the 7th Foot, the Royal Fusiliers, an old and famous regiment. He was an intimate in literary and aristocratic circles and his drawings were always popular.

He was at Quebec with his regiment when he heard of the fall of Fort Ticonderoga, and was sent to St John's, a dreary military post south of Montreal. But the British force at St John's was badly supplied and, surrounded by Americans, the Commanding Officer had little option but to negotiate for surrender. It was André who was sent with the flag of truce, and he finally had to suffer the shame of grounding arms in the presence of a despised foe.

His long journey to internment carried him through Philadelphia which, after the wilds of Canada, was a civilised city to him and he could hardly bear to leave. There were girls there, and among them he was able to flirt with a moody blonde of fifteen called Peggy Shippen. Moving to Carlisle, he found a different brand of American – rough men who no longer thought of themselves as English – but André himself was admired for his urbanity, his engaging manners, and 'the goodness of his heart'.

The prisoners were finally exchanged at New Brunswick and, with the war apparently almost won, the 7th Foot were ordered home. Preferring to stay where the action was, André exchanged into the 26th Foot as a Captain and, because he could speak French, German and some Dutch, offered his services as an interpreter for the German mercenaries employed by the British. He joined his new regiment at Staten Island, on the staff of General Sir William Howe, and spent a quiet winter there. In 1777 he joined the staff of Major-General Charles Grey and he was with the General as aide-de-camp when the British fought their way back into Philadelphia. The new occupants of the town suited the Loyalist families, among which was that of Margaret (Peggy) Shippen with whom André had flirted briefly during his captivity there.

Margaret Shippen had been born in 1760, into one of Philadelphia's leading families, and was used to luxury and gracious living. Now seventeen, she was highly-strung but dainty of features and figure, and she also had a good head for business. Her father had been a Crown official before the war and from him she learned political sophistication. Very feminine and very young, she seemed gentle and timorous but she had great strength of mind and was determined to do well for herself. When war broke out her father had wished the family to stay neutral and emigrated to New Jersey where he bought a farm and a store.

His daughter found the idea of living in the country painful, especially in the reduced circumstances brought on by the move and the war. After a while the family returned to Philadelphia, but it was an uncertain city now, occupied by the Americans but always in constant fear of a Loyalist uprising, and as the tide of battle ebbed and flowed, with Philadelphia reoccupied, eventually the family found themselves behind the British lines.

The new occupants suited Peggy Shippen excellently. She was greatly admired and once more met John André, who again fell under her spell and took her driving, escorted her to the theatre, to balls, dinner parties, and cotillons, and even gave her a lock of his hair. When Howe was recalled to England it was André who arranged a colourful extravaganza in his honour.

Meanwhile Benedict Arnold had advanced considerably in rank and reputation. He had distinguished himself in the fighting and in 1777 was with the American force sent against General John Burgoyne, an able British officer, who had arrived to command an expedition that was to march south from Canada. Due to the indifference of the Government and the slackness of other British generals, however, instead he found himself, at the end of 1777, trapped by an American force 20,000 strong at Saratoga and was obliged to surrender. The success surprised the world, and though the winter that followed was a severe one and the American Army shivered and starved at Valley Forge, support for the Colonists came in 1778 from the French, who were always happy to see their traditional enemy, Britain, in trouble. Spain and Holland followed, while Russia, Denmark and Sweden formed an armed neutrality.

Arnold's part in the defeat of Burgoyne had not been small. He had quarrelled with his commanding officer and during a lull in the fighting was removed from his command. But, allowed to remain in camp, as usual angry and embittered at his fate, when the fighting started again he couldn't resist appearing and, while rallying troops, was severely wounded. As the news of Saratoga reached Philadelphia, the British were obliged to retreat, and as André disappeared the crippled Arnold arrived.

22

By now Arnold was considered to be a very successful soldier. His moody personality had made many enemies and at one point in his career he had resigned his commission. But his resignation had been ignored and now, after the part he had played at Saratoga, his fortunes were rising again. His convalescence was long but, as he began to recover, in 1778 he was made Military Governor of the newly-occupied Philadelphia.

He was still convalescent, his leg and shattered hip immobilised in a fracture box, and he was a bad patient, always revolving in his mind his imagined hurts. The one thing of which Arnold's mental arsenal was devoid was the one weapon that would have helped – dispassionate reason – and he could see no further than his own personal situation. But a suitably elegant house was found for him and he was quick to notice that the European goods, with which the city had been crammed during the British occupation, could be used to his personal advantage. Bought for what they had cost during the British occupation, if they were sold to the blockaded patriots they could yield good profits. What was more, the girls of Philadelphia clustered round the wounded warrior, now widowed. Among them he didn't fail to notice the same Peggy Shippen who had caught the eye of John André.

Unable to resist the chance to make money, Arnold was soon involved with trade, and not always honestly, and he became the storm centre of a rift in the patriot party. When the Executive Council of Pensylvania sentenced to death two Quakers for collaboration during the British occupation of Philadelphia, he injected himself into the controversy which the trials aroused by giving, on the day of the executions, a public entertainment at which Tories and wives and daughters of people proscribed by the state and now with the enemy, formed a considerable part.

His speculations did not go well and he had lived beyond his means for years. Now he found himself accused by the Executive Council of almost everything that plagued the infant republic, and gossip foreshadowed the future when rumours spread that he had gone over to the enemy. Arnold felt that, though he was guilty, so were many respected citizens, and when he learned he was to be tried by court martial he felt he was being made the scapegoat.

But there was still Peggy Shippen and he was seeing a lot of her. He longed to be a pillar of society and admired her because, through her father, she already possessed the position he hoped to achieve for himself. At seventeen she was beautiful and gay and loved luxury, and Arnold concentrated on changing himself from a cripple to a healthy man worthy of a young and attractive bride. On 8 April 1779, they were married, and treason flowered almost at once, the bride in the affair from the start.

Intelligence was as old as war but somehow it had remained a stepchild of the army, considered tainted, linked to spies, turncoats and outright rogues. But Washington was keen to use what intelligence he could gather, and British Intelligence had been stepped up under Howe, so that the list of spies and informants had grown considerably. A few were executed on both sides and on the board that condemned one Thomas Shanks of spying for the English was Benedict Arnold, so he was fully aware of the meaning of what he had begun to contemplate.

It was believed by Captain Robert Donkin, a British officer who was stationed in America throughout the war and wrote a military manual on the subject, that spies could be drawn from all walks of society and every rank and station, old and young, rich and poor, women as well as men; and British spies were everywhere from the Hudson to the Delaware, from Vermont to the Rhode Island coast, using invisible inks and codes assigning proper names to numbers.

Arnold had always believed in self-preservation and, surrounded as he was by disgruntled men, he felt that if he changed sides a whole flood of unhappy patriots would follow him. Feeling they would be fools to impoverish

24

themselves, however, he and his wife decided that the British would need to promise them the equivalent of all they held and hoped for, and, beginning his search for a safe way to offer his services to the enemy, in May 1779, Arnold confessed his aims to a crockery dealer and versifier called Joseph Stansbury, who had dealings with André. Stansbury was able to cross the lines to do business and Arnold asked him to convey his offer to British headquarters.

New York, by this time the only metropolis on the American continent left to the British, was crowded with soldiers, and corruption was rife among civilians and military alike. In April 1779, André, a favourite of the new General in command, Sir Henry Clinton, had been put in charge of Intelligence and for some time had been going through the list of men who might be persuaded to change sides. However, though his own name was already on the lips of the traitorous American couple, as he ran over the names of important Colonists who might be seduced to the royal cause, he never in his wildest dreams considered that of Arnold whose patriotism seemed beyond question.

Unknown to André, though, Arnold had many grievances. Although advanced to Major-General in 1777, he was junior to five lacklustre officers promoted earlier in the year, and though, after Saratoga, where he was the hero of the day, he had been advanced over the five, the hurt still festered. He also considered he had not been reimbursed for personal debts incurred during the Canadian campaign, and now the Executive Council were accusing him of a series of offences, among them those of favouring the Loyalists, demeaning patriots, using government waggons to convey privately owned merchandise, and issuing a questionable pass to a ship in which he subsequently acquired a share. Although cleared on all counts, four of the charges were referred to a court martial, so that he was faced with the humiliation of being tried by a group of men, none of whom had a military record to equal his.

Though the revolution had made possible his greatest

opportunities, it had also brought unhappiness and, for his new nineteen-year-old wife, daughter of a Loyalist family, it had brought exile, disillusionment, and social and economic downgrading. She had enjoyed the company of British officers like André when Philadelphia had been captured and, since she was a convinced Tory, it is even possible that the first suggestion that they change sides came from her lips. Her arguments and his own anger had inclined Arnold increasingly to the British cause.

The Arnolds were well aware of their danger but, although Clinton was unapproachable, Peggy felt she could vouch for André's discretion and, with Joseph Stansbury as the intermediary, the first letters were exchanged. Arnold wanted suitable pay for his treachery and André agreed, but suggested that Arnold should also make possible the seizing of a large body of men or send information on despatches, the discussions in Congress, plans and military organisations. Various methods of communications were offered, then André suggested that he should write a letter to a friend, urging that the letter be shown to Peggy, Arnold's wife, and that when it was answered Peggy should add her own messages in invisible ink between the lines. He would reply in the same way, the letters crossing the lines by means of exchanged officers or a flag of truce, the couriers ignorant of what they were carrying. The innocent mutual friend they chose to involve in treason was a girl called Peggy Chew, who was an intimate of Peggy Shippen and had been in love with André.

Arnold's court martial started on 1 June but was almost immediately postponed because the British were advancing up the Hudson, so that Arnold had to return hurriedly to Philadelphia. The letters continued but the negotiations did not proceed quickly because Arnold wanted his reward spelled out in cold cash and was hinting at a peerage.

Unimportant information was passed, among the letters a shopping list from Peggy Arnold for dress material, ribbons, etc, that might have been coded information. André, not satisfied, wanted more information but, in the end, Peggy, who was now pregnant, sent her respects and, in a round-about way, again as if talking about millinery, brought the negotiations to a close.

The winter of Arnold's court martial had been one of success for the British. Clinton had sailed from New York after Christmas 1779, and Washington, not knowing his destination but fearing an assault on Rhode Island, had deployed his troops north of New York. But the British were landing their men in the Carolinas where the ragtag American troops were no match for them. By spring the British were in possession of Charleston and threatening Savannah; and practically all the Carolinas, as well as Georgia, had been lost to the Americans. Re-embarking for New York, Clinton's plan now was to take advantage of the summer weather to repeat his success in the north.

Several months had passed since Arnold had made his first offer to become a traitor. His court martial had cleared him of all the charges against him but two, those of using government waggons to convey private property, and of issuing a pass for the ship, and his sentence had been nominal, nothing but a mild reprimand. Nevertheless, his character being what it was, he felt outraged and mistreated. He had endured cold and hunger, been wounded at Quebec and crippled at Saratoga and still felt he was owed money. Early in May 1780, he began to move assets to London and the letters started again. By this time Arnold was expecting to have something real to offer because he was hoping for the command of West Point, the main rebel depot and fort on the Hudson, whose loss would threaten Washington's army. Finally in August 1780, Arnold was given the command.

André was excited. The surrender of West Point could prevent Washington crossing and recrossing the Hudson and could mean the subjugation of the North and the end of the war. But by this time communication by letter with Arnold was growing complicated and André suggested a parley face to face, feeling that if such a parley resulted in half of what it promised, he could win high rank, perhaps even the plaudits of the King. There was something in it also that appealed to his sense of theatre, a high drama that could change the course of the war, and he felt he must be part of it. He was also probably spurred on by being in some financial difficulty at the time because the Grenada holdings, from which his family had derived wealth, had fallen to the French and he had to get by on a captain's pay, as well as keeping his mother and three sisters, and a younger brother, William, who had joined the army and run up considerable debts.

William wanted to return to England and since John's regiment, the 26th Foot, was due shortly for home service, he suggested that they swap commissions. William would transfer to the 26th, while John would enroll in William's regiment, the 44th, the Essex Regiment. But as the 44th was being sent to Canada, John arranged another transfer, this time to the 54th, the Dorsetshires, who were to remain in New York. It meant loss of seniority, but when two resignations made vacant the post of Adjutant-General, John André was appointed, with the rank of Major, and became the trusted servant of Sir Henry Clinton. Three days after the appointment was announced, Arnold received André's acceptance of the price he had suggested for West Point.

The moment for the crucial parley seemed to have arrived. Clinton didn't like the idea but in the end he agreed, providing André went with Colonel Beverly Robinson, a Tory in whose confiscated house Arnold was living. Arnold went to the meeting by river, but, almost trapped by a British gunboat, he had to disappear in a hurry. André, who had gone to the rendezvous on horseback, had to return to the British lines.

About this time Arnold was joined by his wife. Her hysterical nature was well known and he was in constant fear that she would let slip an indiscreet word, so that instead of the peerage he hoped for he would end up on the gallows. A new parley had been suggested and after a meeting with Washington at which the latter announced his intention of staying with the Arnolds to inspect West Point, it clearly became necessary to hurry the meeting, and a letter was sent by Arnold, making arrangements.

Arnold was well aware that the success of the meeting depended on its secrecy. Unmoved by Washington's trust in him, he sent on information about his impending visit to André, pointing out that within Clinton's grasp was now not only West Point but probably also the Commander-in-Chief of the American Army and his entire staff, as well as the Marquis de Lafayette, the French nobleman who had joined the American cause. The bargain could spell the doom of the Americans and perhaps the end of the new United States. After all the vacillations, Clinton had begun to suspect the whole affair was a hoax, but he agreed to the meeting on condition that André would have the protection of a flag of truce. He also warned André never to cross the enemy lines, always to wear uniform and not to carry any incriminating documents.

André sped up the Hudson in the sloop, *Vulture*, and a man called Joshua Hett Smith, a local landowner and undercover Loyalist, largely unaware of what was going on, went out at Arnold's request in a boat to bring him ashore. André wore a long blue coat over his uniform and carried passes in the name of John Anderson. As the boat reached shore, Smith led him to a clump of evergreens where Arnold waited.

Arnold insisted there must be no quibbling over terms and demanded £20,000 if he turned over West Point with 3000 American troops, and £10,000 no matter what happened. André had been instructed to offer less but he agreed. Arnold also insisted that a British attack should be synchronised with his own manoeuvring, which would have to appear plausible up to the last moment.

The two men were still talking when Smith, shaking with

29

an attack of the ague, mentioned that it was nearly daybreak. Since André could not be returned to the *Vulture* that night, Arnold said he would take him to Smith's house, a mansion overlooking the Hudson which was to go down in history as Treason House. Three horses were produced and André, Arnold and a negro servant cantered in silence along the road. André was worried. He not only faced a whole day ashore but he realised that against his wishes he had crossed enemy lines.

Taken to Smith's house, they waited in an upstairs room and when Smith arrived, Arnold ordered him to serve breakfast. André had taken off his greatcoat by this time and for the first time Smith saw him in the uniform of a British officer. He joined the others for breakfast and, as they talked, the *Vulture*, which had carried André upriver, was obliged to withdraw. Arnold felt he had to return to his headquarters but he gave André a pass and insisted on showing him papers he had written relating to West Point, which included an estimate of the troops there, a return of the ordnance and the minutes of a recent Council of War. With the weak spots itemised, the information would make the capture of the fortress easy, especially with Arnold's secret co-operation. André placed the papers between his stockings and his feet. He was taking a tremendous risk trying to sneak the incriminating documents through the lines and was disregarding Clinton's orders for the second time.

Late in the afternoon, with no sign of the ship returning for André, it was decided that he would have to return to the British lines by land, and he was given a beaver hat and a claret-coloured coat trimmed with gold lace. He parted with his scarlet tunic with reluctance and watched it folded and placed in a drawer by Smith. Once more he had ignored Clinton's warning – this time that on no account should he part with his uniform.

André, Smith and the servant travelled through the night, negotiating road blocks with the passes signed by Arnold.

Because there were Cowboys in the vicinity – Tory cut-throats who took prisoners and stole cattle – they spent the night at a farm. They started again the next morning, but when Smith refused to go any further, André was left on his own. But he felt confident. His disguise seemed to be working and he was growing close to safety. Near Tarrytown and close to his own lines, he was about to cross a bridge spanning a stream when three shabbily-dressed men wielding muskets emerged from the thickets bordering the road.

One, wearing the green red-trimmed coat of a mercenary German sharpshooter, pointed his gun at André, who took the men for Cowboys. 'Gentlemen,' he said, 'I hope you belong to our party.'

'What party?' he was asked.

'The lower,' he replied, referring to the King's party. He showed his watch to indicate he was a man of substance. 'I am an officer in the British service,' he went on, 'and have now been on particular business in the country. I hope you will not detain me.'

The three men, John Paulding, Isaac van Wart and David Williams, were part of an eight-strong local party out looking for Cowboys and suspicious-looking strangers. All three were young and all had been enrolled in the Westchester Militia. Paulding had once been a prisoner of the British and had escaped in the German sharpshooter's coat that had deceived André.

André had no sooner declared himself when he realised that the three men were no friends of Britain. 'My God,' he said, trying to make a joke of the situation, 'I must do anything to get along.' He produced the pass with Arnold's signature. 'My lads,' he said, 'you had best let me go or you will bring yourselves in trouble, for, by stopping me, you will detain the General's business. I am going to Dobbs Ferry to meet a person there and get information for him.' Paulding seemed cowed and hoped that André wouldn't be offended, but Van Wart was not impressed. 'Damn Arnold's pass!' he said. 'You said you were a British officer. Where's your money?'

They hustled André into the bushes and stripped him to his boots. Two watches were discovered and taken with a few dollars loaned to him by Joshua Hett Smith. It did not represent much but then their eyes fell on André's boots. They were excellent officer's boots and worth having and they made André remove them. It was then they noticed there was something inside André's hose and he was forced to reveal the papers.

Paulding was the only one of the three men who could read, but he knew he had found something valuable and when he had finished reading the papers, he looked up at his companions. 'This is a spy,' he said.

André then asked a price to set him free and offered to remain with two of his captors while the third carried a message to the nearest British post. A sum was agreed on, either 500 or 1000 guineas, but the three militiamen then felt that if they did as André asked they would be put in prison.

There are various versions of the capture and the motives of the captors have been called in question. Congress was told that they had refused to free André 'notwithstanding the most earnest importunities and assurances of a liberal reward'. Yet both Lieutenant Joshua King, of the Continental Dragoons, to whom André was delivered, and his Commanding Officer, Major Benjamin Tallmadge, who had worked in Intelligence, maintained that the three captors had had only robbery in mind as they lurked at the bridge. Tallmadge even said he would have arrested them as readily as he would André.

It has often been wondered why André didn't put spurs to his horse. But he had mistaken the men for pro-British Cowboys and by the time he realised his mistake he had three guns trained on him, so that he felt his chances would be better if he allowed himself to be taken to West Point, where Arnold would surely arrange his release. As they started for Wright's Mills, six miles away, one of the men led André's horse and the other two walked alongside. Soon they were joined by the other five who had been with them when they had first set out, and whom Paulding summoned by firing his musket.

'Big drops of sweat' fell from André's brow, Van Wart said. 'Only a few moments before he was uncommonly gay in his looks but after we made him prisoner you could read in his face that he thought it was all over with him. After travelling one or two miles he said, "I would to God you had blown my brains out when you stopped me."'

The prisoner was exhibited to friends at taverns along the route and at one he was given bread and milk. At Wright's Mills they learned the Dragoons had moved to North Castle, six miles away, and the group plodded on, arriving around five o'clock in the afternoon. The Post Commander, Colonel John Jameson, decided that the incriminating papers that had been found should be sent to General Washington and that André should be taken to Arnold's headquarters. André's hopes soared, feeling that Arnold would certainly set him free, but en route in the custody of Lieutenant Solomon Allen and four militiamen, his arms strapped behind him and with one of the guards holding the horse's bridle, a courier from Jameson brought an order to deliver the prisoner to Lieutenant Joshua King at South Salem. There was a long discussion, in which André joined, between the militiamen who wished to continue, and the officer who wished to turn back. In the end, instead of going direct to South Salem, they went by way of North Castle where they were met by Major Tallmadge.

It had been Tallmadge who had urged Jameson to issue the countermand order, but Jameson had nevertheless insisted on despatching a letter to Arnold informing him what had happened. André was confined under heavy guard in the bedroom of a surgeon's mate, Dr Isaac Bronson, whom he amused by drawing a sketch of himself in the custody of Lieutenant Allen and his men. He also wrote to Washington, admitting his identity and acknowledging that he had been 'betrayed into the vile condition of an enemy in disguise within your posts'. He wrote, he said, to clear his name and defend his honour, insisting that the letter was to vindicate himself, not to solicit security. He asked permission to get in touch with Clinton and to have a change of clothing sent to him. He also pointed out that the British had several South Carolinians accused of parole violation in their custody. It was a threat that was not lost on Washington.

By this time, André had completely dropped the guise of a seedy civilian and was again a British officer who had undertaken a perilous duty. He had come in uniform, not as a spy, and the change into civilian attire, he felt, had not been his idea. He remained unruffled and those who talked with him were impressed by the confidence he had in the rectitude of his mission.

While André sat in Dr Bronson's room, Arnold was busy saving his own skin. When he received Jameson's letter, he had been thrown into a panic and rushed to his wife's room. Even as they talked, they were told that Washington, who was due to arrive that morning, was not far away. There was no time to lose and Arnold rushed downstairs, mounted and galloped to the riverbank where he kept a barge in readiness. He ordered the oarsmen to row him to the *Vulture*, tying a white handkerchief to the flagstaff as protection against the American gunboats and shore batteries and as a signal to the British Captain. He promised the oarsmen two gallons of rum to extend themselves but, as they reached the *Vulture*, he endeavoured to persuade them to change sides and when they refused had them placed under arrest. His escape was André's death warrant.

Back at his home, his wife was throwing a fit of hysterics, putting on a show as a soul of innocence so effectively it convinced everybody. Joshua Hett Smith, without such gifts, was rousted from bed and marched to headquarters between fixed bayonets.

That night André was taken to Arnold's house, guarded by 100 Continental Dragoons. A hard rain had set in and, unshaven, his face covered with stubble, he was already a bedraggled spectacle when they left. Like Lieutenant King, Dr Bronson found himself in sympathy with the soaked prisoner and even Tallmadge felt resentment against the men who had captured him.

Washington directed that André should not be treated harshly but, since it did not seem he could be regarded as a common prisoner, he was to be closely guarded. Headquarters was reached as day was breaking with no let-up in the downpour. Smith was already there but André was kept away from him. Although Washington was also there throughout the whole of the next week, he avoided seeing André so as not to let his personal feelings affect his handling of the case.

When he had arrived at noon the day before, Arnold had already vanished and at West Point he was told that the Commandant had not appeared at the fort that morning. When Washington returned to headquarters, the packet from Jameson had arrived containing the treasonable letters André had carried and the letter from André admitting his identity.

Washington immediately sent men in pursuit of Arnold but it was already too late and Arnold was aboard the *Vulture*. The men returned with three letters sent ashore under a flag of truce. One, addressed to Washington, insisted that André could not be detained as he was a British officer on duty. The other two were from Arnold, one for his wife and one for Washington asking that his wife should be allowed to return to her family. Arnold also exonerated Joshua Hett Smith of treason but made no mention of André, whom he left to bear the brunt of the conspiracy.

Late that day the prisoners were taken separately to West Point, André to Fort Putnam, Smith to a dingy provost guardroom. Tallmadge stayed nearby, writing to a friend that, although André might be 'the greatest rogue that we have ever taken,' he had found him a 'very genteel sensible man'. He added, nevertheless, that he wished 'he had been about a more honourable employment'.

The prisoners remained overnight at West Point, André merely stared at by passers-by, Smith taunted and reviled. The following morning they were taken separately by barge to Stony Point. André talked candidly to Tallmadge who realised that 'Military glory was all he sought, and the thanks of his General, and the approbation of his King'. At Stony Point, another formidable escort was gathered and the group set off – Smith at the front of the column, André at the rear – to Tappan, headquarters of the Continental Army.

Four years before, an American officer, Nathan Hale, had been captured by the British in similar circumstances to André's. He had been a friend of Tallmadge's, and Tallmadge asked André if he remembered the sequel of the story. 'He was hanged as a spy,' André said. 'But surely you don't consider his case and mine alike?' Tallmadge replied that they were 'precisely similar' and, he said, 'similar will be your fate.'

In farmyards and on village greens, crowds had gathered to see the spy, and André, still in the beaver hat and claret-coloured coat, complained about the conspicuousness of his attire. Tallmadge offered him his dragoon cloak and, after a little persuasion, André put it on, wearing it during the rest of the journey.

At Tappan, Smith was taken to a room in the Old Dutch Church, while André was given sleeping quarters in a stone-built tavern, every attention being paid to his rank and character. That night home-made coffins were paraded by the townspeople through the town to remind the prisoners of what lay in store.

André had made many blunders. He had underestimated the complexities that had faced him. The Revolutionary War was in effect a civil war and the fact that Tories and Patriots all looked and behaved alike had created a situation in which seasoned spies had always managed to survive. But, though late in the war the administration of the secret services had grown efficient, André had divided his time between supervising Intelligence and fulfilling his duties as Adjutant-General, and in this lax atmosphere had failed to master certain basic rules. As Intelligence Chief he should never have gone in person to meet Arnold, and he had not chosen the ground himself or provided the means of a safe return. He lost control of the situation and his most grievous mistake came at the very end. He should never have declared himself a British officer when stopped by the three irregulars at Tarrytown; he should simply have produced his pass. If they had been Cowboys, they would have taken him to the British lines; if irregulars, they would have hesitated to hold anyone vouched for by General Arnold.

Making his headquarters in Tappan, Washington arrived the same day as the prisoners, to receive a letter from Clinton, insisting that André had gone ashore at Arnold's bidding and under the protection of a flag of truce. He enclosed a letter from Arnold informing him of André's capture and putting great stress on the flag of truce. Washington was unmoved. Flag or no flag, André had been carrying concealed papers and was disguised as a civilian.

Although Washington could have dispensed summary justice, as General Howe had with Nathan Hale, instead he kept everything legal and named fourteen officers for a court of enquiry, known as a Board of General Officers. The function of a board of enquiry was to assist in reaching a conclusion on any subject on which it was felt necessary to be informed, and they were often held to decide if the circumstances surrounding some incident were such as to require a court martial. Though he did not have to, Washington chose to be guided by the findings of the court. General Nathaniel Greene was president and its members included five major generals, among them the Marquis de Lafayette. They convened in the Old Dutch Church at Tappan on 29 September, their task to examine the accused, weigh the evidence and submit an opinion. Their task was not to return a verdict, though that is exactly what they did.

*

André was brought into court under a heavy guard. He was respectful, even courtly, and always at ease. He did not deny the charges that he had crossed the American lines under an assumed name, carried a pass for one John Anderson, had secret papers concealed on his person, and had adopted a disguise for his journey through Westchester. When questioned, he refused to name Smith as a 'helper' and, to the astonishment of the Board, made no claim to having the protection of a flag of truce.

The Board had before them letters from Captain Sutherland, the Captain of the *Vulture*, Beverly Robinson and Clinton, all stating that he had had the protection of such a flag, and Arnold had written saying that everything André had done was under his express orders. A letter he had written to Colonel Elisha Sheldon, of the Continental Dragoons, an unwitting liaison officer between himself and Arnold, also made it clear that he would arrive for his meeting with Arnold as a British officer under a flag of truce. Taken by André's demeanour, the Board tried for his own sake to get him to agree to the facts.

'Did you consider that you came ashore under the sanction of a flag?' he was asked.

André refused to dissemble. It was impossible, he said with devastating honesty, for him to suppose he came on shore under a sanction, and added that 'if he came on shore under that sanction, he certainly might now have returned under it.' Questioned further, he said he first realised he had crossed enemy lines when he and Arnold had been challenged by a sentry near Haverstraw.

Arnold, he said, had pressed the papers on him but perhaps he claimed this to lessen his own culpability and, when asked if he had come ashore as a private citizen, he said, 'I wore my uniform and undoubtedly esteemed myself to be what indeed I was, a British officer.' He had changed into civilian clothes against his wishes.

At the end of the enquiry, André thanked the board for the respect shown him. His dignity and composure had impressed the fourteen officers but they were nonplussed by his candour in admitting the charges, quite unable to understand why he had never thought of himself as a spy. He was, he clearly felt, only a spy by accident, while wearing disguise had been to his 'great mortification' and he 'had objected much against it.' There was, throughout, a certain naivety about him but not once during his testimony did he mention Joshua Hett Smith, and this point was not lost on the Board.

After he had left the court, the judges were shown the letters from Arnold, Sir Henry Clinton, and Colonel Beverly Robinson, all of which stressed the flag of truce. Their job was to choose between these three and André, who had admitted there had been *no* flag. They had no option but to believe the word of an honourable man like André rather than that of Robinson or Clinton, who were not present, and certainly rather than that of a traitor and liar like Arnold.

As one judge said, 'He put us to no proof but in an open, manly manner confessed everything but a premeditated design to deceive.'

No witnesses were called and the judges' opinion was unanimous. They decided that André should be considered a spy and that he should suffer death. Washington's verdict was announced the following day. On Sunday, 1 October, at five o'clock, André must die.

Washington made a point of writing to Clinton informing him that the case had been referred to a Board of General Officers who had reached the unanimous decision that André was indeed a spy. 'From these proceedings,' he wrote, 'it is evident that Major André was employed in the execution of measures very foreign to the objects of flags of truce.' He maintained also that, even had there been a flag of truce, by no stretch of the law could André's actions entitle him to protection. Enclosed with Washington's letter was a message from André himself, and a letter from Peggy Arnold to her husband.

There was another letter, too, written by Alexander

Hamilton, one of the men who had most to do with the shaping of the constitution and politics of the new American nation, indicating the admiration André had roused, and pointing out that Benedict Arnold was the real guilty party and ought more properly to be the victim. It suggested the two might be exchanged and pointed out that no time should be lost.

André's American judges were very impressed by him and by the fact that he had not once dissembled. They knew he was guilty – as by this time, doubtless so did he – but they were not after revenge. They would undoubtedly have let him go if they could have got hold of Arnold. To the Colonists, Arnold was as much loathed as Vidkun Quisling was by the Norwegians, William Joyce (Lord Haw Haw) by the British, and Tokyo Rose by the Americans in World War II. They wanted Arnold and doubtless hoped right to the end that they would get him.

But the offer of an exchange placed General Clinton in a terrible dilemma. There is little doubt that his attitude to the traitor Arnold was much the same as that of Arnold's own countrymen – no one admires a man who is prepared to sell his country for silver – but obviously he could never agree to an exchange or there would be no more men to follow in Arnold's footsteps. Instead, he suggested that the men who had examined André could not have been rightly informed of the true facts and offered three deputies to confer. Washington had no faith in such a parley but he named General Greene as his deputy and put the execution off until midday, 2 October.

Clinton's deputies proved to be ill-chosen and when Greene appeared he consented to see only one, General James Robertson, a fellow soldier. They argued about whether or not André had been protected by a flag of truce but, no matter what Robertson said, Greene remained adamant. Washington would release André on one condition only – the surrender of Benedict Arnold. As Greene left to consult Washington, Robertson sent a personal appeal with him, reiterating that André had taken no step ashore except by the direction of General Arnold, and pointing out that if André were released, any named prisoner of the British would be set at liberty. He also enclosed a communication from Arnold, now safely in New York, who warned that if André were executed, he would feel bound to retaliate against any Americans who might fall into his hands, and made specific reference to the forty South Carolinians in custody for parole violation.

This letter sealed André's fate. Already despised by his fellow countrymen, Arnold's vengeful reply showed the Americans at once that they could expect nothing in the way of honour from him, and their fury and contempt increased. There was clearly going to be no exchange unless Arnold himself agreed to it and that he was obviously not going to do. There was no alternative but for André to stand in his place.

André's friend, Captain John Simcoe, produced a plan to rescue him and contacted an American acquaintance, Major Harry Lee. Lee's reply at first gave grounds for hope, saying that there was a possibility of André 'being restored to his country . . .' but before despatching the letter Lee had added a postscript saying that Robertson's offers had not come up to what was expected and the view had since changed.

André might have blamed Arnold, or even Joshua Hett Smith, who after all between them had landed him in his present straits, but he still made no mention of either, feeling that he had yielded to their urging and that the mission had been badly planned and recklessly carried out. His silence continued to impress the American officers and Alexander Hamilton wrote to his fiancée, 'I wished myself possessed of André's accomplishments for your sake, for I would wish to charm you in every sense.'

With the aid of Hamilton, André was allowed to write again to Clinton. He readily admitted that what he had done was contrary to Clinton's instructions and concluded by expressing his devotion and gratitude to the man who had so advanced his military career, saying, 'I am perfectly tranquil in mind and prepared for any fate to which an honest zeal for my King's service may have devoted me.'

He expressed concern for his mother and sisters and trusted they would receive the value of his commission. He was resigned to suffering a spy's fate, he said, but hoped that he would die 'in a manner that would do honour to British arms'. He also wrote to Washington asking to be shot, not hanged as a spy and, out of respect for his feelings, Washington did not answer. Policy ordained the gibbet for convicted spies and he wished to leave no one in any doubt about André's status. There was still talk of an exchange for Arnold, and Hamilton was asked to enlist André's help to urge it on General Clinton. Hamilton would have none of the idea.

To pass the hours, André turned out pen and ink sketches, but a personal matter weighed on his mind. André had willed the more valuable of his two watches to an old friend but both his watches had been taken from him. Could the one he had bequeathed to his friend be recovered? One of the watches was found and returned but the one which had been willed to the friend did not turn up, until it appeared in New York in 1923.

On his last night André slept little and, when awakened, seemed on the verge of tears but soon regained his composure. He was shaved, given fresh linen and, as a mark of respect, was given breakfast from Washington's own table. He donned his regimentals, the scarlet coat with green facings proclaiming him an officer in the 54th. When he was warned of the time of the execution, his servant broke into sobs and André sent him away. 'There must be no show of weakness during these last hours,' he said, then, thanking his guards, he announced himself ready.

Tappan swarmed with troops and onlookers flooded the village. At the stroke of twelve André was brought out into the sunshine. He smiled faintly as he faced the escort, and ran down the steps to his place with a light step. A command was shouted and the fifes and drums broke into the Dead

March as the column passed the Old Dutch Church where Joshua Hett Smith's court martial had just been convened.

Turning left, the procession toiled up the long hill towards the place of execution where the gallows had been erected. According to a witness, André's face was deathly pale, but he managed a most agreeable smile, acknowledging anyone he recognised with a courtly bow and commenting on the excellent discipline of the American troops and the music of the fifes and drums.

Near the top of the hill the column turned into an open field and André recoiled visibly at the sight of the gallows. He had expected to be shot like a soldier, not hanged like a common criminal. 'Gentlemen, I am disappointed,' he said. 'I expected my request would have been granted.' But he recovered quickly. 'I am reconciled to my death,' he said, continuing his walk, 'but not to the mode.'

A hush descended as he was led to the cleared space round the gibbet. On one side stood a two-horse baggage cart holding a black coffin. Near it was an open grave. The hill top was packed with spectators, including rank on rank of American troops. The guard formed three circles round the gallows, with their backs to it and bayonets fixed. As André passed the members of the Board of General Officers, waiting together on horseback, he bowed respectfully to each, showing enormous calmness. 'To see a man go out of time without fear but all the time smiling, is a matter I could not conceive of,' said one witness. The Officer of the Day waited on horseback near the scaffold with Colonel Alexander Scammell, Washington's Adjutant. The three men who had captured André stood close by, near to André's servant who was weeping unashamedly.

At André's request, Major Tallmadge stepped forward and they shook hands like old friends. Tallmadge had become so deeply attached to André, he said later, he could remember no instance where 'my affections were so fully absorbed in any man'.

After Tallmadge withdrew, Scammell read the death

sentence. André listened impassively, though it was noticed that he had placed his foot on a stone and was rolling it over and over, choking in his throat as if attempting to swallow. A small flush was also noticed moving over his left cheek. The spectators seemed to be overwhelmed and many were in tears.

As Scammell finished, André was ordered to take his place in the waggon. Hoisting himself on to the tailboard, he stepped to the coffin, stood on top of it and, with his hands on his hips, paced back and forth. He removed his hat and laid it on the coffin, and one witness noticed that he had 'a beautiful head of hair ... wound with a black ribbon and hung down his back'. Then he removed his neckcloth and tucked it into a pocket and, with a forefinger, turned back his shirt collar. 'It will be but a momentary pang,' he told himself, but audibly enough to be overheard.

To hide his identity, the hangman, a Tory who had been promised his freedom in return for hanging André, had smeared his face and hands with soot. As he was about to adjust the halter, André took it from him and lowered it over his own head, knotting it under the right ear.

'Major André,' he was told, 'if you have anything to say, you now have the opportunity.'

André raised the blindfold. 'I have nothing more than this,' he said. 'That I would have you gentlemen bear me witness that I die like a brave man.'

His arms were ordered to be pinioned and, in a deathly stillness, he brought out a second handkerchief which the hangman knotted round his arms above the elbows. The signal was given, a whip cracked like a pistol shot and, as the waggon lurched from beneath his feet, the world ended for John André.

André lay in his grave at Tappan for more than 40 years then, in 1821, at the request of the Duke of York, his remains were dug up and returned to England to be buried in Westminster Abbey. A pension was awarded to his mother, and his brother William was made a baronet.

44

Clinton was said to be 'crushed' by his death. His own fortunes did not improve either, as he, too, was made a scapegoat – for the defeat at Yorktown. He always believed that if André had managed to return to the British lines, Britain would not have lost America.

Even Washington agonised over André, whom he considered 'more unfortunate than criminal'. When he signed the death sentence his hand was said to have shaken uncontrollably. But Tallmadge insisted that he could not have let André be shot without casting doubt on the validity of the sentence, 'the universal usage of nations having affixed to the crime of a spy death by the gibbet.'

Arnold was paid handsomely for his treachery and was commissioned as a Brigadier in the British Army. But no leading Americans ever followed his example and he was never entirely trusted by the British. During the attack on New London, Connecticut, he behaved against his erstwhile comrades with cruelty, and the hatred he aroused in Americans and the keen dislike among the English made Clinton feel he could no longer rely on him. Joined by his wife, he drifted into exile and set up house in London. But he failed to prosper and died heavily in debt in 1801. His wife died two years later.

But he has never been forgotten by Americans. His treachery came at a time of struggle and of the high idealism of a young republic and he might well have destroyed it. His name became a household word for betrayal and cropped up whenever the subject was mentioned. Even in 1941, almost 160 years after André's death, when President Franklin D Roosevelt was struggling to give all the help he could to a Britain embattled against the Nazi might, one of the placards brandished by the bitter isolationist members of the American Women's Neutrality League, fighting to stop him, was 'Benedict Arnold Helped England, Too.'

Joshua Hett Smith was acquitted at his court martial and fled to England but returned later to his native New York. Tallmadge became a Congressman, but he could never forget André, and when John Paulding, one of the men who had captured him, asked for an increase in his pension in 1817, Tallmadge opposed the application. Even after nearly 40 years, his high regard for André had not diminished.

In the long sweep of British military history, André was a very small cog in a very large wheel but to the Americans in a war fought on the American Continent he appears more important. Indeed, to the Americans he has become almost a hero, not for what he did but for the way he conducted himself during his ordeal.

On the 200th anniversary in 1980, the whole incident was reconstructed at Tappan, with American uniforms and an actor dressed as John André undergoing his trial and eventual death – though, as the local paper pointed out, it was not considered necessary to carry this to the final conclusion. André had never married but a descendant of his brother, Major John André, an officer of the Devon and Dorset Regiment – one of the regiments in which André himself had served – but at the time serving in Norway as a Commando, was invited with his whole family to be present to watch the re-enactment of his ancestor's death. This took place at Tappan and the trial was held in the Reform Church which, though not the same building, stood on the exact spot where the Dutch Colonial Church had stood when André's trial had taken place.

Without doubt John André died as the scapegoat for a far guiltier, far less honourable man, but the hatred for Arnold, the passions aroused by the war, Arnold's vengeful 'reprisals' letter, and the hanging of Nathan Hale, made it impossible that he could survive.

Michel Ney

Though, like Benedict Arnold, Michel Ney, Marshal of France, changed sides, he was in essence an intensely patriotic man. His change of sides was not deliberate; he was caught up in the sweeping emotions of a confused period in French history in which there was a King, a Republic, a Directorate, an Emperor, another King and once more an Emperor. It was a difficult time for any Frenchman to understand where his loyalties should lie, and Ney was, above all, a victim of royal spite.

Ney never appeared to be an indecisive man and, in fact, his behaviour always gave the impression of enormous self-confidence. Yet he was often unsure of himself. He was a soldier first and last, with little interest in political affairs, and the tragedy of his trial was that it was that of a man of action bewildered by a political intrigue he failed to understand, and that it was stage-managed specifically for his downfall. Throughout his life he always spoke without thinking, acting always on impulse, and his violent temperament and poor judgement of a situation made him an easy victim when the time came to make difficult decisions.

Ney was born in January 1769, the same year as Napoleon, in the town of Saarlouis, in Lorraine, the son of an old soldier who had become a barrel cooper. By 1788, already tall and strongly-built with red hair, he had enlisted in the Duke of Chartres' Regiment of Hussars. In those days, the French army was officcred entirely by men of rank, but the

French Revolution, which began with the storming of the Bastille in 1789, changed all that and position in the army no longer depended on privilege or connection but on courage and skill. Nevertheless, it took Ney two years to reach the rank of Corporal and another year to reach Sergeant, and when he fought at Valmy, one of the first victories of the French revolutionary armies, in 1792, he was a Sergeant Major. He already had a reputation for reckless courage and a hot temper, and was known as a man who was a hater of injustice, who was always ready to settle a matter of honour with a duel.

Poor but proud as Lucifer, all he wanted was to be recognised as a man who won battles for France, a soldier who went into action ten paces ahead of his men. Fearless, hot-blooded, always quick to take offence, he remained a simple man who was just as quick to forgive anything, save an insult touching his honour. He was the epitome of all that made up the Napoleonic legend and the spirit of the men who jingled across Europe behind the indefatigable Corsican adventurer.

Ney was ambitious but was aware of his limitations, and his advancement, compared with that of other soldiers of the revolution, was not rapid. But by 1794, he was a Captain in the Army of the Sambre-et-Meuse and in 1796 he was made a General of Brigade on the field of battle. He was taken prisoner in 1797 but was released by the Treaty of Leoben. By this time, his hot temper was well known and all too often he was prevented, by the understanding of his associates, from committing some act of folly caused by his concern with his honour. Except when he was fighting, he often seemed uncertain of himself and, like many insecure people, often took refuge in loud bursts of anger and self-assertiveness. To his soldiers, however, he always remained a hero and with them he was always at ease. He was appointed General of Division in 1799 with the Army of the Rhine and eventually given temporary command of the Army. He was with this army at the victory of Hohenlinden which drew attention to him as a soldier of the future.

He met Napoleon for the first time in 1801 and Napoleon's wife, Joséphine, set out to find a wife for him in Aglaé Auguié, a close friend of her daughter, Hortense. Her mother had been a lady-in-waiting to Marie Antoinette and Ney's reaction on their first meeting was one of tongue-tied admiration. Aglaé saw a large young man with red hair, red whiskers, a red face and an awkward bearing, but the marriage was very successful and produced four sons. In the company of his wife, Ney seemed to shed his uncertainty, but he was never happy at the balls and receptions they were obliged to attend as part of Napoleon's Court.

Of all the Republican rankers destined for high rank, he was probably the most modest. Known as the Bravest of the Brave, he was famous for his personal courage and followed the tricolour through most of Napoleon's campaigns, receiving wounds to the hand, arm, thigh, knee, foot, chest and neck. By the establishment of the Empire, he had become Inspector-General of Cavalry, and on his elevation to Emperor, Napoleon recreated the Marshalate and with thirteen others made Ney a Marshal of France.

With the plan for the invasion of England abandoned because his fleet could not guarantee a safe passage, Napoleon turned his eyes eastwards and what followed were the greatest days of the Napoleonic glory – the campaigns of Ulm, Jena and Friedland. Ney distinguished himself, again and again heading the advance or standing between the enemy and the Grand Army. His relations with his fellow Marshals were often difficult, however, but his red hair was always seen in the thick of every battle and 'Le Rougeaud's ' popularity with the rank and file was enormous. He was created Duke of Elchingen after the battle that led to the bloodless victory of Ulm, rendered important services to France in the Tyrol and contributed much to French successes in 1806 and 1807.

He was the acknowledged hero of Friedland, and was

singled out by Napoleon for special praise, but, while he was always genial in his own home, his new title made him more jealous of his honour than ever. By this time, after twenty years of warfare, he was beginning to long for peace and the chance to enjoy his wealth, but when at home he soon became bored with the life his position obliged him to lead. In August, 1808, he was ordered to Vitoria, in Spain, and in that absurd blunder, the Peninsular War, which became three years of intrigues and jealousies, spent much of his time quarrelling with his fellow Marshals, particularly Soult. Yet he served Napoleon well and never lost his popularity with his men.

He was back in Paris in 1811, glad to be shot of Spain, and in January 1812, was given the 3rd Corps of the Grand Army with orders to proceed to Mainz, an instruction which was to lead him to Russia where he was to achieve undying fame as the Commander of the rearguard during the retreat.

He distinguished himself more than once during the advance and at the Battle of the Moscowa was the hero of the day, for which Napoleon made him Prince of the Moscowa. For a month Napoleon waited in Moscow, expecting the Czar to make peace, but when he failed to do so, he was obliged to retreat. On 13 October the first snow fell and on 1 November, Ney was given the rearguard, and so began the story that made him immortal in the history of warfare. It was a demonstration of how much the force of one man's personality and will could accomplish.

He had 10,000 men when his task began but no more than a few hundred when it ended. In the agonising cold, with starving men dropping and dying in the snow, Ney made a fighting force out of the sufferers, boasting and joking in their midst so that they forgot their misery.

Smolensk, they felt, would save them, but when they reached it, it had been gutted by the main army moving ahead of them. At Krasnoie, at Orcha, at a dozen small engagements, Ney kept his force active, and at the Beresina he held the Russians from the only bridge that allowed a passage across the river. At Vilna and Korvo he repeated his successes and finally, on 15 December, he brought his men out of Russia into Prussia. A man with dishevelled red hair and a matted beard appeared, totally unrecognisable.

'I am Michel Ney,' he said. 'I am the rearguard of the Grand Army.' He had saved not only the army but also its honour, and he became the hero of France.

With his army lost, Napoleon was already engaged in raising a new force to face the advancing allies, but by now the attitude in France was sullen. The French felt that too much was being asked of them and the mood began to affect the Marshals, who began to complain that the honours and riches they had won were worthless if they were never to have peace to enjoy them. The campaigns of 1813 and 1814 were fought as fiercely as ever but the troops the Marshals commanded now were often mere boys with little training. During one battle Marshal Marmont saw one of them standing immobile under fire and when he asked him why he didn't fire back he received the answer, 'I don't know how to load my gun.' To these boys, whose fathers had fought in the first battles of the Revolution, and whose elder brothers had fought at Austerlitz and Jena, Ney was a legend and he gave them confidence.

He led them well but Napoleon was now being deserted by the allies he had made through conquest, and one retreat followed another. Napoleon explained them away by saying his recruits were not the men of 1796, but the Marshals were growing old, too, and their disinclination to continue the fight began to show. When Napoleon met them in October, he found them quiet and gloomy and when he appealed to them to remember their great deeds, they returned to their duty without enthusiasm, and Ney was wounded yet again. He was growing weary and was probably even suffering from what these days would be called 'shell shock' or 'battle fatigue'. The retreat from Moscow had taken an enormous amount out of him; there had been no rest ever since and always he had been in the thick of the fighting.

Like all the Marshals, he was eager to retain what he had gained. But he was also moved by a deep devotion to his country, and he began to see that Napoleon and France were not the same thing, and that eventually a choice would have to be made between them. When he rejoined the army in 1814 it was without ardour.

Napoleon continued to be enthusiastic and ebullient, confident of a final victory, but his Marshals were suffering from foreboding. In the campaign of 1814, Ney lived up to his reputation in the field but between engagements the despair of the other senior officers took hold of him, and he began to talk openly of the insanity of continuing the struggle. He seemed even to be seeking death and fought with a frenzy because his mind was troubled by the fact that he was fighting for a cause he no longer believed in; and knowing less of politics than most of his colleagues, he suffered more.

By this time the Royalist agents in Paris were active, not only with agents of the advancing allies but also with the wavering supporters of Napoleon. By 27 March, it was learned that the march on Paris had begun and that Marshals Marmont and Mortier, who were guarding it, were having to fall back. The allies were cautious but in the end the two Marshals had to leave Paris to the invaders and move southwards to Villejuif, Corbeil and Essonnes on the road to Fontainebleau.

Still Napoleon refused to acknowledge defeat, his mind full of plans to regain the capital, and orders were issued for a concentration at Fontainebleau. Napoleon was discussing the situation with Marshals Berthier, Oudinot, Lefêbvre and Moncey and, with Marmont and Mortier still only twenty miles from the capital, was convinced that the magic of his name would turn the tide. None of the Marshals dared say what was in his mind.

When Ney arrived he was ignorant of their demoralisation but he was dispirited and uncertain. Though he was weary of fighting, if the other Marshals had been agreeable, he was more than willing to continue, but with every hour that passed the turbulence of his mind increased.

Meanwhile the Royalist agents had contacted Marmont, a vain and ambitious man who, forgetting he was a soldier not a politician, began to see himself as the voice of France and on 4 April he led his troops over to the enemy, marching them at night so they might believe they were heading the Napoleonic advance on Paris.

The deposition of the Emperor had already been decreed by the Senate on 2 April and this encouraged the Marshals to make a move to end the fighting. Although the soldiers were still crying 'To Paris', there was now nobody to lead them. Ney suggested abdication but Napoleon jeered at the Senate's decree. In reply, the Marshals told him there *must* be peace and Marshal MacDonald said, 'Paris must not be exposed to the fate of Moscow.'

'I shall appeal to the army,' Napoleon said.

'The army,' Ney replied, 'will not march.'

'The army will obey me,' Napoleon snapped.

Ney took a deep breath. 'The army,' he insisted, 'will follow its leaders.'

Napoleon knew he was beaten and, as they watched, he wrote out his abdication, insisting that his infant son, the King of Rome, should succeed him. Ney, with Caulaincourt and Marshal MacDonald, took it to Paris. The choice of the impulsive Ney was an odd one but perhaps Napoleon feared that he might do something foolish if he remained at Fontainebleau. Telling Caulaincourt to keep an eye on him, he said, 'He is as weak as he is brave.'

When the three men reached Essones, they learned that Marmont had already gone over to the enemy, nullifying Napoleon's demands that his son should follow him. There would now be no regency and no Imperial title for the King of Rome.

*

53

Ney had been deeply affected by the spirit of revolt. Many of the Marshals were worried that, if they remained too long on the side of Napoleon, the returning Bourbons might not allow them to keep what they had won. Ney floundered. He didn't give a fig for the Bourbons but he cared for his honour, represented by all he had gained with his sword. Yet the circumstances at Fontainebleau had made it appear that Ney, and Ney alone, had been responsible for forcing the abdication of Napoleon. When Napoleon was informed of what had happened, he made a bitter comment which was to prove prophetic. 'I know him,' he said of Ney. 'He was against me yesterday, but he'd give his life for me tomorrow.'

As Napoleon went into exile on Elba, Ney was welcoming the Comte d'Artois, the heir to the Bourbon throne. He was still wearing the tricolour cockade and Artois commented on it, so that Ney left the meeting with a surly face. Two weeks later, with seven other Marshals, he welcomed Louis XVIII who, anxious for a united country, spoke flatteringly of their victories to set them at ease.

Those about Louis, however, could not be bothered with such a policy. The returning old nobility could not accept these soldiers of the Revolution as their equals, and Ney, whose quick temper set him always looking for an insult, was aware of patronising words, whispers and disdainful smiles. The Duke of Angoulême, wearing a British uniform, asked 'What's that fellow's name?' At the banquets and balls that were given, Ney found himself trying to behave like the courtiers of Versailles before the Revolution. He hated the life, he was bored, and his wife was treated with frigid politeness or even ignored, so that he was soon asking himself if he had been over-hasty in speeding the departure of Napoleon. But the more he abused the Court the more he grew dissatisfied with himself. He was struggling with his conscience, he was unsure, resentful and suspicious, and began to feel he ought to have gone into exile as Marshal Davout had. Talks with his old soldiers increased his rancour but, though his indiscreet outbursts attracted the attention of the Secret Police, he joined none of the conspiracies to bring back Napoleon.

By 1815, Ney was in command of the 6th Division at Besançon and happy to be away from Paris. France was full of rumours of a possible return of the Emperor but Ney had little to hope for from such an event. Despite his dissatisfaction with the Monarchy, he had lost faith with Napoleonism, yet he could not help but compare Napoleon with fat old Louis. In addition, France was full of discharged soldiers and officers on half-pay, and Louis made the mistake of recreating the old Royalist regiments and officering them with the old nobility, men who had seen no service or had even fought with foreign armies against their own country.

When the news came of Napoleon's landing at Fréjus from Elba on 1 March 1815, the position of anybody suspected of plotting against the King became perilous, but there had been no real plots and Ney himself only lost control of his tongue when he was among friends. But his actions at Fontainebleau had lost him popularity and he had begun to feel he had acted dishonourably, and that the present Government, which he despised, had been helped into office by his actions.

On 6 March he was ordered to return to his Corps at Besançon. As yet, no one was panicking about Napoleon but then news arrived that he was at Grenoble and that Marshal Masséna, who had been expected to stop him, had not stirred himself.

Ney's reaction, as usual, was with loud words to reassure himself, and when he saw Louis XVIII he swore to bring Napoleon back in an iron cage. Louis was not impressed. 'That would indeed be a singular sort of canary,' he said.

By now, news had arrived of further progress by Napoleon and Ney gave orders for a march on Lons-le-Saulnier, feeling that failure to stop him would mean disgrace and possible death because of his conduct at Fontainebleau. Ney, in fact, was genuinely anxious to do his duty, not because he revered Louis, but because he didn't wish to incur the stigma of disloyalty a second time. As he approached Lons, he learned that many of his men had no stomach for opposing Napoleon, yet he was still confident of his own ability as a leader. But at Lons, he received Napoleon's proclamation and realised at once the magnetic power of his words. 'Nobody,' he said, 'can write like that nowadays. That is how the King should address us. It is the way to talk to soldiers and move their hearts.' He was already half-persuaded by the famous words, 'Victory will march at the pas de charge ... The eagle with the national colours will fly from steeple to steeple even to the towers of Notre Dame.'

All next day news arrived of Napoleon's progress. He was being received with delight everywhere and whole regiments were deserting at the rumour of his approach. 'I cannot,' Ney said, in despair, 'stop the movement of the sea with my hands.'

But no one came to his help with advice. He was left entirely alone with his responsibility – never something to inflict on a man as volatile and impulsive as Ney.

In the early hours of 14 March, two of Napoleon's officers were brought to Ney. What they said is not known but they carried a letter in Napoleon's own hand. 'I shall receive you as I received you on the day after the Battle of the Moscowa,' he said. Harking back to past triumphs, as Napoleon well knew, was the surest way to win Ney over and inevitably Ney regarded it as forgiveness for his conduct at Fontainebleau.

Ney was not a shrewd man, rash and sometimes not even sensible. Magnificent as a soldier but no judge of men, he found himself driven into a political trap from which he couldn't extricate himself. If he had insisted on fighting Napoleon at Lons he could have plunged the country into bloodshed and civil war. But, having set off with the expressed intention of capturing Napoleon, if he didn't now fight him he would be branded as a traitor. Nevertheless, it was typical of his sense of honour that at his trial he gallantly refused to name the two envoys who had appeared before him and thus saved them from a court martial of their own.

Believing the Royalist cause lost, he could see no alternative but to accept Napoleon, and he read the proclamation to the troops. The effect was instantaneous. There were few protests and enormous enthusiasm, and Napoleon's reaction when they met four days later was friendly. Ney was lost – and so was the King.

On the heels of the departing Bourbons, Napoleon entered Paris on 20 March without a shot being fired. The only objection seems to have come from an old woman selling chestnuts who shouted 'Vive le Roi!' and when challenged by a man shouting 'Vive l'Empereur,' she attacked him with her ladle. Napoleon was carried shoulder-high into the Tuileries and the campaign of the Hundred Days began.

The Congress of Vienna, which had been debating how to reorganise Europe after Napoleon's depredations, ceased its bickerings and, declaring him an outlaw, began to assemble its armies. As the British, Belgians, Hanoverians and Prussians began to gather and the Russians and Austrians grouped at the frontiers, Napoleon collected his forces. But only Marshals Davout, Mortier, Brune, Soult, Jourdan, Suchet, Ney and Murat had declared for him, most of the others wisely remaining out of sight.

In addition, Murat was occupied with hanging on by his fingertips to his kingdom of Naples, Jourdan had grown too old for active service, Brune was commanding in the south and Suchet was with the Army of the Alps. Davout remained in charge in Paris, Soult became a very incompetent Chief of Staff, while Mortier had to drop out almost immediately with crippling sciatica. A new Marshal had been added to the other twenty-five when General Grouchy had been raised in rank but, with defections, illnesses, age and weariness, Ney was the only Marshal to have an active command at Waterloo. Yet even this seemed a haphazard appointment. He received a message from Napoleon via Davout: 'Tell him that if he wants to take part in the first engagement to be at . . . my headquarters on 14 June.' It was less an order than an invitation and there was no offer of a command. But fighting was Ney's trade and he didn't hesitate for a moment.

Napoleon was not at his best at Waterloo and, plagued by illness, he was indecisive. Between the two of them, mistakes were made; Ney furious at Napoleon's slowness in reinforcing him at Quatre Bras, Napoleon equally enraged that Ney had allowed the half-beaten Prussians under Blücher to escape at Ligny.

But Ney had to retain his command because there was no one to replace him and at Waterloo he fought like a madman, always in advance of the shock battalions. He had five horses shot from under him but always remained miraculously untouched himself. Once again it seemed as if he were deliberately seeking death, as if a tortured conscience were driving him on. The battle closed as Ney knew it would close, in dispersal and utter disaster. The Imperial Guard melted away but, as always in battle, Ney didn't panic. His face blackened with powder, an epaulette shot away, his uniform torn and smeared with mud, waving a broken sword, he tried to rally the retreating Frenchmen. 'Come and see how a Marshal of France can die,' he roared. But he was well aware of what would happen if he survived. 'We shall be hanged if we live through this,' he said. As he shouted for a rally, even in their extremity of terror, a few Frenchmen retained their self-respect and were able to shout 'Long live Ney!' Only when it was dark did he limp away, leaning on the shoulder of a corporal, the last senior officer to leave the field.

Tumbled from his throne a second time, Napoleon once again refused to acknowledge defeat and tried in Paris to gloss over the disaster. But once again he was destroyed by Ney, who had arrived in Paris to find himself unjustly accused of losing the battle. Napoleon was blaming him for over-caution but, though in command of one-third of Napoleon's army, he had been given so little information about what was happening, he knew no more than the newest-joined private and, knowing the Prussians to be hovering somewhere on his flank, the caution he had shown was manifestly wise.

Never the man to take such accusations lying down, he made clear how untrue Napoleon's claims were and bluntly insisted he was deceiving the Chamber of Peers. 'Wellington is advancing,' he insisted. 'Blücher has not been defeated . . . The enemy will be at the gates of Paris in a week.'

Napoleon was forced to surrender and as soon as Louis and his courtiers reappeared at the Tuileries, they began a witch-hunt, and a long list was drawn up of the names of Marshals, generals, ministers and officials for whose blood the émigrés were howling. The first name on it was that of Ney, the one man they wanted, the man who had promised Napoleon in an iron cage.

Paris was in a turmoil with the politicians wondering why on earth they had ever accepted Napoleon again. The Royalist white cockade, once again supported by foreign bayonets, reappeared. Only one man prevented the émigrés from shooting every prominent man who had declared for Napoleon, and that was Davout at the Ministry of War. They couldn't put Davout on trial because he had never declared for Louis and, with his threats from the Ministry of War to continue the struggle if a blanket amnesty were not granted, he forced the allies to accept his terms. The peace treaty, or convention, known as the Capitulation of Paris, was drawn up, its most important paragraph Article XII which stated quite clearly that those who had been involved with Napoleon should continue to enjoy their rights and that there should be no thoughts of vengeance.

Ney was persuaded to leave Paris on 6 July, the day the allies marched in. Soult had managed to slip away and go into exile, assisted by a British officer with a warm respect for his old Peninsular opponent. As the summer wore on, with the Royalists noisy in their cries for vengeance, Brune was murdered by a hysterical Royalist mob and Murat was shot by his own people. Finally, Ney, who had taken refuge in the Cantal, was recognised and arrested.

He was very unlucky. A local man who rode to warn him of the approach of the gendarmes suffered a heavy fall from his horse and was unable to complete the ride. Ney received the police agents calmly, however. Though they had been ordered to take him to Paris in manacles, he gave his parole and, despite two offers to allow him to escape, as a man of honour he refused. On arrival in the capital, he was lodged in the Concièrgerie. The Bourbons ordered a court martial and Louis, never a vindictive man, wrung his hands in dismay.

'Why did he let himself be caught?' he wailed. 'We gave him every chance to get away.'

Because of his conduct, it was assumed that Ney would allow himself to be condemned without defending himself, but the mere suggestion that he had tarnished his precious honour put him on his mettle. He at once challenged the right to try him by an ordinary court martial and demanded to be tried by his peers. Desperate to save him and furious at the flagrant violation of the terms of the armistice, Davout did everything in his power to get Ney's decision reversed. Marshal St Cyr, who had taken over from Davout at the Ministry of War, carefully convened a special court known as a Council of War with no fewer than four of Ney's fellow Marshals as judges – Moncey, named as Chairman, Augereau, Masséna and Mortier. Though Moncey, Augereau and Masséna had not supported Napoleon, they had also not supported the King, and in Mortier's case, only a fortuitous attack of sciatica had prevented him from standing alongside the prisoner in the dock. Ney had even bought his horses as he had ridden up to Waterloo.

Not one of the Marshals accepted the position. Mortier said he would sooner be cashiered, Masséna more craftily pleaded a personal quarrel, and Augereau claimed he was ill. Moncey took the honourable course of declaring himself at once, and categorically refused to sit in judgement on a man he revered for his courage. 'Where were those who accuse Ney while he was on the field of battle?' he wrote to the King. He pointed out that in Russia it was Ney who had saved the remnants of the army. 'I myself,' he said, 'had relatives, friends, soldiers there who loved their leaders, and it is I who am called upon to condemn to death a man to whom so many Frenchmen owe their lives, so many families their sons, husbands, fathers . . . If I am not to be allowed to save either my country or my own life, I will at any rate save my honour.'

The letter enraged the courtiers round Louis, and Moncey was dismissed from the army and sentenced to three months imprisonment in the Castle of Ham. His place was taken by Jourdan, who had also deserted the Bourbons for Napoleon, and the legal farce designed to destroy the bravest man in France commenced in the Palais de Justice on 9 November. Mortier had backed down and Jourdan had replaced Moncey, but three other high-ranking officers made up the court.

Davout had always insisted that Ney was safer in the hands of a military court martial instead of a court of peers, claiming that no one could condemn such a man. At first it seemed he might be right because the judges were most respectful to the prisoner.

Ney made no bones about the fact that he had offered his services to the King on receiving the news of Bonaparte's landing but he insisted he had never promised to bring Napoleon to Paris in an iron cage, claiming that he said he *deserved* to be brought to Paris in an iron cage. He dismissed with contempt the suggestion that he had received 500,000 francs from the King to do the job.

He described what had happened at Lons-le-Saulnier and insisted that his about-face had never been premeditated. He had not at any time been in contact with Napoleon, but had been swept along by the atmosphere and by Napoleon's words. 'I have often been tempted to blow out my brains,' he said, 'but I have not done it because I wish to vindicate

61

myself ... I have done much wrong ... but I am not a traitor ...'

'A dyke,' he continued, had broken, 'and I lost my head.' On meeting Napoleon, he had been reminded of his campaigns and Napoleon had addressed him as the Bravest of the Brave. 'I left Paris with the intention of sacrificing my life for the King,' Ney insisted. 'I lost myself.'

He stuck to his claim that the court was not competent to try him, and after a lot of legal wrangling, the judges agreed with him. 'We were cowards,' Augereau said afterwards. 'We ought to have insisted on our right to save him from himself.' By five votes to two, the judges decided that Ney's claim should be upheld and his fellow Marshals retired with relief.

Furious at the delay, the Royalist Government immediately prepared a new trial. Ney's wife, Aglaé, appealed to people in high places, among them the Duke of Wellington, but Wellington told her that Britain could not interfere in the affairs of France. Having played a major rôle in reinstating the Bourbons, it was a lame excuse. She then tried the Duc de Berry, younger son of the Comte d'Artois, who was to succeed gouty old Louis XVIII as Charles X. He was quite without sympathy, even claiming that the throne was unsafe 'so long as one of those soldiers was left alive.' The Czar returned the same answer as Wellington. Appeals and excuses there were in plenty but no one was prepared to come forward to save the life of France's bravest soldier.

The Bourbons – always excepting the King himself – grew impatient and a new trial was commenced on 4 December. Though this time Ney was to be tried by the Chamber of Peers it was no more than a continuation of the court martial, with the same evidence and the same witnesses. The difference this time was that Ney was not being tried by soldiers who understood him and understood the pressures that had been put upon him, but by a court composed largely of civilians led by émigrés who felt they had been humiliated.

The Chamber of Peers, from which those who had been created peers by Napoleon or who had sat during his reign had been removed, had become a Royalist Chamber and contained many for whom the trial was a foregone conclusion. Between returned émigrés and Royalists hoping for favour and position, there was no hope of a fair trial. In royalist circles there was only anger at the action of the Council of War which had declared to the world that it wanted Ney to escape, and the King could do nothing to control the fury of his supporters. Cool deliberations were out of the question, and the only effect of the Council of War's decision was to make Ney's enemies more ruthless.

A basis of the prosecution's argument was that Ney had not only gone over to Napoleon at Lons-le-Saulnier but that a pre-arranged plan to do so had been formed while Napoleon was still in Elba. It was utter nonsense, because as Ney rightly claimed, he had abandoned the Bourbons only when it was clear his troops would not fight for them. He also insisted he was protected by the amnesty arranged by Davout.

At first the trial seemed to go Ney's way. The prosecution's witnesses seemed unsatisfactory and one of them, the prosecution's principal witness, General Bourmont, had changed sides three times before Waterloo and again during the battle. Ney was contemptuous. He was no orator but his bearing, his anger, and his obvious sincerity made a great impression. He conducted himself with great dignity and when Bourmont, who had been with him when Napoleon's proclamation had been read to the troops, said that the only way he could have stopped the Marshal would have been to kill him, Ney exclaimed, 'You would have done me a great service. Perhaps it was your duty.'

Other witnesses gave no consolation to the Royalists. The Prefect of Ain deposed that when he had told Ney that Swiss troops were on the march to defend the King, he had replied that if foreign troops intervened, French troops would support Napoleon to a man. The Marquis de Vaulchier said that Ney had deplored the ineffectual measures taken to stop Napoleon. General Grivel had no doubt of Ney's fidelity as late as 13 March and was shocked that no one had opposed the reading by Ney of Napoleon's proclamation to the troops. Another officer described the tremendous enthusiasm when it was read.

The bad start only made the Royalists more determined. Ney had given warning that he intended to appeal to Article XII but, with no longer any fear of allied intervention, nothing stood in their way.

Ney was firmly of the opinion that Article XII would save him, and it was an indication of his political immaturity that of the whole list of people considered by the Royalists to be guilty of treason, he was the only one who regarded the convention arranged by Davout as binding on Louis XVIII. His life depended on the famous Article but it was interpreted in one sense by Davout, the then Minister of War, and the plenipotentiaries who had signed it, but in another way by the Allies and the Government of Louis XVIII. There was obviously room for discussion but this was refused by those who were trying Ney, who dared not allow his counsel to use a means of defence which would have saved his life.

Davout claimed that, but for the Article, the French Army would have continued to fight, but the prosecution maintained that his interpretation was out of order. Ney protested in vain. 'I remained in France on the strength of it,' he said, and Louis XVIII, who owed his throne to the Convention, was too weak to oppose his family who were bent on vengeance.

With sympathy for Ney beginning to build up throughout France, the Royalists were in a hurry. Article XII had been arranged, they claimed, only between armies and not between governments. In fact, the French negotiators trying to arrange peace after Waterloo had been instructed to yield on any article of the Convention but this one, and nothing had been said to make them suspect that there was more

than one way of interpreting the words which to them seemed a guarantee. What Wellington had not told them was that he intended the Article to be binding with England, Prussia and Austria until Louis's return, but not to be binding
on Louis, and he had felt it was the only way to come to a quick agreement and prevent the impatient and vengeful Blücher attacking Paris.

It made no difference. Although Louis had made use of the agreement on one occasion, the interpretation put on the article by Ney's accusers was the only one that was allowed. In secret session the Peers decided there must be no further mention of Article XII and from then on Ney's trial became a travesty of justice.

Why, Ney's counsel asked, out of all the mass of defectors, should Ney stand isolated from the rest? And in a last desperate attempt to save the Marshal, he suggested that since, under the Treaty, Saarlouis, where Ney had been born, was no longer French, then Ney himself was no longer a Frenchman. But Ney would have none of this. He jumped up and, in that great voice of his which had rallied troops through the thunder of battle, he roared, 'I am a Frenchman! I will die a Frenchman!'

By 5 p.m. on 7 December, the trial was over and the Chamber commenced its deliberations. At 11.30 p.m., the vote of the 161 peers was announced. By 107 to 47 Ney was found quilty of receiving Napoleon's emissaries; by unanimous vote (with one abstention) guilty of reading the proclamation to his troops and thus inciting them to mutiny and desertions, and of himself re-enlisting under Napoleon. 109 voted for the death sentence, seventeen for deportation, five abstaining.

Davout had said with withering scorn that no one could condemn Ney to death, not even Marmont. But Marmont did and with him were Marshals Victor, Kellerman, Pérignon and Sérurier, all men who had fought alongside Ney since the first campaigns of the Revolution. But none of them were men who had ever greatly distinguished themselves, and the Marshals had never been a band of brothers like Nelson's captains. They were quarrelsome and possessed every vice except cowardice, and none of the men who voted against Ney possessed the magic to inspire troops that the man they were condemning did. One peer, the young Duc de Broglié, refused to be borne along, claiming that Ney had been carried away by what was happening around him. He noticed the atmosphere of intimidation and claimed that the determination of those peers who wanted Ney punished influenced those who were uncertain, and that he himself had required considerable courage to disagree.

Taken back to the Luxembourg Prison, Ney called for dinner and ate with a good appetite. Then, having smoked a cigar, he lay down on his bed fully dressed and fell into a sleep that was not that of a tormented or exhausted prisoner but the normal quiet sleep of a healthy man.

There was still time for Louis to commute the death sentence to one of deportation, but he was still unable to withstand the demands of his family, of whom the Duc de Berry and the Duchesse d'Angoulême, the sole survivor of the Royal family imprisoned in the Temple during the Terror, were the most implacable. It was said that if only it had been generally known what Ney had done during the retreat from Moscow the French people would have *forced* a pardon, but Napoleon's propaganda had glossed over the disaster and only the army knew the truth of that, while Ney's enemies were totally unaware because they had been living safely in exile during the great years of France's glory.

At 4 a.m., Ney was awakened by the arrival of his wife and children. Aglaé was in a distressed condition but Ney managed to calm her and begged her to leave him. She still had not given up hope but Ney knew there was none and he was as calm as he had always been in Russia. Left alone with his guards, he walked up and down until one of the guards suggested fetching a priest.

The priest remained with Ney for some time, promising to return for the last moments. When he came, Ney, who had dressed himself neatly in blue coat and black breeches, helped him into the fiacre.

'Get in first, Father,' he said. 'I shall be above sooner than you.'

They rode to the Closérie des Lilas near the Observatory in the Luxembourg Gardens. Fearing an attempt at a rescue, the Government had changed the place of execution at the last moment. Embracing his confessor, Ney gave him his snuff box to be handed to his wife, and handed out a few pieces of gold he had in his pocket to be given to the poor.

A captain indicated where he should stand and Ney moved with a brisk step to the spot. Taking off his hat, he began a protest against his condemnation but as the officer in command of the firing squad made ready to give the signal to fire, he called out loudly, 'Comrades, straight to the heart, fire!' As he repeated the words, the officer gave the signal and at 9.20 a.m. Ney fell dead. As Rochechouart said, 'That was a wonderful lesson in how to die.'

The body was taken to the Hospice de la Maternité where many distinguished people came to look at it. To a group of Englishmen who appeared, an old soldier said grimly, 'You did not look on him so calmly at Waterloo.' On 8 December, the body was taken to the cemetery of Père Lachaise where Ney now lies buried, surrounded by his fellow Marshals.

Despite the hatred of the émigrés, as Ségur's account of the retreat from Moscow became known, there was a change in public opinion. Yet still the Court and family of Louis could not hold their tongues, and at a dinner party when they were vilifying Ney in their usual manner, a Russian soldier spoke up for him. 'I don't know where you gentlemen were in 1812,' he said, 'but I can see you were not with the French Army.'

The wall against which Ney was shot became a shrine and in 1853, his faults forgotten and only his courage remembered, a statue to him was unveiled close to the spot where

67

he died. The bravest of men, he had been a victim of circumstances and the vengeance of lesser men than himself.

A strange footnote to Ney's story came with the arrival in North Carolina in 1819 of a ruddy-faced man of about fifty years of age. He said he was a French refugee and that his name was Peter Stuart Ney. There was some mystery about him and, when questioned, he said he was Marshal Ney and that the execution had been faked. There was some reason to believe it might be so. He had scars where Ney had received his wounds and because both Ney and Wellington were Freemasons it was assumed that Wellington had interceded on his behalf. Peter Stuart Ney became a schoolmaster and taught until his death in 1846, but he was an excellent horseman, a first-class shot, and was always ready to discuss military matters.

His pupils were convinced he was the Marshal and he explained that the French Government had granted him his life in return for exile and that the firing squad had used blank ammunition, while he had been warned to fall as though dead. Even on his death bed, he continued to claim to be the Marshal. The story was taken so seriously that an American historian in 1886 asked the French Government to clear up the mystery. Their negative answer failed to end the matter, and in 1895 a book was published by a clergyman who had been a soldier in the Confederate Army during the American Civil War. He claimed that he had compared the schoolmaster's writing with that of the Marshal and was completely convinced that the exile was Marshal Ney. Doubts regarding his true identity persist to the present day but whoever Peter Stuart Ney was, he was not the Prince of the Moscowa. *That* Ney died under the wall of the Luxembourg in December 1815.

Among those who later deeply regretted his shameful death was the Duchesse d'Angoulême. Her father, mother and brother had died during the Revolution and she was understandably frigid toward the Bonapartists, but when she was given a copy of Ségur's account of the Russian campaign and she read of Ney's example to the rearguard, she put it down with tears in her eyes. 'If only we had known,' she said.

France was always inclined, after a period of warfare, to vent her spite for a defeat on her soldiers. The courts martial of two other French Marshals who, like Ney, became objects of hatred to their countrymen further illustrate this.

Like Ney, François-Achille Bazaine lived through difficult times. Born in 1811 under the first Napoleon, he was a child during the return of the Bourbons and was just entering manhood and about to join the army when they were deposed by the revolution of 1830 – to be replaced by the Orléanist branch of the royal family, who were removed in their turn in 1848 by another revolution. In 1851, a nephew of the Great Napoleon, elected president of the Second Republic, made himself Emperor with the title of Napoleon III, the man who was deemed to be Napoleon II, the Great Napoleon's son, having died young. Before his career as a soldier ended, however, Bazaine was once more living in a Republic.

Like Ney, he began his military life as a private soldier. He served in Algeria and in four years became a Lieutenant with the Cross of the Legion of Honour. In 1839 he was a Captain and a few years later a Brigadier-General. He distinguished himself in the Crimean War and was made Governor of Sebastopol after its capture. Gaining fresh laurels in Italy in 1859, when Napoleon III tried to impose the Archduke Maximilian of Austria as Emperor on the Mexican people, Bazaine was in command. He was accused there of mixing political and personal interests with his generalship and, on returning to France in 1867, was coolly received by Napoleon. As an ex-private soldier, he had always been regarded with some contempt by his better-educated, fellow senior officers who had passed through St Cyr or the École Polytechnique and had not served in the ranks, but, nevertheless he was created a Marshal and in 1870, on the outbreak of the Franco-Prussian War, was given command of the 3rd Corps. When Napoleon III proved less able as a soldier than his famous uncle, Bazaine was given the Army of the Rhine.

But Napoleon III's Marshals were not the Marshals of Napoleon I, the French Army was poorly trained and Bazaine was never really of the quality of a Marshal, anyway, and always behaved in battle more like a brigadier. After a series of French defeats, he could think of nothing better to do than retreat to Metz where he allowed himself to be besieged. Marshal MacMahon's attempt to relieve him ended in the French disaster at Sedan, and a series of obscure negotiations at Metz resulted in Bazaine surrendering the city with 140,000 men, thus freeing the German besiegers to crush the great effort that was being made to raise the siege of Paris.

After their defeat, the French went through a period of humiliation and bitterness. It was always a French habit to claim they were betrayed and nail their fallen heroes to a cross and in their anger and despair, they sought a scapegoat. Napoleon III could be blamed for the surrender at Sedan; the Communards for the surrender of Paris; it needed only Bazaine to be found guilty for Metz and France felt she could hold her head up again.

In 1873 Bazaine was court martialled for dereliction of duty, and a group of undistinguished soldiers was found to sit in judgement, headed by a royal prince of no military experience. Throughout the trial Bazaine maintained that the Government of National Defence, which had taken over when Napoleon III was captured at Sedan, had never established relations with him and his chances of being acquitted seemed good. But he had made enemies, and it was a consolation to many well-connected French leaders who had not come out of the war with much honour to blame the ex-private – even for MacMahon's defeat at Sedan – because it left unimpaired their own military reputations.

There were a lot of high-flown sentiments from both accusers and judges, with the other Marshals entering the witness box to give each other warm testimonials at Bazaine's expense. The prosecution's final speech made no mention of the defeat at Wörth of the well-connected MacMahon and gracefully explained his savaging by the Germans at Sedan by suggesting he had been moved only by his eagerness to relieve Bazaine. Bazaine had never enjoyed the aura of heroism that surrounded Ney but, like Ney, he was the victim of the shortcomings of his own country and the moral cowardice of his fellow generals.

The court returned a verdict of guilty and Bazaine was condemned to death, the sentence commuted later to imprisonment for twenty years. The final decision, ironically enough, was left to MacMahon, who had just become President of France. Bazaine was taken to the Ile St Marguérite, near Cannes, but, despite his age of sixty-three and his considerable bulk, he escaped by descending from the high walls of his prison on the end of a home-made rope to a boat in which was waiting his wife, a Mexican girl he had married at the age of fifty-four. He landed at Genoa and spent his last years in Madrid, where he died in 1888, aged seventy-seven.

Marshal Henri Philippe Benoni Omer Joseph Pétain, the man who held Verdun against all the German onslaughts in 1915 and 1916 and gave the French Army back its dignity after its mutinies in 1917, was also tried on a charge of treason. Despite Verdun, Pétain, who became a Marshal in 1918, was always inclined to defeatism. Like Ney, like Bazaine, he had grown up in very difficult times, when France was never certain of the road it should take. Born under the Emperor Napoleon III, he was old enough to see and understand the disasters of 1870, and the Third Republic that followed, always unstable, and Pétain reached manhood in an atmosphere of defeat, ever-changing governments, and political and financial scandal.

It was on Pétain that fell the responsibility for asking

Hitler for an armistice after the disastrous campaign of 1940, and though the Germans were always the controlling force, he became head of the French Government. By the end of the war, his name was spoken with detestation, though he always claimed he had acted in the best interests of his country.

At the age of eighty-seven, when the allied invasion took place in 1944, he appealed to the French not to be involved and was taken to Germany by the retreating Wehrmacht, returning voluntarily to France in 1945. Once again, France had been humiliated by its leaders and cried out for a scapegoat. The finger pointed immediately to Pétain and at his trial he was sentenced to death and spent the rest of his life as a prisoner on the Ile d'Yeu off the Vendéan coast.

Despite their position, the Marshals of France had often failed to live up to the high regard to which their rank entitled them. When asked at Waterloo if he expected any of the French to change sides, Wellington had retorted 'No,' adding, 'We might pick up a Marshal or two, but nothing worth a damn.'

Captain Carey

The court martial of Jaheel Brenton Carey in 1879 was one which divided England. By some, Carey was execrated as a coward who had panicked and left the patrol he had been leading when it had been surprised by a party of Zulus in South Africa. By others he was considered to be a martyr to staff mismanagement who had been singularly unlucky in that one of the three men who had been lost in the ambush had been the heir to a throne. There had been surprise ambushes of patrols in every war, but the importance of one of the victims in Carey's case raised the question to a point of importance when it was discussed again and again in the Press. It was the biggest story of 1879 and roused such a fury in France, English travellers on the Continent had to bolt for the safety of the Channel ports.

Born in 1847 in Leicester, Jaheel Brenton Carey was the son of a Devon clergyman and had been named after an ancestor of his mother, one of Nelson's sailors who had won a baronetcy for distinguished service. He was educated in France and passed through Sandhurst before receiving a free commission – it was still the days of purchased commissions – in the 3rd West India Regiment, a unit regarded as a notch rather below a regiment of regular infantry, but nevertheless a unit of the British Army. In 1867, after service in West Africa, he accompanied an expedition to Honduras which had become a British colony only five years before. There, the Mayan tribes from the Yucatan were in the habit of appearing to raid and kill, and they were ravaging the country above Corozal. It fell to Carey to go forward with another officer as escort to a civil official trying to arrange a parley, but they were soon surrounded and, as the official raised his hand in a gesture of peace, the Indians surged forward and dragged him from the saddle. The glory went out of soldiering for Carey as he saw the official hacked to death, then, as the two officers managed to make their escape, he found himself taking part in a wild stampede for safety.

Ordered back to Jamaica to give evidence in the court of enquiry which followed, he married Annie Isabella Vine in 1869. Then returning to England in 1870, he took advantage of being on half pay to serve with an English ambulance in France during the Franco-Prussian War. Near Longueville, under fire from Prussian batteries, the Englishman chanced across the French Emperor, Napoleon III, a thin, weary, defeated figure. By his side was a slight young officer, little more than a boy, whom Carey recognised as the Emperor's son, Louis, the heir to the Imperial Throne. It was not to be the last time they would meet.

During this war, Carey was captured three times by the Germans but was always released when it was realised that he and his friends succoured German as well as French wounded. He went through the siege of Paris and when he left at the end of January 1871, he took with him a decoration for his services. In April, having gained a first class certificate from the School of Musketry, he was posted to the 81st Foot, but in 1873 transferred to the 98th Foot and after further service in the West Indies, applied for the Staff College, which he entered in 1877.

Tall, well-built and good looking, cursed with the name Jaheel, without a public school background, and with a wealth of Gallic gestures springing from his French upbringing which left him curiously un-English, at Sandhurst Carey had to endure more than the normal amount of ragging. But he was not unpopular with his fellow officers, though they disliked his ostentatious piety and his public adulation of his mother, wife and two young daughters, which seemed excessive even in that age of heavy sentimentality.

When he left Staff College for leave at the end of 1878 he heard rumours that there was a war brewing against the Zulus in South Africa. The High Commissioner there, convinced that the powerful Zulu nation should be curbed, imposed impossible conditions on them and at the beginning of 1879, Britain went to war. Preparations had been in hand for some time in Natal. The Army, divided into five columns, was to march to the Zulu capital, Ulundi, and command was given to Lord Chelmsford. Chelmsford had commenced his career in the Rifle Brigade, had served in the Crimea, both as a regimental officer and on the staff, and in the last stages of the Indian Mutiny, before moving on to a post on Sir Robert Napier's staff in the Abyssinian campaign. He was far from enthusiastic about the war in the Eastern Cape.

His campaign started with a disaster. While he was reconnoitring the ground for a move forward by the strongest of his columns, due to the mistakes of subordinates, 800 British and an equal number of native troops in camp at Isandhlwana were surprised and massacred by 20,000 Zulus. It was only redeemed by the magnificent defence of Rorke's Drift by a handful of men against overwhelming numbers. When the news reached England it was decided to send out reinforcements and with them went Carey – and Louis, the French Prince Imperial, the youth on whom the Napoleonists' dream of a return to the Empire rested.

Napoleon Eugène Louis was twenty-three years old and before he was six hours old he had been draped with the ribbon of the Legion of Honour. Known as Lou-Lou, he was heavily indulged by his father who saw in him the hopes of the Napoleonic dynasty. Inevitably, to follow in the foot-steps of his great-uncle, Napoleon, he had to be a soldier and he was enrolled as a Grenadier of the Guard at birth, given the Grand Cross of the Legion of Honour at two days old, and commissioned at nine months. He attended his first military review, mounted, before he could walk, so that he became extrovert, daring and generous, always living in a dream of future military glory.

When the war with Prussia came in 1870, he accompanied his father to the army on the frontier and rode through the initial action at Saarbrücken where 60,000 Frenchmen dislodged 1000 Prussians and then nervously retired again. The sight of battle thrilled the boy but almost immediately the unprepared, badly-led French Army began to crumble and Louis saw his world break apart as the French went down to defeat. While he was being escorted to safety in Belgium, his father was captured at Sedan and Louis returned to his mother, the Empress Eugénie, in England, where she had been obliged to flee when the Empire had collapsed.

In England, he went to the Royal Military Academy at Woolwich – the Shop, the place where artillery and engineering officers received their training. He was accepted as an equal by the other cadets and, though he enjoyed showing off, he wasn't a boaster. His partisan views on Waterloo naturally caused problems and even disrupted classes, but he graduated in 1875, first in riding, first in fencing, and seventh overall. He might have come fourth but he refused to take an unfair advantage by sitting for the examination in French. In fact, he sat unofficially and, to his surprise, was beaten by an English cadet. Claiming he came from a family of gunners, he opted for the artillery. He was popular in England and always welcomed as a guest at weekend parties. But, without a political future, he felt life was hollow, and when the news came of Isandhlwana and reinforcements were mustered, he immediately begged the Duke of Cambridge, Queen Victoria's cousin and Commander-in-Chief of the British Army, to be allowed to go. As a Napoleon, he felt he could never face his countrymen without experience in battle.

Disraeli disliked the idea but in the end Eugénie enlisted the aid of the Queen, and it was decided that Louis should go to Zululand as a 'spectator'. Not for a moment did anyone think there was any risk involved.

The French weren't happy. To the Napoleonists, to whom Louis was already Napoleon IV, he was risking his valuable neck. To the rest he was serving as a rankless member of the army of the hated British.

Arriving in Durban, his first need was for a horse and he managed to persuade the owner of a splendid grey, over fifteen hands and known as Percy, to sell to him. The owner wasn't very willing and told Louis's agent to inform his master that the horse was inclined to be skittish and had a hard mouth. Soon afterwards, Louis faced Chelmsford who, to say the least, didn't fancy the idea of his presence at all. He had little time to spare for a French Prince and knew perfectly well he couldn't be given a job with a battery, the one job he wanted. For safety he took him on his personal staff.

Having withdrawn to reorganise after Isandhlwana, Chelmsford started his second invasion of Zululand in April. Behind the confidence given by the reinforcements there was a certain nervousness. The Zulus had proved themselves relentless and ruthless enemies and their habit of mutilating the dead meant that while the army *en masse* felt it could handle them, individual patrols were always uneasy affairs because of the Zulus' unpleasant habit of appearing suddenly out of the long grass with their murderous assegais.

The man responsible for supplies and transport was Colonel Richard Harrison, Royal Engineers, Acting Quartermaster-General, a stolid, experienced officer who had served in the Indian Mutiny and in China. One of his duties was to find a suitable route forward but, unfortunately, he had no staff beyond a single lance-corporal and was obliged to use the Special Service Officers unattached to regiments who were available for odd jobs. Those who had arrived for the invasion of Zululand in January 1879, became known as aasvogels, or vultures, because they had eaten up all the good assignments. Those who arrived with the

77

reinforcements in April to make good the losses after Isandhlwana were known as boomvogels because it was said they were 'up a tree', and on the whole they were assigned to transport duties.

After fourteen years in the army, Carey was well suited for staff duties and he became a boomvogel but, even with his assignment, Harrison's staff was still weak and Chelmsford realised he had found a suitable place for the Prince Imperial. The appointment would remove him from Chelmford's back and place him under supervision in a job that would entail a minimum amount of risk. Louis threw himself into the work with an infectious enthusiasm, glorying in roughing it and willing to volunteer for anything.

With Major Redvers Buller (later General Sir Redvers Buller) trying to find a way forward, Harrison decided to accompany him on the next foray, for which 200 men were to be supplied as an escort. Louis asked to go and Chelmsford decided that, with an escort of that size, there was no danger. South Africa and Zululand is magnificent country for horsemen and Louis, a splendid rider, was delighted. But he was still immature and, as a foreigner with no special responsibilities, was difficult to control. When a group of Zulu scouts were seen ahead, he charged after them, sword in hand, looking for a straggler to engage. Troopers were sent after him, but before they could catch up with him, he had spotted another lone Zulu.

Buller, a normally impassive man, was disgusted. They were, he said, on a patrol, not a Zulu hunt, and he knew that if Louis became involved with a large force of Zulus he would draw the others in after him. He determined to get rid of him as soon as possible and, when he categorically refused to assume responsibility for him, Harrison ordered the Prince back to camp where a fortification had been built and, to Louis's delight, named Fort Napoleon. Louis managed to persuade Chelmsford to intercede and when Harrison started forward again, Louis was with him once more.

Although Harrison was the senior officer, the man in practical control was Commandant Bettington, an Irregular of the Natal Horse, a New Zealander who startled Louis because he disdained the use of swords and carried only a revolver and a riding crop. His men were armed with Martini-Henry carbines which, while capable of a hot fire on foot, since they had no safety catch were habitually carried empty and were difficult to use mounted or in an emergency. Nevertheless, Louis managed to be involved in a few exciting incidents and behaved well under fire. That he was being indulged was obvious from the fact that kopjes and trenches continued to be named after him.

By this time, however, Chelmsford had received Buller's complaint and he ordered Harrison to keep Louis in camp at all times unless he was accompanied by a strong escort. A French journalist by the name of Deléage, who admired Louis, berated the English officers he met for their indifference to the value of a Prince Imperial. To his surprise, they agreed with him, and one of them even came after him to discuss Louis in fluent French. This was Carey, whom Deléage found most un-English. Carey had become friendly with Louis and was an admirer of his ardent spirits.

On Sunday, 1 June, orders called for the cavalry to scout ahead and choose a campsite for the following day, and Louis requested permission to go with them to make sketches beyond the projected site of the new camp. Harrison decided that, since the ground had been pronounced free of Zulus and that Louis would be all the time virtually in sight of the main column, there could be no harm. He insisted, however, on an escort of at least six of Bettington's experienced troopers and six native troopers who were quick at spotting movement. Carey asked to accompany the Prince. Harrison didn't like the idea but Louis's sketches were by no means the best and, thinking Carey might supervise them, he gave in. He was under the impression that Louis had arranged for an escort under an officer whom he assumed would be Bettington, and that Carey was simply to accompany the party.

The next morning six troopers reported to the staff tent. The six Basutus who should also have turned up failed to do so, and orders were left for them to follow. There was no officer because the cavalry Brigade-Major had not provided one, thinking that, since Carey was present, everything would be satisfactory. As the group left, they passed Harrison, who assumed that Carey had replaced Bettington. As the two groups went their separate ways, an officer called a warning to Louis, and he shouted back, 'Carey will take good care that nothing happens to me.' Carey was still smarting under the jibes of fellow officers who had been teasing him about the size of an escort he had demanded for an earlier patrol which had proved quite safe.

At noon the party, with a Zulu guide and with Louis's terrier trotting behind, reached the end of a ridge near Itelezi Hill, then Louis decided to head for a deserted kraal a mile or two ahead where he said they would find fuel to make fires to boil their coffee. Carey disagreed because the kraal stood near a deep donga and was surrounded on three sides by tall grass. But Louis over-ruled him. Reaching the kraal during the afternoon, they noticed the huts showed signs of recent occupation.

Off-saddling and knee-haltering the horses, they made a fire and began to boil coffee. Searching the huts, the men found freshly-chewed sugar cane and a mound of warm ashes, and one of them, noticing three native dogs slinking around, observed that where there were dogs there must be men. But the two officers were stretched on the ground by this time, at their ease. Neither of them had bothered to perform the first essential – scouting the vicinity or posting a look-out. The flattering friendship of the Prince seems to have banished all Carey's commonsense, experience and training.

At 3.30 p.m. Carey suggested re-saddling. Louis wanted another ten minutes but just then the guide reported that he had seen a Zulu on a nearby rise. Carey could not understand what was being said and one of the troopers, Corporal

80

Grubb, a man with sixteen years in the Royal Artillery and a decade of farming in Natal behind him, who spoke fluent Zulu, interpreted. Louis ordered the men to collect the horses but they had scattered in grazing and it was another ten minutes before they were all saddled. Louis said, 'Prepare to mount!' then, as either Louis or Carey shouted 'Mount!' the command was lost in an earsplitting volley from the grass a few yards away, frightening the horses and stampeding the men. Forty Zulus burst from the grass screaming '*uSuthu!*' and the panic was complete.

Doubtless in Carey's mind was the horror of the killing and stampede he had witnessed in Honduras, and still fresh in the memory of everyone was the horror of the hundreds of mutilated corpses that had been found among the waggons and tents on the scene of the massacre at Isandhlwana.

The horses carried the frightened men out of the donga but one of them, Rogers, lost his horse and, as he dodged into the huts to shelter, he was skewered by an assegai. Corporal Grubb had mounted but was far from secure in the saddle. Trooper Le Tocq, a Channel Islander, managed to mount his frightened horse but in doing so he dropped his carbine. He managed to retrieve it and flung himself belly-down across the saddle as the horse bounded away. A third man, Trooper Abel, was shot in the back and fell from his horse. As Le Tocq, the Channel Islander, galloped past the Prince he called out in French. 'Dépêchez-vous, Votre Altesse, s'il vous plaît!' he yelled.

But Louis had been unable to mount. His foot had been raised as the command to mount was given, but few horses will stand still when other horses are galloping and the skittish Percy shied violently and bolted. Only his grip on the saddle holster saved Louis from a fall but he could neither get his foot in the swinging stirrup nor slow the horse. For over a hundred yards, he clung on but then the holster collapsed under his grip. To a rider of Louis's skill, it wasn't a disaster and he gathered himself to vault into the saddle, a

81

showy trick he had often performed but, as he did so, the holster gave way completely and Louis fell. As Le Tocq passed Grubb, he shouted, 'Stick firm to your horse, boy, and put in the spurs! The Prince is down!'

As he had fallen under his mount, Louis's right arm had been trampled on and now, as he rose to his feet, he found he was alone.

He groped for his sword, which had once been owned by the Great Napoleon, but it had slipped from the scabbard. Drawing his revolver with his left hand, he ran down the donga, but the Zulus caught him and, as he turned at bay, a man called Langabalele pierced his thigh with a thrown assegai. A second assegai struck his shoulder and the Zulus were on him. As he sank to a sitting position, there was a brief hacking fury then it was over.

The panic caused by the stampeding horses lasted until the riders were fifty yards from Louis. Nobody knew what was happening and no one was in a position to give commands. Carey reined in, in a dilemma. Neither he nor Louis had stopped to help Rogers or Abel, if indeed they had seen them fall, and he *had* seen Louis moving away from the kraal; although not mounted, it had looked as though he was about to mount. The conduct of all of them had been less than heroic, but the situation was of the sort that could happen to any group of men suddenly surprised, and in Zululand often had. As they drew together from widely separate points, a riderless Percy appeared. There was no sign of Louis, the Zulu guide, or of the two missing troopers. With an awful certainty Carey knew they were dead.

Carey carried a sword and a revolver but the four men with him had only three carbines between them because Grubb had dropped his as he had regained his seat on his plunging horse, and, shrinking from the idea of riding back to face an unknown number of Zulus, Carey realised he could do nothing but try to rescue the living. As they rode away, Corporal Grubb riding the Prince's horse, Carey was horribly aware of the mistakes that had been made – the inadequate size of the escort and the failure to scout the ground or post a look-out. His soul shuddered at what he would have to face.

As they neared the camp, they saw a column of riders approaching, led by two officers, and changed direction towards them at a gallop, Carey riding ahead of his men to give a warning. Of all the men in Africa, it was Carey's misfortune that the ones he met at that moment were Brigadier-General Sir Evelyn Wood and Colonel Redvers Buller, both men of fearsome courage. Wood already held the VC and Buller was to win it soon afterwards. What they are supposed to have said is based on the words of their escort who heard it.

As Carey's group approached, Buller observed to the man alongside him that they were riding as if the Zulus were after them.

'Whatever is the matter with you?' he asked sharply as the group reined in.

'The Prince Imperial is killed,' Carey said.

'Where? Where is his body?'

Carey pointed behind him to a hill some three miles away. Through his glasses, Buller could see a party of Zulus leading three horses.

'Where are your men, sir?' he demanded. 'How many did you lose?'

Carey still seemed to be in shock. 'They're behind me,' he said. 'I don't know.'

'You ought to be shot,' Buller snapped. 'And I hope you will be! I could shoot you myself.'

As General Wood rode up, he asked for the Prince, and Buller said he had been killed. Wood turned to Carey. 'Is that the case?' he asked, and when Carey said it was, Wood snapped, 'Then, sir, what are you doing here?'

But neither Buller nor Wood could see any sense in returning to the donga in the failing light and Carey was ordered on to the camp. He was greeted cheerfully at first but his announcement about the Prince shocked his listeners to silence. The stunned Harrison informed Chelmsford who couldn't believe the news at first. Cancelling the move to the next campsite, he ordered a major force to make a search at daybreak. Carey was left white and trembling, slumped at his desk with his head buried in his arms. During the night, he bared his soul in a letter to his wife.

'I am a ruined man, I fear,' were almost his first words, but he claimed he could not have done anything other than what he did. He pointed out that, having been laughed at for his cautiousness, he had grown reckless and would have gone on the patrol with only two men. 'No doubt they will say I should have remained by him,' he went on, 'but I had no idea he was wounded and thought he was after me . . . I was such a fool to stop in that camp; I feel it now, though at the time I did not see it.'

The searchers the next morning found Abel near the kraal, with Rogers propped up near him. Both were naked with their bellies ripped open. Louis lay on his back, also naked. There were no less than seventeen separate wounds on the body, at least two of them mortal and all were in front, showing he had died facing his enemies. The fingers of his right hand clutched a fistful of Zulu hair but, though the Zulus had slashed at his belly as they always did, they had barely grazed the skin. His terrier, also speared, lay close by. He was carried from the donga on a stretcher made from four of the lances carried by men of the 17th Lancers.

There was a funeral service, the first of many to come. Louis had been wrapped in the Union Jack and strapped to a gun barrel and the entire force turned out to pay their respects. That night the body was embalmed as well as could be under the circumstances and the following day started on its way back to Durban.

The news shocked England, more even than Isandhlwana, but in France the storm burst in all its fury. Alive, Louis had been a threat to the Republican Government; dead, he was a tragic and romantic figure. Anglophobia burst out in a frenzied rage and travelling Englishmen bolted for the

Channel ports while English firms shuttered their windows. When the body reached England it was found that the improvised embalming had not worked and the ravaged face was unrecognisable, while some officious ass sent Louis's uniform to his mother so that she was faced with her son's clothing, slashed, muddied and smeared with blood.

Meanwhile Carey was being blamed by his fellow Regular officers for what they considered a stain on their honour. The Irregular officers, used to campaigning in South Africa, took the more realistic view that when a small party was surprised by Zulus, flight was the only sensible course. There was also a feeling that Harrison had not taken as much care with the patrol as he might have done.

Because of the rumours that were flying about and the suggestion of faint-heartedness, Carey requested a court of enquiry. On 11 June, he was suspended from duty and the court recommended a court martial which met the following day. The charge was one of misbehaviour before the enemy, and of galloping away when surprised by the Zulus, without attempting to defend the Prince or rally the escort.

In evidence, the experienced Corporal Grubb said he had not thought the precautions taken for safety at the kraal were sufficient. At the moment of flight, he said, Carey led, and he claimed that no orders were given about rallying or firing on the Zulus. It was he, Grubb, who had beckoned the fleeing riders to stop and take stock. Nevertheless, he said that if they had hesitated at the kraal every man would have been killed, and he felt that any man falling from his horse would have had no chance. He had no idea who was in command of the patrol.

Sergeant Robert Willis also admitted that no attempt had been made to help the Prince, but he wasn't surprised and didn't think any rescue could have been made, though he felt they might have rallied 200 yards from the donga. He had thought the Prince was in command.

Colonel Harrison admitted that he had given no orders to

Carey to command the escort but that, according to Queen's Regulations, the senior combatant officer, Carey, would normally be in command. He was glad Carey had volunteered as he felt he could look after the Prince. If Carey had not gone he would have directed another staff officer to go. Later, recalled by Carey, he said he regarded the Prince as a civilian attached to the staff and was not aware that he had any status in the British Army. Bettington said the four survivors of the escort were among his best men.

Carey claimed that the charge against him could only be interpreted as a charge of cowardice. The escort, he insisted, had never been placed under his command and he had believed he was merely accompanying the Prince. He said that bolting from the kraal as they had when attacked was the only sensible thing to do and, having seen the Prince with his foot in the air about to place it in the stirrup when the first shots were fired, he reasonably assumed he had mounted. He pointed out the impossibility of rallying in the kraal with unloaded carbines, no swords and bolting horses. There had been no other course open to them, he claimed, but to flee, especially since the horses were almost out of control.

The patrol, he went on, had been led by the Prince while he had been present only to correct Louis's sketches. The panic, he said, was common to every man present but he himself had remained calm and attempted to guide the rout. Louis, he claimed, had insisted on the patrol moving out, although half the escort had failed to turn up; it was Louis who had chosen the resting place; and Louis who had failed to post a look-out.

Yet Louis had held neither rank nor position in the British Army while Carey was a commissioned officer with full authority, though it had to be admitted – and the defence made sure it was – that Louis had habitually worn the uniform of an officer in the Royal Artillery and had acted and been treated as if he were an officer. Louis, in fact, had always been only a boy playing at soldiers, yet everybody had let him play, and though he had not held official command of the patrol, he had held de facto command because of his position, and had given orders which Carey, influenced by his growing friendship, had permitted without a murmur. It was also pointed out that Harrison had not specifically charged Carey with command and, as he had met the patrol leaving camp, had even said something about not interfering with the Prince's plans.

Captain Brander, prosecuting, in his summing up, insisted, however, that Carey could not evade the responsibility of the command on the grounds that the Prince had no status in the British Army; and that Colonel Harrison had charged him specifically with looking after the Prince. Carey, he claimed, far from doing all he could to rescue the Prince, had done nothing at all. In fact, he had been the first man away after the Zulus' volley and gave no orders to rally or fire, although the trooper, Le Tocq, had said it might have been possible. Carey, he insisted, could take no credit for saving *any* of the escort because it had been a clear case of every man for himself. Though the Prince had managed to run two hundred and fifty yards after the vanishing horsemen, he had been left to his death. Not a shot had been fired in his defence, though it was clearly Carey's duty to see he was mounted and safe.

The court closed to consider its findings and Carey's arguments were rejected at once. His readiness to shift the blame to Louis acted against him and when the court reopened it was to take formal evidence of Carey's service, the usual sign that a verdict of guilty had been returned. However, the findings could not be published until they had been reviewed, and Carey was sent home under arrest. He asked to be allowed to remain and fight until the war ended but his request was refused. Although the verdict had not been published and could not be until the case had been reviewed, Carey knew he had been found guilty, and in fact, Chelmsford had given the only sentence that would cleanse the slate: Carey was to be cashiered.

By this time a number of writers had rushed into print, and in England much of the Press sprang to Carey's defence. The blame, they said, must lie with Harrison, Chelmsford, or the Duke of Cambridge, who had let Louis go to Africa. The *United Services Gazette* condemned Carey, but the *Army and Navy Gazette*, though it admitted that as the only commissioned British officer present Carey ought to have shown more coolness and brought up the rear instead of leading the flight, was more sympathetic. A writer in its columns signing himself 'A soldier' wrote 'Although ... Captain Carey lost a most brilliant chance of distinguishing himself, I cannot see why he should be held responsible for an occurrence which ... is bound to happen in every campaign, for the simple reason that the victim was in this case a person of rank ... To condemn a man, as the civilian Press seems disposed to do, because he got away and a brother-officer had the bad luck to be killed in a surprise, appears to be monstrous and adds a new danger to the profession of a soldier.'

In the same journal a little later, a writer who signed himself 'A Sergeant', really got to the crux of the matter. 'If the Prince had got away safe,' he wrote, 'it would have been considered a fortunate affair, even if all the remainder (Lieutenant Carey included) had perished. As, however, it was as it happened ... it is deemed necessary to hang someone for it, and the scapegoat fixed upon is Lieutenant Carey.'

There is a great deal of truth in the Sergeant's comments. In all wars, groups of men are surprised and save their lives by bolting, and the old adage about running away to fight another day is often very apt. No fuss was raised about other instances of men being killed in Zulu ambushes and it was simply the Prince's rank that made this particular ambush important. The Italian newspaper, *Italie*, in a leading article, pointed out that competent military critics in England, Germany and Austria were unanimous in justifying Carey's conduct and continued, 'If the officer who fell had been an ordinary mortal, instead of being Prince Louis Napoleon, no one would have dreamed of blaming Carey.'

The sentence of the court martial had to be reviewed before it could be published and when Carey arrived in Plymouth in August – after the war had ended – although he knew he had been found guilty, he was still uncertain about his fate and, to his astonishment, his ship was met by a brass band and a deputation with a public address. Once ashore, led on by the sympathy he was being shown, he foolishly made himself available to any reporter who wanted to see him, always seeking to criticise the court martial and justify his actions.

While he was still aboard ship, the Assistant Adjutant-General at Portsmouth appeared and took Carey to his office ashore. There he had an interview with Prince Edward of Saxe-Weimar, the General commanding the Southern District, who was acting on instructions from the Duke of Cambridge.

A week later in the same office Carey was informed that he had been found guilty and sentenced to be cashiered. However, the court had recommended mercy on the grounds that Carey had not understood the position in which he stood with regard to Louis and had therefore failed to estimate correctly his responsibility. It had also drawn attention to, among other things, the smallness of the escort, the poor arms of the escort and the fact that the men with him were not regular soldiers accustomed to military discipline. Lord Chelmsford had added that he considered Carey not deficient in personal bravery but that he 'might have lost his head in a crisis'. An official despatch from the Horse Guards dated 16 August, advised him finally that the charge had been submitted to the Queen who had been advised that it had not been sustained by the evidence, and had decided not to confirm the proceedings, so that Carey was to be released from arrest and would rejoin his regiment for duty. The announcement also exonerated Chelmsford but said that Harrison's orders had not been explicit enough and that Carey's experience should have rectified the error.

It was a compromise and satisfied no one, except perhaps Carey. Gazetted Captain before the news of the tragedy had reached England, for some time he played the ill-used hero whose career had been saved only by the Press and public opinion. In fact, it had been saved by neither, but by Louis's mother, the Empress Eugénie. She had spurned recriminations and had appealed to Queen Victoria that no one should suffer for her son's death. Victoria had hesitated but had finally written to the reviewing authorities.

By then, however, Eugénie had read the frantic letter Carey had written home to his wife on the night of the tragedy. A friend had offered to collect a few details of her son's last days and had applied to Carey's wife who, without realising its importance, had sent the letter. It seemed to indicate that Carey had known all along that he was in command and in a way virtually admitted his guilt, but Eugénie was not vengeful and accepted it only as a plea for mercy from Annie Carey.

The public were still taking Carey's side. Harrison had cleared himself with the War Office and, in fact, came out of the campaign with distinction, but those who had wrongly blamed Chelmsford for Isandhlwana now wrongly blamed him for the death of the Prince Imperial. Aristocratic generals had not been popular since the Crimea and the rumour was that Carey was paying for the mistakes of his superiors.

Unwisely he began to court the Press, and his statements were sometimes in bad taste, especially when he suggested that it was his prayers to God that had caused the quashing of his sentence and his release from arrest. In September the *United Services Gazette* pointed out that two privates of the 8th Foot had been sentenced to five years penal servitude and dismissal with ignominy from the army for running from their posts in a similar sudden panic in Afghanistan. Refusing the recommendation for mercy, Sir Frederick

Haines had observed, 'They must regret they ran away in Afghanistan and not in Zululand. Had (they) taken flight ... there, they might have been sent under easy arrest to England ... had congratulatory addresses presented ... been interviewed by ... the Press, their likeness put in the illustrated papers and, after the announcement that their court martial proceedings had been quashed, have been played home in triumph by a volunteer band.' He ended up with a sentence of bitter sarcasm. 'It is said that there is a scheme on foot to get up a subscription ... to present Captain Carey with a sword. Would not a pair of spurs be a more appropriate compliment?'

Carey continued to try to justify himself, but his statements were often contradictory. He began to suggest that Louis was not only immature, but had presumed on his birth and been insubordinate, and he even wrote to Eugénie, and without being aware that she had seen his letter, suggested she receive him. He was fended off and asked if he would publicly disclaim some of the things he had said about Louis. Carey ignored the appeal.

The public continued to cheer the mention of his name, and he began to grow arrogant, taking the view that his character was stainless. The Empress remained aloof. To her Carey remained always the officer 'who had run away as fast as his horse could carry him, leaving behind a comrade and two men.' In the end he was informed that she considered the pursuit of his correspondence useless, and when he still persisted, she passed the letters to Queen Victoria who showed them to Disraeli. Reading them, the Queen felt surprised that Carey had got off so lightly, while Disraeli blamed the mismanagement of the court martial and observed that if their verdict had been sanctioned '... this mean wretch might have been transfigured into a hero or a martyr.'

The case continued to be argued. Some officers took the view that if Carey had kept his men together, faced about and opened fire on the Zulus the Prince might have been saved, and that it was only the stampede in terror that had

91

encouraged the Zulus to emerge from their hiding place. Nobody seemed to notice when they accused Carey of leaving the Prince to his fate that the Prince, like the others, had been leaving to *his* fate Trooper Rogers, who had lost his horse.

Carey rejoined his regiment, still championed by the *Army and Navy Gazette* and receiving sympathetic letters from serving soldiers. He went with the 98th to India and by 1882 was Senior Captain in his battalion. They were stationed at Karachi but, with malaria rife in 1881, it had been decided to relieve a three-company detachment at Hyderabad. In 1883 orders were received to move on to Quetta and on 21 February Carey was involved in the dismantling and packing of equipment when a sudden noise startled a horse which lashed out with its hind leg and caught him in the stomach. Put to bed he was given hot fomentations to relieve the pain and for the rest of the day lay with his knees drawn up in agony. The next morning he was no better and towards afternoon he lapsed into unconsciousness. The doctor said he had a ruptured intestine which had caused peritonitis. He died soon afterwards.

Perhaps Carey didn't end up as the pariah legend says he did. If he had, he must have been a tough-minded individual indeed to endure, as is suggested, having his fellow officers turn their backs on him whenever he entered a room. In fact, he was a highly-strung emotional man and, with a family who were comfortably off, had no need to tolerate such humiliation when he could simply have left the army. Yet it is true that the *Army and Navy Gazette*, which had always championed him, in its note on his death did refer to him being a 'victim of persecution'.

Carey's case was one of panic and this would have been acceptable if he had made some attempt to recover the situation. But he failed to do so. There had been a similar case in March 1879, when a convoy of twenty waggons and a company of the 80th Foot, which had been sent to escort it, had been caught at Myer's Drift on the Intombe River by a large force of Zulus.

The river was swollen by heavy rains and only two waggons had been able to cross, but Lieutenant H H Harwood was sent across to prepare for the crossing of the rest the following day. Virtually in sight of the garrison at Luneberg, Harwood decided against entrenching the two waggons and on both sides of the river the men turned in. In a fog at 5 a.m. the following morning, the whole valley was seen to be swarming with Zulus who surrounded the camp on the northern bank and butchered every single man. Harwood placed his thirty-four men under cover of a solitary waggon but their fire revealed their presence and several hundred Zulus crossed the river and began to attack.

Seeing his party was not strong enough to keep off the Zulus, Harwood ordered them to fall back on a farmhouse in their rear, then, mounting his horse, galloped off to Luneberg for help. Colour-Sergeant Anthony Booth, with only eleven men, moved in good order to a farmhouse two miles south of the river, keeping his group well in hand and holding off the Zulus with a skill that gained him the Victoria Cross.

On 20 February 1880, Harwood was tried by a general court martial at Pietermaritzburg, accused of abandoning his men while under attack and of having failed to take proper precautions for the safety of his camp. Harwood claimed he had taken every possible precaution but that it was not possible to form a laager with only two waggons. He was, he said, better prepared for the attack than the northern party which had more waggons and more men, and he had ridden for help because he was the only man with a horse.

The court found him not guilty and acquitted him, but Sir Garnet Wolseley, by this time Commander-in-Chief in Zululand in succession to Chelmsford, would have none of it. Unable to reverse the verdict, he let it be known what his feelings were on an officer who, under any pretext whatsoever, could desert his men while engaged with the enemy. 'The more helpless a position...' he said, 'the more it is his bounden duty to stay with them.' Because British officers had always done that, he said, the soldier had learned to feel that '... he can in the direst moment of danger look with implicit faith to his officer...'

The court martial verdict, he concluded, struck at the roots of this faith and he felt it necessary to mark officially his emphatic dissent. In England, the Duke of Cambridge so strongly approved of Wolseley's remarks, he ordered the findings and comments to be read at the head of every regiment in Her Majesty's service.

Wolseley's comments are particularly apt with regard to Carey, but it is perhaps ironic that the Duke of Cambridge had allowed himself to be led from the hard-fought field of Inkerman in the Crimea in 1854 with no more than a badly grazed arm, while his men remained behind to continue the fight and while other desperately wounded officers remained with their soldiers throughout. In fact, when conditions in the Crimea had worsened, he had even gone home, leaving his men to the mercy of the winter. Queen Victoria was said to have been very angry and when the Duke went to Sheffield to unveil a war memorial, he was greeted with cries of, 'Who ran away from the Crimea?' Perhaps he was hardly the man to sit in judgement of others.

Carey's case was the reverse of the usual order. He was not made the scapegoat for the action or lack of action of the staff, but the Press, who chose unwisely to champion him, tried hard to make the staff – or at least Harrison and Chelmsford – the scapegoats for Carey's moment of panic.

Nevertheless Carey *was* unlucky. Other men had been assegaied in ambushes when the Zulus had risen like spectres from the long grass, and other parties had been put to abrupt flight in which some of them had been lost. There were no court martials for Hlobane, which was an ambush on a grand scale. Rupert Lonsdale, who had ridden into the camp at Isandhlwana on a stumbling worn-out horse after a long ride and, finding it destroyed, had turned round in precipitate flight, was not accused of cowardice. There were also no courts martial for the men who fled precipitately from the massacre and none for other parties who had been put to abrupt flight in which some of them had been lost. Carey was unlucky in that his group had included an heir to a throne and that this heir had been among those who were lost.

Alfred Dreyfus

The Dreyfus court martial was less a court martial than a whole series of trials lasting over a period of years, which completely divided the French nation and brought down one government after another. The Dreyfus Affair was a case of bigotry and anti-Semitism triumphant, with one man sacrificed for the collective honour of one élitist group – the top echelons of the army. The whole world became interested and indignant, and in 1899, long before it was finished, an Australian newspaper commented, 'When the Dreyfus Case is ended ... there will be a relief to mankind all the world over.' The comment was true, because the Dreyfus Affair was that of a people acquiescing in a denial of justice for political or military expediency.

When the Affair started in 1894, France was already an unhappy country. Still suffering from the humiliation of the defeat by the Prussians in 1870, it was undergoing a depression with falling prices, unemployment and hunger, and a series of bad financial crashes which had hampered the Government. Some fifteen cabinets had fallen since 1881 but the new ones always seemed to contain the same faces, and the majority group in Parliament were the Republicans who had been in power since 1877. When the case ended the Party had split into a dozen minor factions and their power had waned, but so also had that of the ultra Right and the anti-Semitic groups, and the Socialists were beginning to flex their muscles.

Because there was the belief that a clerico-military plot lay behind it, the Affair also broke the power of the Catholic Church in France and crumbled the legendary élitism of the army. During its course there were constant changes of ministers – Ministers of War especially – coalitions fell, politicians compromised and adjusted their consciences, people refused to accept responsibility and there was a lot of loose talk about the Republic being in danger. There were cover-ups, lies, resignations by the dozen and almost all the major figures intimately connected with the Affair seemed to appear in one capacity or another before a court of some sort – courts of enquiry, civil courts, criminal courts, assize courts, appeal courts or courts martial – and almost everybody was accused of the falsification of documents.

There are many versions and many views of the case. Even those who supported Dreyfus fell into two camps, those who merely wanted justice and those who tried to make political capital out of injustice. The case became the plaything of politicians so that it becomes impossible to describe every twist and turn, and as one author concerned with the Affair says, the more the evidence is examined the less heroic – or less odious – the chief characters become.

The Affair passed through three phases, the first concerning only the handful of those who wanted the sentence revised. The second followed the trial of Emile Zola, the novelist, when the intellectuals became involved. The third was that of the professional politicians who behaved throughout with the opportunism of their kind. Whatever else is said, however, the working classes, the mobs who appeared noisily from time to time on the streets, were never able to differentiate between the three phases or the two groups and in the end what had been the secret actions of a minor official had transformed the French political scene.

Born in 1859, Alfred Dreyfus was the fourth son of a wealthy Jewish family of textile merchants from Mulhouse in Alsace, who were obliged to witness the entrance into their city of German troops after the débâcle of the Franco-Prussian War, which resulted in the annexation of most of Alsace and part of Lorraine to the new German Empire. With their home town now German, the Dreyfus family settled in Switzerland, from where the father could oversee the affairs of his Mulhouse factory, and in 1874 they moved to Carpentras in France, where they were recognised as French. One son, Jacques, remained behind in Mulhouse.

Alfred, a solemn youngster with poor vision and a lustreless voice, while being expected to follow his brothers into the family firm, decided instead to enter the army. He was an unlikely candidate, though – as an Alsatian – he felt his move was entirely logical, and he entered the École Polytechnique, France's prestigious engineering school, in 1882, a curiously unimpressive young man despite his good results. Graduating, he was promoted to First Lieutenant and spent a year on garrison duty with the artillery before being posted in 1883 to a battery of the First Cavalry Division. He was considered a good officer, though he was regarded as a bit of a prig and a prude. In 1890 he married Lucie Hadamard, the granddaughter of an Alsatian Jew who had served in the Army of King Louis-Philippe.

Alfred Dreyfus had been toying with the idea of applying for admission to the War College, something few Jews had considered and fewer had achieved, and in 1890 he was accepted. It was a tremendous achievement. Top graduates of the college were guaranteed an assignment to the General Staff, on which no acknowledged Jew in the history of the army had ever served. His classmates were the sons of French nobility, and, although French aristocratic families had lost much of their power, they were still determined to keep the upper ranks of the army their private territory. Dreyfus finished near the top of his class but he was judged by one instructor, Major Georges Picquart, a Catholic, a member of an ancient Lorraine family and brilliant himself, as being somewhat narrow-minded, lacking in imagination and possessing an unjustified pushy self-confidence.

Nevertheless all seemed set fair for Dreyfus, but in his final weeks at the War College, following a series of financial scandals involving Jews, there was an outbreak of anti-Semitism in France. Though Jewish statesmen had helped create a republic out of the shambles of 1870 and the mighty Rothschilds had provided the indemnity imposed by the Germans – something which allowed the French to hold up their heads again – the first anti-Semitic newspaper appeared in 1881. When, in January 1893, Dreyfus received orders to report to staff headquarters the aristocratic Picquart, who had preceded him, felt uneasy at having a Jew in such a sensitive position.

According to regulations, Dreyfus had to be assigned to the Staff's four bureaux, the first of which dealt with mobilisation; the second (the famous Deuxième Bureau) with intelligence; the third with operations and training; the fourth with communications and transport. The Chief of Staff was Lieutenant-General Raoul le Mouton de Boisdeffre. Dreyfus took up his duties with the First Bureau, from which he received a superior rating, and eventually moved on to the Fourth Bureau. Behaving as a *bon vivant*, he managed to impress by the amount of money he possessed. Moving to the Deuxième Bureau in 1894, he received a commendation of 'exemplary' and finally moved on to the Third Bureau.

In the climate of distrust that existed between France and Germany after 1870, war plans were constantly being drafted and new weapons produced by both sides, and spies and counter-spies were employed. In the French War Office a section to deal with this part of the business of war was created under the cover name of the Statistical Section. It had no relation to the Second Bureau and existed only to study papers handed in by agents or prepare papers to be used by counter-agents. With no records kept of the movement of documents or photographs, it was very inefficiently run by Colonel Jean-Conrad Sandherr, who in 1894 was a sick man.

The Minister of War, General Auguste Mercier, had been

appointed by the Prime Minister, Jean Casimir-Périer, but when the President of the Republic, Sadi Carnot, was assassinated in Lyon by an anarchist in 1894, Casimir-Périer became President and his place as Prime Minister was taken by Charles Dupuy. Mercier was practically the only man Dupuy retained from Casimir-Périer's Cabinet but, during his term of office, he made a series of mistakes which shattered the reputation he had for commonsense, so that he became aware that he needed a genuine coup to restore confidence in him. It was at this time that he learned of the bordereau, a hand-written list naming five purportedly classified military items known to have been passed to the Germans by a French officer.

The bordereau had been discovered in the German Embassy waste basket by a cleaning woman who was a French agent, and Lieutenant-Colonel Albert d'Aboville, of the Bureau of Communications and Transport, and his chief, Colonel Pierre-Elié Fabre, decided that, because it seemed to indicate an encyclopaedic military knowledge, its author must be a staff trainee. Examining the list of such men, they came up with the name of Alfred Dreyfus. To the aristocratic D'Aboville, Dreyfus, a Jew, was an obvious choice and, when they compared the bordereau with his reports, the handwriting seemed to be the same. Sandherr was convinced, and took the evidence to General de Boisdeffre who saw Mercier, and the two of them concurred with the decision of Sandherr, Fabre and D'Aboville. It was then that De Boisdeffre asked his cousin, and a member of the staff, Major Armand du Paty de Clam, to conduct the necessary enquiry. Du Paty pored over the bordereau and examples of Dreyfus's handwriting. His report was restrained by the inconclusive nature of the evidence and his own inexperience of such things, but he felt there were adequate grounds for an investigation and Mercier obtained the services of an official handwriting expert, Alfred Gobert of the Bank of France. The demand for haste worried Gobert and he asked for the name of the suspect. This was refused but he was able from the limited information at his disposal to identify Dreyfus.

On 14 October Mercier told De Boisdeffre, Brigadier-General Charles Gonse, Assistant-Chief of Staff, Colonel Sandherr and Du Paty that he wanted evidence of Dreyfus's guilt by the following evening. Gonse was already having doubts and he knew that Gobert had doubts, so he rushed photocopies of the bordereau and specimens of Dreyfus's handwriting to four more experts, one of whom, Alphonse Bertillon, of the Préfecture of the Police, was not really an expert at all. Later, that night, Boisdeffre summoned Du Paty and told him that he would have charge of the investigation. Du Paty was worried about his mission and when he received the verdicts of the handwriting experts he grew even more worried. Gobert did not believe Dreyfus was guilty, and of the other four experts, one doubted very strongly, one gave a qualified yes, one affirmed, and Bertillon had no doubt.

That Sunday, 14 October 1894, Dreyfus, now thirty-five, received a message to report to the Chief of Staff the following morning. He was met by Du Paty. Du Paty didn't enjoy summoning Dreyfus. Although he was vain and often silly, Du Paty had a brilliant service record and, not wanting the investigation to backfire in his face, he tried to get an annulment of the order for arrest. Mercier insisted. The lack of real evidence also worried Sandherr and he and Felix Gribelin, the archivist of the General staff, searched the files until they came up with a note that the cleaning woman-agent had produced earlier. It referred to 'that scoundrel D'(*le canaille de D*) having passed over plans. The note, in fact, was part of a regular correspondence being carried on between the German and Italian military attachés in Paris, Colonel Maximilian von Schwartzkoppen and Colonel Alessandro Panizzardi, who worked hand in hand, often employing the same agents, sharing the spoils and usually signing their letters with the code names 'Maximilienne' and

'Alexandrine'. 'Alexandrine' was the name on the letter. It was known that 'D' was a civilian clerk whose career Sandherr had terminated, but the letter was nevertheless added to the others, a move that was to be fatal to Dreyfus.

With Du Paty, when Dreyfus arrived, were Gribelin, the archivist, two policemen, and Major Hubert Joseph Henry, second-in-command of the Statistical Section who for some reason was hiding behind the curtains. Dreyfus was asked to fill in an inspection form and then, with Du Paty claiming that he had injured his right hand, was asked to take dictation. After only a minute or two Du Paty said, 'You are trembling, Captain.' Dreyfus said his fingers were cold. A few moments later, after a few sentences of dictation, Du Paty leapt to his feet shouting, 'Dreyfus, in the name of the law I arrest you! You are accused of the crime of high treason!'

The bewildered Dreyfus was searched, Du Paty claiming the evidence was overwhelming, and a loaded revolver was placed on the table. The inference was obvious. Dreyfus was expected to shoot himself to save the honour of the army. He made it clear he wasn't interested. 'I will live,' he said, 'in order to prove my innocence.' Henry was assigned as guard for his trip to prison.

Dreyfus's apartment was searched but, despite demands from the Minister of War and the Chief of Staff for a confession, a suicide, which would have been tantamount to a confession, or incontrovertible proof of treason, nothing was found.

Still protesting his innocence, Dreyfus was escorted to the Cherche-Midi Prison by a Captain Lebrun-Renault, of the Garde Republicaine, who that evening, either because he had misunderstood or was deliberately twisting what Dreyfus had said, informed a group of journalists that Dreyfus had admitted his guilt.

Since Dreyfus was clearly not in need of money, the absence of motive worried the General Staff. A mistaken jailing could destroy careers and Sandherr asked Maurice

Paléologue, of the Ministry of Foreign Affairs, if he could find anything that might be of help. Eventually Paléologue produced a decoded message from Colonel Panizzardi to his Chief of Staff which suggested that if Dreyfus had never been in contact with him it would be convenient to instruct the Italian ambassador in Paris to publish an official denial. With Sandherr's permission, Henry subtly changed the message so that it appeared to show Dreyfus's guilt. The altered note was sent to the Chief of Staff and the Minister of War. With it went the Italian Chief of Staff's reply to Panizzardi denying all knowledge of Dreyfus.

Pressed by Boisdeffre, Du Paty admitted his doubts about Dreyfus's guilt, but the Press, which so far had had to be content only with rumours, finally came out with Dreyfus's name and the fact that he was Jewish. Maître Edgar Demange, one of France's most distinguished lawyers, was engaged to defend him.

The central document in the army's case was the undated handwritten bordereau. Dreyfus argued that the handwriting was not his and that anyway it could not have been written by an artillery officer because of its inaccuracies. It also ended 'I'm off to manoeuvres', and it was a matter of record that the General Staff had cancelled the manoeuvres which its trainees were scheduled to attend in the summer of 1894.

Between his arrest on 15 October and an interrogation on 4 November, no member of the Dreyfus family was allowed to communicate with the prisoner, so that Dreyfus's brother, Mathieu, was convinced there was a plot to force him out of the army because he was Jewish.

During the two months Dreyfus was in prison, the Paris Press never doubted there was sufficient evidence to convict but they were united in the belief that any trial should be public. The Jewish Press, though basically convinced of Dreyfus's guilt, suggested there might have been a frame-up.

The seven officers who constituted the court martial that started on 19 December tried to be fair and it was not their fault that, despite the portions of evidence which clearly called for special knowledge, there was no artillery officer among them. Nor was it their fault that the Minister of War, General Mercier, insisted on a closed trial at the first mention of military secrets. France was still suffering from a nervous fear of Germany and, when Demange rose to speak on behalf of Dreyfus on 19 December, he was quickly silenced by the president of the court and the public removed from the room. Demange still remained confident of an acquittal.

Du Paty's evidence seemed to help Dreyfus even further. His reference to trembling puzzled the judges. There was no indication in the handwriting that Dreyfus had trembled and nothing in the dictation Du Paty had given to make him tremble. Demange insisted that the prosecution had failed to establish that the defendant was the author of the bordereau. But to the defence Dreyfus was a disappointment. He was neither vigorous in his denunciations nor did he offer any challenges to duels, which, it was felt, any officer worth his salt would have demanded long before.

Wearing the rosette of the Legion of Honour, Major Henry, of the Statistical Section, claimed he had been told there was a spy on the General Staff and, indicating Dreyfus, he shouted, 'And that traitor is sitting there!' When it was demanded that he should substantiate his charge, Henry refused. 'There are secrets in an officer's head,' he said, 'which he does not even share with his cap.' It was a statement that greatly impressed the judges.

Nevertheless, an acquittal was still confidently expected but, on the final day, as the five judges retired to deliberate, Du Paty arrived with a small packet of documents from General Headquarters on which Mercier had written, 'For the officers of the court martial.' The packet was handed over, unknown to Dreyfus or his lawyer, and its contents were sufficient to influence the verdict. The judges voted Dreyfus guilty.

The sentence came as a shock. 'My sole crime,' Dreyfus

said bitterly, 'is that I am a Jew!' But the fact was that more officers had given character evidence in Dreyfus's favour than had given it against him, and the anti-Semitic shadow that fell over the case came not from the army who, on the whole, were indifferent, but from the Press.

The unanimous verdict lifted a load from many minds. It was felt Dreyfus *must* be guilty, and Georges Clemenceau, later President of France and at the time against Dreyfus, though opposed to the death penalty, felt that in this case it should be applied. With the Socialists also trying to gain points, Dreyfus had suddenly become politics.

For a while Dreyfus contemplated suicide but in his stiff way he decided he must live to clear his name. On 31 December 1894, his appeal to the Court of Military Review was rejected and on Saturday 5 January, he suffered the torment of the atrocious ceremony of a public degradation, in which his buttons, badges and braid were cut from his uniform and his sword broken in front of him. Nevertheless, despite the shouts of 'Death to the Jew!' and 'Dirty Jew!' coming from outside the parade ground where the ceremony took place, he confounded everybody by marching in perfect step in his ruined uniform, shouting his innocence as he was led away.

Now a civilian and a common criminal in manacles, Dreyfus was taken to his cell and from there to the Ile de Ré in the Bay of Biscay. In March 1895, he was moved to Devil's Island, only four degrees above the equator off the coast of Venezuela, which Napoleon III had once decreed should no longer be used to house criminals. The climate of the island, though healthier than the mainland, registered very high temperatures but its rainy seasons in spring and autumn seemed endless. Escape was virtually impossible, and Dreyfus was incarcerated in a stone hut which gave him a view only of an endless expanse of water. His guards were not supposed to talk to him but they were as bored as Dreyfus and his passion for chess seduced them into becoming partners. But when his wife arranged for him to be able to buy a few small luxuries from Cayenne, the capital of the colony, the other prisoners began to boycott the store, and the merchant was obliged to cease sending supplies.

The convicted man, however, was surprisingly resilient, and his honour was all-important. He kept himself alert with books and magazines sent by his wife and, though he suffered from colic and fever, he was determined that his body shouldn't fail him before he was vindicated. There were times when he didn't even have anything to read and times when anxiety and rage spilled out of his letters home. His righteous anger probably saved him from insanity.

Meanwhile the distasteful spectacle of the degradation had started people thinking, and Dreyfus was not entirely without supporters. It was accepted that somewhere there was a traitor but the army's case had seemed to rest chiefly on a dossier of false gossip about women and gambling, things which, even if true, would normally have resulted only in a commanding officer's reprimand. As for the bordereau, it began to look like a forgery of Dreyfus's handwriting.

Believing Dreyfus the victim of an anti-Semitic plot, his family were at a loss. Prominent Jews counselled them to abandon any ideas of a press campaign on behalf of the convicted man. Others felt that the family was wealthy enough to look after themselves. At the same time, they became the recipients of letters containing spurious information which, as often as not, were documents prepared by the police in an attempt to entrap the family into giving away proof of Dreyfus's guilt.

Each day was a nightmare and their home was constantly watched. One of their few friends was Major Ferdinand Forzinetti, the commandant of the Cherche Midi Prison where Dreyfus had been lodged, who had never felt that Dreyfus was guilty. There was only one promising point – the irregularity of the court martial evidence. English private detectives were employed and, in an attempt to force their enemies' hand, Mathieu persuaded the *Daily Chronicle* to

106

print an article which reported that Dreyfus had escaped. Eleven days later, an anonymous article appeared in the sensationalist Paris journal, *Eclair*, which revealed the existence of the secret documents which had been presented to the judges of the court in closed session. The author was Du Paty de Clam and the article had been written with official sanction because someone high in the army or Ministry had thought that this sort of counter-attack might sweep the Dreyfus sympathisers from the field. Unfortunately, it rebounded because for the first time it informed the indefatigable Mathieu that evidence had been produced at the court martial without the accused or his lawyer having any knowledge of it. With Maître Demange's assistance, a request for a retrial was prepared.

It was an unfortunate fact for the Dreyfus family that during this time France was going through a period of instability when governments rarely lasted more than a few months and no one Prime Minister, no one Minister of War, was able to deal with the Affair at length. In April 1896, André Lebon, the Minister of Colonies in a new government under the leadership of Jules Méline, received what seemed to be an intercepted letter to Dreyfus which appeared to indicate that Dreyfus had an accomplice and that somewhere there was a whole host of undiscovered secrets vital to France's security. Lebon had the letter copied and forwarded to Cayenne with instructions that Dreyfus should be watched when he read it. The answer proved only that Dreyfus had been as puzzled by it as the Minister, but Lebon gave instructions so severe that he became the only man out of all his persecutors whom Dreyfus came to hate. Wooden palisades were erected round his hut, cutting off not only the view but also the breeze, and he was placed in irons and immobilised on his bed.

Even the commandant in Cayenne was moved to protest, but he was immediately recalled and a harsher gaoler appointed. During the day Dreyfus fought against the heat, the ants and the mosquitoes; at night the manacles rubbed his flesh raw and the guards had instructions to shoot if he acted suspiciously. Despite a weakening of the body, however, Dreyfus's spirit remained unbroken. A visit by the Governor of the island produced shouted protests. 'Someone wants a scandal,' Dreyfus yelled. 'He'll have it.'

By December 1897, however, he had almost reached the end of his tether when suddenly things began to change. The illness of the Chief of the Statistical Section, Sandherr, had obliged him in 1895 to give up his post, and his place had been taken by Major Picquart, the man who had once judged Dreyfus narrow-minded and pushy. Picquart was not a virulent anti-Semite. Like Du Paty de Clam, he was politely indifferent to Jews. Nevertheless, he had had little sympathy for Dreyfus at his degradation and always grew angry if anyone called him 'Picard', which was a name borne by many Jews. He had doubted Dreyfus's guilt and had expected an acquittal but had accepted that the secret evidence submitted to the court must have contained clear proof of his crime.

He had had no wish to run the Statistical Section because he felt that it forced him, an officer of breeding, into reading other people's mail or spying through keyholes, but, since he spoke and wrote Italian, German, English, and Russian, his familiarity with foreign armies made him essential. The Marquis Gaston de Gallifet, a hero of the war of 1870 and a permanent member of the Army's Superior War Council, added his flattery to that of the then Minister of War, General Jean-Baptiste Billot, and Picquart reluctantly accepted the post, assuming control six months after Dreyfus's degradation.

Finding the Section in some confusion, he tightened up procedures and got rid of some of Sandherr's agents who had been corrupt and far from clever. Major Henry told him nothing about the Dreyfus Case, and what Henry knew might have startled him. After the revelation of Dreyfus's arrest, the Italian Chief of Staff had wired Panizzardi that Italy had no knowledge of a Captain Dreyfus, and this was significant because what was known in Berlin was also known in Rome. Picquart was also not informed that the Section had received a message from Berlin revealing that there certainly *was* someone in Paris in the pay of Schwartzkoppen. The message came from one of Sandherr's few reliable agents and even went so far as to describe the contact. 'Forty-five,' it said, 'and decorated with the Legion of Honour.' Why nothing came of the message is one of the mysteries of the case.

A few months after Picquart's arrival at the Statistical Section, he came into possession of a document which became known as the *petit bleu*, a message on blue paper of the sort that passed through the underground pneumatic tube system in use in those days by the Paris postal department. This one, however, had not been transmitted through the system but had been torn up before use. It had been salvaged from the German Embassy waste basket and was addressed to a Major Esterhazy at an address in the Rue de la Bienfaisance. Picquart knew nothing of the mysterious Esterhazy but he made up his mind to find out as much as possible.

There was a lot to find out. Marie-Charles-Ferdinand Walsin-Esterhazy was a Major with the 74th Infantry at Rouen, to the north of Paris, the son of one general and the nephew of another, and his ancestors had arrived in Paris from Hungary, where the Esterhazy name was famous in the reign of Louis XIV. When the Revolution came, they had emigrated to Russia.

One who stayed in France had married a Monsieur Walsin and when she gave birth to a son by a French marquis, the complacent husband had allowed the child to bear his name. This child's children adopted the surname Walsin-Esterhazy, and one of them became the father of Marie-Charles-Ferdinand. By no means poor, Walsin-Esterhazy suffered from tuberculosis and, although far from stupid, he was too lazy to do well at school. In 1867 he tried to get into

109

Saint-Cyr, the military academy, but failed and spent the next two years in clubs, casinos and music halls and on race tracks, calling himself 'Count' Esterhazy. He was soon heavily in debt.

In May 1869, he accepted service in the Papal Legion and, claiming to have been wounded during the defeat of the Papal forces by the Italian monarchy, he persuaded his uncle, General Esterhazy, to arrange a transfer to the French Foreign Legion. He might have done well in North Africa but he was brought back to France to take part in the disastrous campaign of 1870 on the Loire. With half the French Army either besieged by or prisoners of the Germans, promotion was rapid and he became a Captain. But with the end of the war, he was returned to the rank of Lieutenant, though in the regular army, where his spurious title, his name and a few powerful friends seemed to ensure success.

With his greying hair and sunken eyes he even looked like a conspirator, but he was skilled with the pen and wrote offering his service to the *Evening Standard* in London before finally becoming a translator in the Second Bureau. After serving with the staff, he received an appointment with an infantry battalion and in 1881 was sent to Tunisia where his skill with the pen enabled him to doctor an account of a battle which described his own efforts in glowing terms, though he had not even been present. Returning to France, he set about getting himself the coveted Legion of Honour, something he eventually succeeded in doing.

By this time he was heavily in debt and fell back on a series of little frauds, even a little blackmail, before finally marrying a rich wife, whose money he went through so quickly she obtained a court judgement for them to have separate accounts to protect what was left. In December 1892, he was posted to Rouen but his finances were now in a sad state and, like Benedict Arnold, feeling that his superiors had blocked his chances of promotion, he retaliated with a visit to the German Embassy in Paris.

After a nasty espionage scandal, in 1890 the German ambassador had ordered his staff to avoid any more such activities and pledged the French Government that in future they would obtain their information through proper channels. His new military attaché Colonel Maximilian von Schwartzkoppen, however, was secretly under the orders of the German Intelligence Bureau to spy on France. On 20 July 1894, Esterhazy was shown into his office and promptly made an offer to provide secret information. Esterhazy began to call regularly, and documents changed hands. Schwartzkoppen offered a prepared list of twelve items he was interested in, ranging from the composition of regimental batteries at Châlons, through the details of a new 120 mm cannon, to army formations, details of the Manonvillers fortress and the plan of manoeuvres for mounted batteries.

Esterhazy's knowledge of these subjects was scant so he compiled 'official' documents and notes out of his head. What was accurate in them was of limited value and what seemed to be of value was inaccurate. None of it was top secret. The note he wrote to accompany them closed with the comment that the writer was about to leave on manoeuvres. This last sentence was to cause trouble because he did not appear to have attended general manoeuvres in 1894 but, in fact, he had gone at the last moment to command a regiment of reservists and had dropped the packet of documents, along with the explanatory note, into the German Embassy as he passed through Paris. Schwartzkoppen forwarded the documents to Berlin but tore up the covering note and dropped it into the waste paper basket, from which it was neatly removed by the cleaning woman-agent and passed to the Statistical Section, to become known to posterity as the bordereau.

Meanwhile Esterhazy was sinking deeper into debt but ironically, because of help he had given to Jews during a series of duels provoked by *La Libre Parole*, a virulent anti-Jewish journal, some of his debts were paid by prominent Jews, among them the Baron de Rothschild. But he was still in trouble and, feeling he could offer more to Schwartzkoppen if he were on the General Staff, he directed his talents to trying to manoeuvre himself behind a desk at headquarters. The Germans, however, were already beginning to doubt his value as a spy. They wanted to know about the new 75mm gun and about French mobilisation plans, and growing irritated, they ordered Schwartzkoppen, in February 1896, to break the contact. He dictated two messages to Esterhazy, but liking neither of them, tossed them into the waste paper basket from which, as usual, they were retrieved by the cleaning woman-agent. On 1 March 1896, while Henry was on leave, Picquart, now a Lieutenant-Colonel, was handed the torn-up letters. Horrified, he felt he was about to discover a new Dreyfus case with Esterhazy as the guilty man.

Picquart was becoming obsessed by Esterhazy and, while examining an example of his handwriting he suddenly realised he was looking at the same handwriting he had seen on a document produced during the Dreyfus case. Sending for the file, for the first time he learned of the packet of secret documents that had dammed Dreyfus. And, staring at the bordereau, he realised the handwriting was Esterhazy's.

Picquart was an intensely honest man but he was aware of what his discovery could mean. De Boisdeffre would never welcome the suggestion that his judgement had been wrong so, in his report, Picquart merely indicated the need to question Esterhazy and did not mention the man on Devil's Island, though he knew his report would force the army to review its judgement of him. He was risking a lot, but Picquart had a remarkable reputation. Like Dreyfus, he had been born in a city occupied by the Germans after 1870 – Strasbourg – and had been a brilliant student at St Cyr and the War College. He had been wounded in colonial wars, his background was impeccable, and he was a favourite of the Marquis de Gallifet, the hero of the Battle of Sedan, who was a mighty figure in the French Army. De Boisdeffre was stunned by what he learned, reminding Picquart that it was more important to prove the guilt of Esterhazy than the innocence of Dreyfus.

General Billot, by now the Minister of War, was equally horrified, especially when he learned of the secret file which had been handed to Dreyfus's judges. He had heard of Esterhazy because of his demand for a position on the staff and knew that he had a powerful friend in Deputy Jules Roche, who was at the moment heading a commission studying the military budget. It was clearly a bad time to arrest Roche's friend as a suspected spy, so he sent Picquart away believing he would soon be able to arrest a spy and free an innocent man.

The matter was passed among a succession of senior officers, all of whom had been involved in the Dreyfus case and were eager to protect their rear. They refused to change their views of Dreyfus's guilt but, despite their rebuffs, Picquart, like Mathieu Dreyfus, began to feel that something must be done to repair the damage. Attempts were made by various people, among them Major Henry, to persuade him to drop the case, but Picquart refused and General Gonse, the Assistant-Chief of Staff, exploded. 'What is it to you if that Jew stays on Devil's Island?' he snapped.

'But, General,' Picquart protested, 'he is innocent!'

Gonse insisted that the case couldn't be reopened because of the generals who were involved in it and, when Picquart continued to insist, Gonse replied, 'If you say nothing, no one will be any the wiser.' It was too much for Picquart. 'General,' he retorted, 'what you have just said is an abomination. I don't know what I shall do, but . . . I shall not carry this secret to my grave!'

For a while, in fact, he could do nothing because of a visit of the Czar of Russia to Paris. Much of the pomp was being organised by De Boisdeffre, who had one eye on the St Petersburg Embassy and was one of the major figures in the case. Meanwhile the Dreyfus family's attempt to restart the case was running counter to the counsels of the Jewish leaders who preferred to avoid trouble. But they had the backing of Forzinetti, Dreyfus's first gaoler, who never wavered in his support, and of Bernard Lazare, a forceful Jewish journalist who prepared a pamphlet claiming the trial had been a judicial error and that Dreyfus's guilt had never been proved. Members of the Chamber and the Senate, journalists, academics and high ranking officers received copies. A lot that had been kept quiet was revealed and Lazare ended by demanding a review of Dreyfus's trial.

It was useless. The gutter press came out with a virulent opposition and Henri de Rochefort, a deranged patriot who ran the newspaper, *L'Intransigéant*, went back on a promise to help and joined the counter-blast.

But then, on 10 November, one of the discredited hand-writing experts who had felt that Dreyfus had written the bordereau sold his copy of the document to the newspaper, *Le Matin*, whose owner saw at once that, though the writing was similar to that of Dreyfus, it was not the same. Until then Schwartzkoppen had not even known what it was that the Dreyfus case was based on and when he saw the copy in the newspaper, he and Panizzardi, the Italian Military Attaché, felt that they had to disclose at least some of the truth.

Esterhazy was shocked by the appearance of the border-eau. Another newspaper began to throw its weight behind the Dreyfuses so that General Gonse, beginning to believe that Picquart was leaking information, ordered him to inspect the Intelligence organisation on France's border with Germany. As a result, Major Henry became acting head of his department.

Henry, a burly ex-NCO fiercely loyal to the army, had always been jealous of Picquart, and felt that he, Henry, should have taken Sandherr's place. In an attempt to ingratiate himself with Gonse and encouraged by De Boisdeffre to find more weapons for the army in the fight against the Dreyfus family, with the aid of a forger, Leeman, who passed under the name of Lemercier-Picard, he doctored the evidence.

Loyal to his superiors, who had made him a gentleman by elevating him to commissioned rank and giving him a post on the staff, Henry began editing Panizzardi's inoccuous 'Alexandrine' telegrams to Schwartzkoppen. In one, found long before the Dreyfus case broke, he changed the phrase 'P . . . has brought me a lot of very interesting things' to 'D . . . has brought me a lot of very interesting things,' thus incriminating Dreyfus. Finally, using a very ordinary message from Panizzardi found by the cleaning woman-agent, he worked into the small hours of the night to alter it. The original document was written in blue pencil on ruled blue paper and, tearing it carefully to separate the body of the note from its greeting and its signature, he discarded the original message and inserted a carefully forged passage in what appeared to be Panizzardi's handwriting, even taking care to make use of the Italian's faulty French. The passage contained Dreyfus's name and references to 'this Jew'. Henry then taped the original end of the letter to this new body and placed them in the original postmarked envelope. This letter was to become known as the False Henry.

When the Vice-Chief of Staff, Gonse, was shown Henry's 'evidence' he was delighted. Du Paty was not impressed, however. 'General,' he said, 'I am not enthusiastic.' To Henry he was even more blunt. 'Henry,' he said, 'take care. Your papers have a bad smell about them.'

Meanwhile in the east of France, Picquart had a feeling he had been outmanoeuvred. Honesty made him feel that the truth about Dreyfus should be produced, even at a cost to the army, even at a cost to his own career, and he decided to bring the facts to light. But a move was already being made to get rid of him and, just as he was about to return to Paris, he was ordered to Marseilles and then to Algeria and Tunisia, and he recognised it was the War Minister's solution for removing a troublesome officer. In 1897, nearly four months later, he managed to return on leave to Paris. The Minister of War refused to see him and, on his return to Tunisia, he was thrown from his horse. The thought that the accident might have been fatal and that he would have carried the secret he possessed to his grave, troubled him enough for him to write an account of all he knew.

By this time he suspected that his mail was being opened by his subordinates in Counter-Intelligence, probably with the permission of Gonse and even the Minister of War. Soon afterwards he received orders that took him to the Libyan border, a dangerous area where he might well be killed. A letter to Henry protesting about the interference with his mail provoked an accusation of prejudice against Esterhazy and disloyalty to the Statistical Section and, realising how easy it was for an officer to be convicted on false evidence, he determined to do what he could to restore Dreyfus.

Returning to Paris briefly, he gave the account he had written to his lawyer, Louis Leblois, who entrusted it to the Vice-President of the Senate, Auguste Scheurer-Kestner, another Alsatian, who had always been puzzled by aspects of the Dreyfus case. Scheurer-Kestner felt he must help but he also felt the question must not remain one of racial prejudice but one of justice, and confided Picquart's story to Joseph Reinach, a Jewish Deputy.

The members of the General Staff ought by this time to have realised it was time to investigate Dreyfus's story but enough of them, from Henry upwards, were involved for them to decide against it, and a letter was sent to Esterhazy informing him that he was to be accused of writing the bordereau. Esterhazy had meetings with Schwartzkoppen and with a heavily disguised Du Paty, who told him the army was willing to protect him from the Dreyfus 'clique' so long as he co-operated.

Meanwhile Scheurer-Kestner had met the President of the Republic, Félix Faure, who, however, was not convinced that there should be a retrial. Scheurer-Kestner now tried General Billot, another Alsatian and an old friend, but he received no help there at all. Billot agreed with what he said about Esterhazy but felt he was not a traitor and was being accused by the Jews of Dreyfus's crime. He based his beliefs on the dubious story of Captain Lebrun-Renault, the Garde Republicaine officer who had claimed Dreyfus had confessed to him on his way to prison, and on the False Henry, the letter Henry had doctored. When the details of the interview appeared in *Le Matin*, having been passed on by one of Billot's associates, it began to seem that Picquart was the key to the puzzle, and the Statistical Section, under Henry, now began to manufacture evidence to compromise *him* in the scandal.

With stories about his part in the Affair circulating in the salons and diplomatic circles, Schwartzkoppen was growing irritated and, calling on President Faure before leaving for a new assignment in Berlin, he gave his word of honour that he had never known Dreyfus. An increasing number of politicians began to doubt the word of the senior army officers.

The nerveless Esterhazy now actually appeared before Billot and claimed that the Jews had started a campaign against him. His cheek was colossal and all attempts to frighten him failed. Yet things were closing in on him. A Jewish banker recognised the writing on the bordereau as that of one of his most consistently overdrawn depositors; Scheurer-Kestner finally divulged the secret entrusted to him by Picquart's lawyer; and on 15 November Mathieu Dreyfus wrote a letter to the Minister of War exposing Esterhazy. Esterhazy claimed he had close family ties with Schwartzkoppen and even admitted that some of the words of the bordereau were so like his own writing, they might have come from his pen. Billot felt that Esterhazy should be examined, but still refused to accept that Dreyfus was not guilty.

The Chief of the Paris Military Police, General Georges de Pellieux, was selected to whitewash Esterhazy, and Picquart was even returned from Tunisia, still alive because his Commanding General, hearing his story, had counter-manded the orders from Paris and told him to disregard the instructions taking him to Libya. Henry, now a Lieutenant-Colonel and officially in charge of the Statistical Section, told his story and Picquart, finding himself shadowed by police agents, began hourly to expect arrest.

Then, in the middle of this new attempt to obscure the case, a fresh bombshell exploded. A packet of letters written by Esterhazy to a mistress, since discarded for a new one and justifiably embittered, came into the hands of *Le Figaro* and began to appear in its columns. They started a panic among the High Command because they were virulently anti-French. In one of them, known as the 'Uhlan letter,' Esterhazy said the French weren't worth the bullets to kill them, and ended 'If someone came ... to tell me that I am going to be killed as a Captain in the Uhlans tomorrow while sabring the French, I should be perfectly happy.' This time Esterhazy had gone too far.

Apprehension became horror and even Esterhazy was frightened. More people became convinced of Dreyfus's innocence and Esterhazy's guilt and the Italian ambassador even suspended Panizzardi's diplomatic immunity to allow him to give sworn testimony against Dreyfus's alleged relations with the Italian Embassy. It was one thing for Schwartzkoppen to inform the French President in private that Dreyfus was innocent; an official request by the Italian ambassador was another. The reply, which, in effect, impugned the Italians' good faith, rested heavily on Henry's doctored letters, and the Chief of the Military Police absolved Esterhazy from the bordereau and the *petit bleu*, by innuendo even suggesting that Picquart was responsible for the latter and that Esterhazy's infamous letters about France had been written by someone else.

It seemed conclusive, but the French were not stupid. Since 1870, none of France's governments had lasted more than a few months, and the Republic was unstable and rocked by one crisis after another, with the growing power of the Socialists set against the inherited power of the Church, the army and the aristocracy. But France's weakness against Bismarck's Germany was obvious, and the only institution that seemed capable of guarding its ideals was the army and the officer corps. Now, however, despite the efforts of Jules Méline, the Prime Minister, every day the newspapers became more and more critical of the army and the case became known simply as 'The Affair.'

The efforts to whitewash Esterhazy gained momentum. Du Paty was in a panic because he, more than anyone, was involved, and the supporters of Dreyfus were now so numerous the term 'Dreyfusard' was coined, and the Dreyfus family had now recruited their most powerful supporter, Emile Zola, the writer, whose articles had been attacking the Government ever since he had become convinced of Esterhazy's guilt. A meeting with Mathieu on 13 November 1897, had made Zola the most resolute Dreyfusard in France.

Despite the fact that the handwriting experts who had examined the bordereau, surrendering to pressure from the army, had suddenly become unanimous that Esterhazy was not the author of the bordereau, he went on trial on 10 January 1898, in the same room where Dreyfus had been sentenced to life imprisonment. Mathieu Dreyfus argued his connection to the bordereau but Esterhazy was boastful and irrelevant and the court martial was in part in closed session, so that Picquart's evidence on the bordereau and the *petit bleu* was given only after the audience had been removed. It took the judges only three minutes to decide on a verdict of not guilty.

Pandemonium broke out and Esterhazy was treated like a hero. Newspapers in London, New York, Vienna and Budapest took a different view. Zola was disgusted and, writing all night, he came up with an article for *L'Aurore*, the newspaper owned by Georges Clemenceau. This was the famous *J'Accuse*. It was a unique document in which he made clear his disgust with the army, and one after the other accused Du Paty, Mercier, Billot, De Boisdeffre, Gonse and others, even the handwriting experts, of diverting the course of justice.

It started a series of anti-Jewish riots across France, and the uproar forced the Government's hand. Zola himself stood trial on 7 February 1898, on a strange charge of accusing the judges of the Esterhazy court martial of acting on Government instructions. The trial lasted sixteen noisy days. Scheurer-Kestner was called, as were the former President, Casimir-Périer, Henry and Picquart. Picquart explained that the bordereau must have been composed by an officer outside the staff unfamiliar with the artillery, while Maître Fernand Labori, Zola's counsel, explained that staff apprentices had known they were not to attend manoeuvres, thus making it clear that the writer who had referred to going on manoeuvres could not have been Dreyfus.

Pellieux, the Chief of Military Police, who had white-washed Esterhazy, was so angry he shouted that he had seen proof of Dreyfus's guilt and proceeded to quote the False Henry. De Boisdeffre's evidence was almost a demand that Frenchmen should forget Dreyfus and remember only the issue of national honour and survival. He confirmed what Pellieux had said about the False Henry and demanded that the country have confidence in its army chiefs. Zola's counsel was not allowed to cross examine and, when Esterhazy appeared, the result was a foregone conclusion. Zola and Clemenceau were found guilty, fined heavily and sentenced to imprisonment, Zola to one year, Clemenceau to four months. World newspapers expressed their disgust and, in Berlin, the *Berliner Tageblatt* suggested that the French Army had won its first victory since its defeat in 1870.

It was ironic that all these appalling miscarriages of justice took place at the height of what has become known as *La Belle Epoque*, that period when Paris was judged the most exciting, colourful and enlightened city in the world. It was a place of brilliant salons where *bons mots* were prized above jewels, and where the constantly collapsing governments alienated the upper classes trying to protect their wealth. But by now, the Dreyfus case was beginning to erode the pleasurable calm of these soirées, and hostesses, when inviting guests, began to check their views on Dreyfus and Esterhazy. Pandemonium could erupt at any time, either in the home or in the street, or in the Chamber of Deputies. Catholic children began to call a chamber pot a Zola. One duel followed another as people took sides, and in Bordeaux, Nancy, Nantes and Rennes mobs sacked Jewish shops and desecrated synagogues, while in Algeria the army was called out. As many honourable men honestly supported the army as supported Dreyfus. Almost no one could avoid the situation and people more than once found themselves obliged to change sides as their opinions varied.

The army fought back with spirit, attempting to silence Panizzardi who, instead, told the shocked British military attaché everything he knew. An attempt was made to make Picquart out as a homosexual, and De Boisdeffre assisted by pushing rumours that the Kaiser himself had seen the bordereau. Kaiser Wilhelm considered it so absurd and thought De Boisdeffre so incompetent he hoped that, for Germany's sake, he would never be replaced as Chief of Staff.

The summer of 1898 was a sad one for the Dreyfusards, and many of their supporters were defeated in the national elections in May. There was a new Prime Minister, Henri Brisson, however, and there was a hope that he might help. But he was too wary and even appointed Godefroy Cavaignac, a cousin of Du Paty and 'a man of the General Staff', as War Minister. In April a retrial was ordered for Zola but, certain he would lose, the writer fled to England.

Revelations such as Schwartzkoppen's and Panizzardi's kept appearing in the newspapers. By this time Esterhazy had been forcibly retired and in May, his nephew, Christian, whom he had swindled, announced that he was willing to testify before an examining magistrate that his uncle was the author of the two incriminating telegrams. Sensing that he was getting deeper and deeper into the mire, Esterhazy tried to challenge Picquart to a duel but Picquart refused the challenge and when Esterhazy, drunk on absinthe, attacked him in a bar with a walking stick, Picquart picked him up by his collar and his trouser seat and tossed him into the gutter.

With the students rioting, it was becoming essential that the new Minister of War reassure the nation and, his one ambition to end the Affair, Cavaignac spoke in the Chamber, quoting the documents in the case, including the False Henry. He was impressive enough for the Chamber to vote that the speech should be printed and distributed throughout France.

While Dreyfusards mourned, the Socialist, Jean Jaurès, replied with a series of articles in the form of an open letter. The first was published simultaneously with one from Picquart stating that the documents Cavaignac had quoted were inventions. Cavaignac reacted quickly and the following day, Picquart, who had been dismissed from the army earlier in the year, was arrested and imprisoned for divulging official secrets. Cavaignac would have liked to have a lot more people brought to trial but instead decided to have an expert re-examine the Dreyfus dossier. Though it wasn't realised at the time, it was the opening of the door.

Captain Louis Cuignet, who was given the job, pored over the contents of the dossier and, while scrutinising the False Henry, he realised that neither the colour nor the measurement of the lines on the paper matched. The flabbergasted Cavaignac ordered him to examine the sheet once more and on 22 August Cuignet announced that the forgery was unmistakeable. Henry was interviewed by Cavaignac eight days later. Boisdeffre, Pellieux and Gonse were all present and it didn't take long to break down Henry's denials. An officer was summoned to escort him to the prison at Mont Valérien where the following day he cut his throat with a razor.

Still, incredibly, the Government refused to believe in Dreyfus's innocence but on 3 September 1894, when Lucie Dreyfus made a formal request for a revision by the Court of Appeal of the judgement of 1894, Cavaignac resigned and Esterhazy decided that the time had come to bolt. As he caught the train to the Channel steamer to England, Zola was preparing to return.

Taking the view that Henry's suicide made no difference and that what Henry had done was less important than why he had done it, the poet and journalist, Charles-Marie Maurras, now entered the fray with a series of anti-Jewish articles. Picquart was still in prison awaiting trial and he made it clear that if he were found dead in his cell it would mean murder, not the suicide of Henry or of Lemercier-Picard, the man Henry had employed to forge the False Henry, who had recently been found hanged. Brisson's Cabinet was on the point of toppling, there was a danger of insurrection in Paris, the city was flooded with troops, and a mounting crisis arose with England over the possession of Fashoda in East Africa. Then on Tuesday, 25 October, the Minister of War, the third of Brisson's short government, announced his resignation and that was the end of Brisson and the beginning of a belief – quite unreal – that the army intended a *coup d'état* to save its honour. Republican France barely survived. Brisson was replaced by Charles Dupuy, and the crisis with England passed.

The Court of Appeal which Dreyfus's wife had requested started in late October, 1898. The situation in France, with changes of governments and altering cliques, made for thoughts of vengeance, but the injustices against Picquart continued. However, at this time the Germans were feeling friendly towards France and it was believed that a few words from Schwartzkoppen about the *petit bleu* would save not only Picquart and Dreyfus but also European peace. Prodded by Prince Albert of Monaco, the German ambassador took the initiative and Schwartzkoppen finally admitted that the *petit bleu*, the note which had been found in his waste paper basket, was probably from him to Esterhazy. Since it had been dictated and was not in Schwartzkoppen's handwriting, however, the admission was valueless and Panizzardi refused to help if the Germans wouldn't, so nothing came of the attempt to aid Dreyfus.

The French continued to damage themselves. Esterhazy produced a book on the Affair in which he admitted authorship of the bordereau but claimed he was acting as a double agent for Sandherr, and still France refused to accept that Dreyfus was innocent.

With the Court of Appeal still in session, in exchange for a guarantee of immunity from prosecution, Esterhazy returned to Paris to defend himself, his object less to help than to profit. All the old witnesses reappeared; Lebrun-Renault's report of Dreyfus's confession was denounced; and one of the judges of the original court martial admitted that he had been very much influenced by Henry's evidence and now believed that the verdict had been wrong. Once again, the Government, encouraged by President Faure, tried to undo the good that was being done and it began to look as if the drama would have to be replayed all over again. But then President Faure suddenly died in the arms of his mistress and his place was taken by Emile Loubet.

Once again the political situation began to suggest a *coup d'état*, and Paul Déroulède, an erratic patriot and chief of the League of Patriots, called out his followers for exactly that. But it all went wrong and Déroulède found himself in prison instead. It was soon the turn of Du Paty. This unfortunate had become the scapegoat for all the sins of the War Office and was charged with the forgery of many of the documents in the case. He was also accused of passing information to the Press and finally of anything else that might be discovered. He was arrested but the charges were soon proved useless and he wisely retired to a sick bed.

By this time Dreyfus himself was almost beyond caring what became of him, but on 3 June 1899, the Court of

Appeal came to the conclusion that the 1894 court martial had wrongly condemned him and remanded the case to the military authorities at Rennes, and, convinced that Loubet was a Dreyfusard, a gang of young aristocrats attacked the President at the races at Auteuil. In a rage, the French people began to mobilise against the powerful forces of the army, the aristocracy and the Church. It brought about the end of Dupuy's Government and René Waldeck-Rousseau, who was elected in his place, decided his must be a Government of strong personalities. For Minister of War he chose the Marquis de Gallifet, the old leftover hero from the war of 1870 and one of the few who had had the courage to speak up for Picquart and Dreyfus. Loathed by the working classes for putting down the Commune that had followed the Siege of Paris, he was nevertheless trusted as the one man who seemed capable of bending the army to the decision of the Court of Appeal.

Arrangements were made to bring back the condemned man, by now almost a legend in his own time. None was more enthusiastic than Zola who had suffered a great deal by his defence. His royalties had disappeared in libel actions but he was elated by the thought that Dreyfus was to be acquitted. After more than 300 days in prison Picquart was also released and, acquitted by the Court of Appeal of the charges against him, was admired throughout the world for his moral courage.

Despite everything, the cadaverous Dreyfus was not allowed to see his family. Off the coast of Brittany he was transferred to a coastal vessel which took him to a fishing village so small it was unconnected to the rest of France by telephone or telegraph and the following morning he reached the military prison of Rennes. On 1 July 1899, he was reunited with his wife. He knew nothing of what had been happening or of Picquart's martyrdom on his behalf. He learned of the fall of governments and of the intellectuals and politicians who had taken his side, but his health was shaky and he spoke slowly and suffered from malaria, anaemia and recurrent nightmares.

Two eminent counsels, Edgar Demange and Fernand Labori, had been engaged to plead for him and as foreign dignitaries and journalists began to assemble in Rennes, few of them took the side of the army. By this time most of the French Press had been won over, too. The trial began on Monday, 7 August, in the city's high school, Dreyfus entering between two lines of soldiers stationed with their backs to him. He seemed a little old man with a stumbling gate who in no way gave the impression of a soldier, so that even the Dreyfusards were a little disappointed. He was never given his military title and was referred to throughout simply, as 'Dreyfus'. All the old evidence was repeated, and once again an attempt was made to add false documents to the dossier in front of the President of the Court. The evidence revealed only gossip, irrelevance, duplication and forgery. There were closed sessions while the documents were examined, but the friends of Dreyfus began to predict that once more he would be convicted. Paléologue, Casimir-Périer and Mercier were called, Mercier offering the old canard that Dreyfus had written personally to the German Kaiser and trying to suggest that at the time of Dreyfus's accusation France and Germany had been on the verge of war. It was all nonsense.

After a weekend break the court prepared to reconvene but, as Dreyfus's counsel, Labori, set out for the court with Picquart, a man in a black coat fired at him and wounded him. As Picquart tried to catch him, the man shouted, 'I have killed the traitor's lawyer!' Picquart returned to Labori just in time to prevent another man from stealing the lawyer's brief case containing all his documents. General Mercier was believed, by some, to be behind the attempt, the Government by others. When physicians announced that Labori might take months to recover it was decided to continue with the case, and this was a disaster because Demange had never agreed with Labori's aggressive style

126

and did not press or probe, so that the witnesses for the prosecution were allowed to repeat all the old falsehoods. Picquart distinguished himself yet again and Gobert, the handwriting expert, described the pressure put on him by General Gonse in 1894, while another of the experts, who had once decided against Dreyfus, now announced that he believed the bordereau to have been written by Esterhazy. Though witness after witness insisted that the items in the bordereau were classified beyond access to all but a few, Casimir-Périer claimed he had been told by General Mercier that they were of no importance.

After eight days Labori returned but by then the damage had been done. Mercier was dominating the court, speaking without being asked and questioning with impunity. Labori tried to show how the General Staff had tried to ruin the honourable Picquart to protect Esterhazy but, while the prosecution was allowed to produce against Dreyfus a dubious former Austrian officer called Cernuski, Labori's attempt to call Schwartzkoppen on his behalf was deplored as unpatriotic. Even so, the Kaiser allowed the newspaper, *Reichs-Anzeige*, to publish a categorical denial that Germany had ever sought the services of Dreyfus, and Waldeck-Rousseau even tried to seek a deposition from Schwartz-koppen, to which the Kaiser replied stuffily that Germany had already denied dealing with Dreyfus.

With the Prime Minister and the Minister of War finally beginning to exert influence, the Dreyfus family began to believe in an acquittal, but on 9 September the tribunal's verdict was announced. By a vote of five to two Dreyfus had once again been found guilty of high treason with extenuating circumstances. Instead of life, the court imposed a sentence of ten years, five of which he had already served.

A cry of horror and disgust ran round the world and demonstrations began in Berlin, London, New York and Vienna. Clemenceau's *L'Aurore* said France was now a country with 'no security either for the liberty, the life or the honour of her citizens', but when politicians pressed for a third court martial, Gallifet assured the President and Prime Minister that another court martial would only convict Dreyfus again.

France was exhausted by the Affair. Most people believed that the ideal end would be clemency for Dreyfus and, in fact, within twenty-four hours Joseph Reinach informed Mathieu Dreyfus that the rumours of a pardon were accurate. On Sunday, 10 September, a group of Dreyfus supporters met to urge Mathieu to persuade his brother to accept. Jaurès wanted to continue the fight for an honourable acquittal but Mathieu argued his brother's condition. Clemenceau said a pardon wasn't sufficient, though he admitted that if he had been Dreyfus he would accept one. It seemed at first that Dreyfus would indeed refuse a pardon but in the end he withdrew his objections for the sake of his family and on 19 September 1899, he became a free man. It was suggested that the family should go to Jersey to avoid 'incidents'. Instead they went to Bordeaux. An invitation came from Prince Albert of Monaco to join him as guests, but to leave France seemed to admit lack of courage and they didn't go.

Curiously, even for his supporters, Dreyfus remained a poor hero. They had wanted him to demand not a pardon but an acquittal and Charles Péguy, the writer, observed, 'We might have died for Dreyfus, but Dreyfus would not have died for Dreyfus,' which was all very well for someone who had not had to endure Devil's Island.

The Affair had turned the political scene upside down and in the senatorial elections in January 1900, the Left won eighty of the ninety-nine contested seats, though one of those elected was Mercier, recently retired from the army. Prime Minister Waldeck-Rousseau, trying to lead France into the new century without the rancour of the previous years, introduced a general amnesty denying litigation on current and future cases to do with the Affair.

A visit to Switzerland began to restore Dreyfus's health

but he was not satisfied with the pardon or the amnesty because it deprived him of his most cherished hope of having his innocence legally proclaimed. It also made sure that General Mercier, the principal author of the crime of 1894, went scot free. Dreyfusards grew irritated with Dreyfus for his refusal to be the official leader of their cause and even Maître Labori, one of his staunchest supporters, turned against him because the amnesty meant that while Du Paty's indictment and the charges against Esterhazy and Mercier were nullified, Picquart and Zola were denied the right of judicial exoneration. As an author, Zola was fortified by public opinion and increased royalties but Picquart had been disgraced by charges of forgery and betrayal of duty and *his* opinion of the pardon had never been sought. When he met Dreyfus he refused to shake hands.

In the elections of 1902, the Radicals and Socialists turned the Affair to their advantage, claiming that the Church and the aristocrats had been the cause of all the trouble, with the result that for the moderate Republicans, Conservatives and Royalists the elections were a disaster, and Catholic schools, hospitals, monasteries and commercial establishments were closed, while officers' careers suddenly all too often depended on their religion.

A further attempt was made to bring the case before the Court of Appeal and, in a speech to the Chamber of Deputies, the Socialist, Jean Jaurès, told again of the cabals of the generals, the ministers and the clergy. It was a stunning assault and the Minister of War, now General Louis André, was instructed to review the evidence. André squeezed a confession from the archivist, Gribelin, on Henry's chicanery; discovered what must have been a bribe to the Austrian officer, Cernuski, who had given evidence against Dreyfus at Rennes; proved that Lebrun-Renault's story of a confession was quite untrue; and showed that the phrase 'D... has brought me a lot of interesting things' had originally been 'P... has brought me a lot of interesting things.'

The Court of Appeal plodded once more through the mound of evidence and the surviving witnesses but, though Du Paty surrendered the original draft of the Dreyfus commentary prepared for Mercier in 1894, Mercier still continued to insist that Dreyfus was guilty. The verdict was announced on 12 July 1906, nearly twelve years after Dreyfus had first been sentenced. The Rennes verdict was annulled and Dreyfus was finally declared innocent of all charges by an unanimous vote.

A special bill was passed reintegrating him and Picquart into the army, Dreyfus as a Major, Picquart as a Brigadier-General. The ceremony of Dreyfus's return took place in a courtyard adjacent to the one where he had been degraded. He retired from the army in 1907, but returned to command an ammunition column during World War I, dying in 1935.

Picquart, who was soon afterwards given command of a division, served as Minister of War under Clemenceau, but was never forgiven by his fellow officers, and the reforms he attempted were met with hostility. He was given command of an army corps, but, again thrown from his horse in 1914, he died a few days later, an honourable man but always a little too stiff to be entirely likeable. Schwartzkoppen, also by this time a General, died of wounds in Berlin in 1917, deliriously shouting that Dreyfus was innocent. Du Paty fought with great skill and gallantry and fell at the head of his battalion in 1916. Esterhazy remained in England where he served a period in prison for false pretences. During the war he wrote scurrilous articles lambasting the country which had sheltered him. He died in 1923.

Although brilliant, Dreyfus was considered by people who knew him to be of limited spirit and the Affair in the end became too convoluted ever to be easy to understand, even by the people involved in it. As Charles Péguy, one of the few who managed to make a clear distinction between those supporters of Dreyfus who were devoted to the triumph of justice and those who were out to get what they could out of the Affair, said, 'Everything begins in mystique and finishes up in politics.'

Billy Mitchell

The war which removed so many of the protagonists in the Dreyfus Affair from the scene and so much changed the face of France, toppled dynasties and wrecked economies, had also produced a new element to fighting which, despite its extensive use in the great battles of the Western Front, was still by 1919 barely understood by the leaders of the armies. In the same way that they failed to understand the importance of the tank, so also many of them failed to understand the value of the new element – the air – and its instrument of war, the aeroplane, which had bred a new kind of warrior, young, daring and untouched by old loyalties. These men had created a new service and, making their traditions as they went along, were indifferent to old customs. They were highly technical, had none of the old habits of respect for their elders and were never ever hidebound. From the moment the war started, it had thrown up a new style of military thinker.

America had entered the war in 1917, promising to darken the skies of Europe with American aeroplanes but, when the war finished and for some time afterwards, American airmen were still flying British or French machines. Although some were outstanding, on the whole the American fliers had little time to prove their worth. American aviation did not really figure in the war until the last seven months, but those seven months were quite long enough to start American airmen thinking.

There were plenty of Europeans with experience to encourage them. The end of the war in November 1918, came suddenly and unexpectedly when the allies were still thinking in terms of a 1919 campaign and weapons and machines were still being planned for the coming year. For these, America had been regarded as the arsenal of Europe and the leader of the Allied missions converging on Washington to speed up the building of aircraft by the potentially powerful American plants. Major-General William Sefton Brancker, of the British Air Council, in the summer of 1918, told the American Press, 'The progress of aviation during the last four years has been little short of marvellous. War has been the making of aviation.'

It was the expression of a momentous new fact, the truth and significance of which had not yet fully dawned on the people of the United States. Europeans had been living and dying with it since 1914 but for the vast majority of Americans – despite all they read about what was happening in the skies of France – flying was not quite real. Because they were a long way from the fighting, the new weapon had also failed to be understood by many of the senior American officers. For one of them, one of the few who didn't fail to understand, it brought martyrdom and the role of scapegoat to the old attitudes. Billy Mitchell saw too far ahead, as far ahead in fact as World War II, and he paid the price with disgrace for defying the old ways of thinking.

Visionary, unorthodox genius, flying hero, agitator, William E Mitchell stamped his name in the USA across the decade of the 1920s. Almost from the day he discovered the power of the aeroplane he began to head for his court martial. In a sense, the 1920s in America were the Billy Mitchell era. The war had produced hundreds of young men who had learned to fly and wanted to go on flying and they became romanticised as the barnstormers, men who performed with old aeroplanes for the benefit of civilians. With their stunts and wing-walking they were, in fact, motorised trapeze artistes, devil-may-care gypsies who thrived on the thrills they could

132

give their audiences. Wearing tight-fitting helmets with ribbons sewn to the crown, big bug-eyed goggles, tight breeches and leather jackets and spinning wild and untrue yarns about how they had once faced Richthofen over the fields of France, most of them flew Jennies, JN4Ds, American aeroplanes that were as placid as old cows but, in most cases, were all too often old wrecks whose struts looked as if they'd been repaired with stakes from a fence from one of the fields where they put on their displays.

They were part aviators and part showmen and their little circuses were a peculiarly American institution. The military pilots, however, thought these stunt flyers characterised American aviation's undisciplined adolescence and were determined to bring a professionalism to flying through worthwhile achievements. They were aided very much in their object by one man, Billy Mitchell.

During the 1920s, Billy Mitchell's voice cried out for America's need for a strong air defence and disciplined aviation. As America's first great air war strategist, he had helped break the back of Germany's final effort in France in 1918 and, with the vision to understand the potential of air power, he foresaw the possibility of a Japanese sneak attack on Pearl Harbor twenty years before it happened. He believed the aeroplane had replaced the fleet as the first line of defence and saw it as a great strategic weapon that could carry a war to the sources of an enemy's industrial might. Even before World War I had finished, he was demanding equal status with the navy and the army for the air force, and everything that happened in the post-war years strengthened his beliefs.

Born in Nice in 1879, the son of a United States senator and Civil War veteran, he enlisted in the army as a Private on the outbreak of the Spanish-American war in 1898. Offered a commission, he accepted reluctantly because he felt his father's influence had had a hand in it, and served in the Signal Corps in Cuba, the Philippines and Alaska before becoming interested in aviation. As early as 1906, before the

133

US army even possessed an aeroplane, he wrote prophetically 'Conflicts, no doubt, will be carried out in the future in the air. . .'

Since the Air Service came under the jurisdiction of the Signal Corps, he soon became aware of the development of aviation as part of the military scene. As a signals officer, he was involved with the improvement of the kite balloon and the development of aerial observation, and prophesied that dirigibles would one day be able to fly over a battlefield, carry messages out of beleaguered fortresses and, by means of towed balloons loaded with explosive, would drop bombs on enemy fortifications.

The Aeronautical Division of the Signal Corps was formed in 1907, but Mitchell didn't immediately request to join because, as a married man, he was not eligible for flight training. In 1912, now a Captain, he joined the General Staff in Washington, the youngest officer ever to have been appointed to such a prestigious post. When war broke out in 1914, he was never an isolationist and in 1915 he was asked to prepare a report on the needs of American aviation. He did so, arguing that if the navy should ever fail to stop an invading army, aviation would have to take over. He pointed out that aeroplanes could be used for reconnaissance, for preventing enemy reconnaissance, and for offensive action against submarines and ships. The report drew such attention that, although not yet a flyer, he had become the chief exponent of air power and the accepted spokesman for the air service.

Now a 36-year-old Major, he decided he must learn to fly and took lessons at his own expense. When America entered the war in 1917, Mitchell was assigned to the American Expeditionary Force as Aviation Officer. What he saw made him realise the potential of the aeroplane, and he noted that British and French training and tactics were far superior to America's. He flew as a gunner, went up in observation balloons, and became the first army aviator to cross the enemy lines and the first to be decorated.

Though American troops arrived in France by mid-summer 1917, there was no sign of aviation assistance, and Mitchell noted, 'Our air force consists of one (French) Nieuport plane which I use myself.' He made friends with British and French experts and complained about the lack of American planes and pilots. His anger grew with every delay. In March 1918, when the Germans made their last desperate push, Mitchell was given command of all American fighting squadrons at the front.

Using a nucleus of pilots who had flown with the French or British air forces, he 'begged, borrowed or stole' airfields, hangars and French machines, and on 14 April proclaimed America's entry into the air war. His hero was General Hugh Trenchard, who had been responsible for creating the Royal Air Force and, like Mitchell, was years ahead of his contemporaries in his thinking. His beliefs were simple – air power could and should be used offensively and would one day become more important than sea power. A Brigadier-General by the end of the war, Mitchell had become better known than any of the army generals or navy admirals. He personified the American spirit and when he returned home on the last day of February 1919, as the liner *Aquitania*, steamed into New York Harbour carrying 5,800 returning soldiers, a flight of army aeroplanes appeared overhead from Mitchel Field – not as it happened, named after Billy Mitchell but after a Mayor of New York who was killed while serving in the Air Service.

The machines dived over the ship and dipped their wings and the soldiers cheered and waved, thinking the salute was for the returning heroes. But it wasn't. It was a salute to a single man aboard the ship, Billy Mitchell, America's first flying general, and it was from his own men. He was their idol for his courageous flights over the line and, to the people in the States who had read about his exploits, he was a colourful figure in what had been a drab, colourless episode. He had introduced new ideas and had even talked of dropping soldiers on parachutes behind the

135

German lines, an idea that was startling in the days of the First World War.

Soon after the war Mitchell was made Assistant Chief of the Army Air Service, but he was already a controversial personality and never had any hesitation in explaining his opinion on how aeroplanes should be used. With his row of medals, he was an eye-catching figure and popular with the Press, for whom he was a genius at providing headlines. He believed in air power and the need for an independent air force, both themes which did not coincide with the ideas of the old-school officers of the army and navy. Naval officers never seem to have got on with airmen and to the top American army and navy men, although flying men were passionately behind Mitchell almost to a man, he had already become anathema, as much as anything because he struggled constantly to obtain government funds for the air service that the other two services felt should be available to them. The same thing exactly was happening in Britain.

To let people know about aeroplanes and their potential, Mitchell organised a series of spectacular flights – the first, in 1919, a race from coast to coast and back. Unfortunately, it was hardly the success he hoped because nine men lost their lives; but it was followed by the Round-the-Rim Flight, tracing the boundaries of the United States by aeroplane. Despite a crash-landing, the circuit, 9,823 miles long, was completed in seventy-eight days, with 100 landings, no mean achievement considering the shortage in those days of emergency fields. Believing firmly that Alaska was a natural defence outpost against air attack from the east, in 1920 Mitchell organised the New York to Nome flight. Officialdom regarded danger from the east as ridiculous, but the flight was made, taking six weeks with once again rough landings in wheatfields and bush clearings. At Nome, the leader of the flight wired for permission to cross the Bering Strait to Siberia. The request was refused.

In 1922 an attempt was made to fly non-stop from coast to coast. The first attempt, from west to east, ended with the aeroplane having to turn back, but it nevertheless put up a world endurance record. The second try ended with a radiator leak. On the third attempt, trying from east to west, two air force lieutenants, Oakley G Kelly and John A Mcready completed the flight in a Fokker T2 in 1923. In that year, the air service also demonstrated in-flight refuelling despite the danger from petrol falling on hot exhaust pipes, and in 1924 a Curtiss PW8 pursuit plane actually raced the sun across the United States.

Billy Mitchell was behind all these flights, but his big dramatic role came in what became known as the bombing of the battleships, a stunt he forced on the authorities to prove what he had come to believe was Gospel – that the aeroplane was mightier than the warship.

Despite what had been discovered about the possibilities of aerial bombing during the war, the US Navy still considered itself the nation's first line of defence, and the chief bulwark of that line of defence was the battleship. This was despite the fact that in Europe it was already being felt, among thinking junior naval officers, that such huge ships had become a waste of money and men. They were useless for protecting convoys and were so expensive they needed a fleet of smaller ships to protect them every time they moved. The greatest naval battle of the war had ended indecisively and for most of the hostilities the great ships of both sides had swung at anchor in safe harbours.

To the US Navy, however, it seemed impossible that one of their dreadnoughts could be sunk by bombs. Mitchell infuriated the admirals with his assertion that any ship in existence could be destroyed from an aeroplane and his insistence that, while the navy felt the armoured ship was the mistress of the sea, in fact it was just as helpless as an armoured knight had been when firearms had been used against him.

Mitchell was forty now, handsome and extrovert, a skilled pilot and already personifying the difference between the airman and the foot soldier. He was arrogant, flamboyant and possessed too-sharp a tongue, but all these things made people listen to him. Among his most ardent supporters were Eddie Rickenbacker, America's greatest flier of World War I, and other men who were to become famous names in World War II like 'Hap' Arnold, Jimmy Doolittle and 'Tooey' Spaatz. One who opposed him was Richard E Byrd who felt that, although he was sincere, he was a zealot and years ahead of the present state of aviation. But Byrd was a navy man.

Although Mitchell continued to insist he could sink a battleship with bombs and begged for an old one for a trial, the navy ignored him, and the Secretary of the Navy, Josephus Daniels, once complained to the Secretary of War about him.

He was not without his naval supporters, nevertheless. Though 'salt-water' admirals lined up solidly against his infringement of the concept of sea-power as the first line of defence, there were a few who came to Mitchell's side privately. Admiral William S Sims, World War I Commander-in-Chief in European Waters, remarked, 'The average man suffers very severely from the pain of a new idea ... It is my belief that the future will show that the fleet that has twenty aeroplane carriers instead of sixteen battleships and four aeroplanes will inevitably knock the other fleet out.' Another supporter, Admiral W F Fullam, concluded, 'Sea-power will be subordinated to or dependent upon air-power', while in Britain, Admiral Sir John Fisher observed, 'By land and by sea the approaching aircraft development knocks out the present fleet, makes invasion practicable, cancels our country being an island, transforms the atmosphere into a background of the future. There is only one thing to do with the ostriches who are spending their vast millions on what is as useful for the next war as bows and arrows. Sack the lot.'

The official reaction in the navy, of course, was dominated by the sea-going diehards who could not stand the idea of aircraft replacing the vast ships they loved so much and which looked so splendid in review.

Not that the navy was oblivious to the possibilities of aeroplanes but it found it impossible to regard them in any other way but as the eyes of the fleet. After all, they pointed out, it was a naval seaplane which had made the first crossing of the Atlantic in 1919, and in 1929 they had begun converting a collier, *Jupiter*, into an experimental aircraft carrier, to be named *Langley*. When, in 1921, the navy opened a Bureau of Aeronautics, its chief, Rear Admiral William A Moffett, actually agreed with Mitchell on the potential of air power, though not as a separate service.

The argument went on. World naval disarmament was being discussed and it was an important point for Mitchell that for the $45,000,000 that were needed to build a battleship which might even be scrapped under the forthcoming treaty, you could buy 1000 aeroplanes. And, he liked to add, a few of those aeroplanes could sink that ship. Why couldn't he be given an old unwanted battleship to prove his theory?

General Henry H ('Hap') Arnold, Commander-in-Chief of the US Army Air Forces in World War II, described what followed as Mitchell took his case for tests to the public through the newspapers. 'On every sort of pretext, all kinds of people tried to stop the tests. Strong pressure was brought to bear on President Harding and on Congress. But Mr Harding liked the way Billy Mitchell did things, or in any case, sensed, with a good instinct, Billy's appeal to the American public.'

Growing irritated by Mitchell, the navy arranged a small experiment, with Mitchell as an observer. Taking the obsolete battleship, *Indiana*, into Chesapeake Bay in late 1920, they bombed her with dummy bombs filled with sand and exploded stationary bombs on deck and in the water. The deck became a tangle of wreckage but the *Indiana* failed to sink. Appearing before the House Committee on Appropriations in 1921, Mitchell pointed out that from 5000 feet eleven per cent direct hits had been made with the dummy bombs on the *Indiana's* deck. The navy was furious that Mitchell had given away data it considered confidential to the Navy Department, and had made public a report which said the bombing had demonstrated the improbability of a modern battleship being either destroyed or put out of action. Josephus Daniels made sarcastic comments about 'Admiral Mitchell' trying to qualify as a 'naval expert'.

The *London Illustrated News* had published two photographs of the damage done to the *Indiana*'s deck, though none had appeared in the American Press, and Britain was deeply interested in what was going on in the States because, while the uproar was going on in Washington, she had sunk at Spithead the dreadnought, *Baden*, formerly part of the German High Seas Fleet, with a combination of gunnery, bombing and torpedoes dropped from the air, the last-named being the decisive factor.

On its surrender in 1918, the Imperial German Navy had been divided among the victorious allies, to be sunk for test purposes within a given time limit. The biggest of America's share was the battleship, *Ostfriesland*, a squat, powerful vessel that was by no means obsolete. Built in 1909 with a triple hull and watertight compartments, she had survived eighteen shell hits and a mine at the Battle of Jutland, and Admiral von Tirpitz had christened her the 'unsinkable battleship'.

Unwilling to turn over ships to the Air Service, however, the navy arranged a compromise. Both houses of Congress were already willing to place the German ships at the disposal of the Air Service but, before a decision could be made, the Navy and War Departments, acting together, announced that joint army-navy bombing tests were to be conducted, using nine of the German ships as targets. The tests would be under rules fixed by the navy, and naval seaplanes would take their turn at bombing.

Josephus Daniels agreed to the tests, but on behalf of the navy, 'blared forth' defiance. According to Arnold, he said he would 'stand bareheaded on the bridge of any battleship during the bombardment by any airplane, by God, and expected to remain safe.' He only regretted that the eager airmen could not be allowed to attack under actual combat conditions 'to learn how fast would-be bombers would be shot down by battleships in a real war.'

This defiance, instead of arousing derision against the airmen, merely made them more determined, and they began to besiege Mitchell with the request that the navy be allowed to shoot back at them while they sank the battleships.

'Let's do the thing right,' they said. 'It was,' Arnold claimed, 'probably the nearest thing to an undeclared civil war since the Whiskey Rebellion ... in 1794.'

The tests were to be carried out at sea seventy-five miles off the Virginia Capes so that the ships could sink in deep water. This meant that the Air Service bombers would have to fly from Langley Field, twenty-five miles inland, a distance of around 100 miles. This was a severe test for the aeroplanes of the day with their limited range, and there was even a danger that some of them might run out of fuel and come down in the sea.

Mitchell would have preferred a point off Cape Hatteras at a spot only twenty miles offshore, or even Cape Cod where the tests could have been carried out ten miles offshore. Talking to his bombardiers, however, he reminded them that where they were to do their bombing was near where the *Monitor* had once battled with the *Merrimac*, a Civil War contest that had spelled the end of wooden warships, and that with their bombs they could start another naval revolution.

Gathering the best pilots in America at Langley Field, he formed them into the 1st Provisional Air Brigade. They were placed on a war footing and trained rigorously. Targets the size and shape of battleships were marked out for them, and they dropped bombs on the scrapped hulks of the *Indiana* and *Texas* in Chesapeake Bay. For his main attack, Mitchell chose a squadron of Martin bombers powered with twin liberty engines, capable of carrying a ton of bombs and with a range of between 500 and 600 miles. He also had a Handley Page, two Capronis, and a large number of De

Havillands. He was determined to make the operation as significant as he could because he knew if he failed that it would be the end of him and he was well aware that there were plenty of people who would like to see him fail. He later even accused the navy of trying to prevent him sinking the *Ostfriesland*.

Since he had no bombs at the time bigger than 1100 lbs, he persuaded General C C Williams, US Chief of Ordnance, to manufacture 2000 pounders for the occasion. They were the world's largest bombs at the time and were not exceeded until World War II.

The tests began on 21 June 1921, and were spaced over a month, while the whole of America watched. Almost the whole US Atlantic Fleet was in the area, and official observers, high ranking officers, Congressmen, foreign attachés and reporters watched from the transport, *Henderson*. The navy had ruled that only a given number of bombs were to be dropped at one sortie, after which the planes must withdraw to allow a control ship to assess the damage. It was well known that under the agreement made with the other allied powers, the German ships had to be sunk by 24 July and that, if the bombs failed, naval gun-fire was to give the *coup de grâce*. The new battleship, *Pennsylvania*, was at hand, fully expecting to use her broad-sides to finish off the *Ostfriesland*.

Mitchell's men were not allowed to use their bombs until three weeks after the tests had begun. On the first day, a German submarine, U117, was sunk by naval planes from Hampton Roads. Their 163 lb bombs split the submarine open like a pea pod and sank it within sixteen minutes. The speed with which it had been despatched surprised some observers but the anti-Mitchell officers consoled themselves with the thought that a submarine was very different from a battleship. The following day two more submarines were sunk by gunfire from destroyers. On 29 June, the target was the radio-controlled battleship, *Iowa*, but only dummy bombs were to be used because the object of the exercise was to see how many hits could be scored. Of eighty dummy bombs dropped, only two scored direct hits and aboard the *Henderson* there was some gloating.

The first vessel allowed entirely for the use of the Air Service was a destroyer, and Mitchell ordered fifty planes into action. Flying in waves and beginning with small bombs, they worked up to 300 pounders carried by the Martins. The destroyer broke in two after forty-four bombs and sank in nineteen minutes. The navy pointed out she had been a sitting duck and had not been protected by anti-aircraft fire. Mitchell had accompanied every mission in his own DH4, trailing a pennant, and couldn't resist circling the *Henderson* after the sinking.

His orders to the bombardiers for the bigger ships were not to try to hit the armoured decks but to drop their bombs alongside in the water, to crush in the hulls with the water-hammer effect. The turn of the light cruiser, *Frankfurt*, came on 18 July. She resisted assault all day by navy, marine and army planes dropping light bombs and after the sixth attack, a naval officer in *Henderson* observed, 'I'm feeling safer every minute.'

In the late afternoon, however, six Martin bombers left their base. They had to circle the target for an inordinate length of time while the control ship lay alongside the *Frankfurt*, lingering over the damage inspection. Finally the Squadron Commander radioed that his fuel was limited and he must begin bombing in fifteen minutes. The control ship still took another ten minutes to move away, then the Martins swooped down and planted fourteen bombs. The *Frankfurt* reared up and slipped under bow-first.

There was still the *Ostfriesland*. For this General John Pershing, the American Commander in France during the war and now America's most distinguished soldier, and the Secretary of the Navy were watching. With poor visibility and a squall, the first day, 20 July, went poorly for Mitchell. No bomb heavier than 600 lbs had been used before the tests were called off, and the *New York Times* correspondent observed, 'It was a great day for the advocates of the battleship.' Yet seams had been sprung and the ship had settled two feet by the stern during the night.

On the following day, the heavy bombs made their appearance, first the 1100 pounders. The navy had insisted there could be only two direct hits with each major type of bomb, and after three hits the bombers were ordered away and the inspection ship moved in. In the afternoon, six Martins appeared, each carrying one of the new giant bombs, followed by the Handley Page carrying another. One by one the Martins laid their eggs in the water, not on the deck, but alongside, and the 'unsinkable' ship turned turtle and went down by the stern twenty-five minutes after the first bomb had been dropped. The Handley Page dropped its bomb in the oil slick.

There was a dead silence. Everybody who had been watching knew he had seen the beginning of a new era, and some of the naval officers actually had tears in their eyes. That night there was a tremendous celebration at Langley Field.

General Williams, whose skill had produced the giant bombs, said, 'A bomb was fired today that will be heard around the world.' Admiral William A. Moffett, of the Bureau of Naval Aeronautics, was even more blunt. 'The lesson,' he said, 'is that we must put planes on battleships and get aircraft carriers quickly.'

After the sinking of the *Ostfriesland*, in an exhaustive 442-page report to the War Department on 29 August 1921, Mitchell concluded that 'Air forces, with the types of aircraft now in existence or in development, acting from shore bases, can find and destroy all classes of seacraft under war conditions, with a negligible loss to the aircraft' and 'Aircraft acting from suitable floating aerodromes can destroy any class of surface seacraft on the high seas.' He concluded by insisting that 'the problem of the destruction of seacraft by air forces has been solved, and is finished.'

But his opponents had not been entirely convinced. The report of the Joint Army-Navy Board, led by General

144

Pershing, admitted that the aeroplane had 'added to the complexity of naval warfare' and stressed the need for aircraft carriers, but still reached the conclusion that the battleship remained 'the backbone of the fleet and the bulwark of the nation's sea defence'. The Assistant Secretary of the Navy, future President Franklin D Roosevelt, had remarked before the tests that 'the day of the battleship has not passed, and it is highly unlikely that an aeroplane, or a fleet of them, could ever successfully sink a fleet of navy vessels, under battle conditions.' Even after the test, he remained unconvinced. 'I once saw a man kill a lion with a 30–30 rifle under certain conditions,' he remarked. 'But that does not mean a 30–30 is a lion gun.'

Mitchell, of course, was completely vindicated when World War II came, but inevitably, at the time there were loud cries of 'Foul' and some navy officers suggested that he had cut short the assessment of damage at each stage in the tests. In reply, Mitchell charged the navy with making the tests as difficult and dangerous as possible for the bombers.

Being a hardheaded realist, he knew the public would quickly forget what he had demonstrated and that his battle had to be fought over and over again. A week after the test off the Virginia Capes, he staged a simulated bombing attack on New York City. This was followed with simulated bomb runs over eastern cities and, as before, he let the Press carry his message to the people. He wrote many articles expounding his theories and demanding a new national awareness of the air. He took to the air himself, and demanded that his pilots do the same, to prove that aeroplanes could perform the feats he said they could. In air races at Detroit in 1922 he established a new speed record of 224.38 miles an hour, almost unthinkable in those days.

With vessels about to be scrapped under the disarmament treaty, Mitchell was given another battleship, the *Alabama*, which his airmen polished off with a 2000 lb bomb. In 1923, two more battleships the *New Jersey* and the *Virginia*, were handed over. *Virginia* was sunk by a 1100 bomb from 3000 feet. The second ship, the War Department ruled, was to be bombed from 10,000 feet. At that time, no bomber could climb that high with a bomb load, but Mitchell had just acquired a few new superchargers and, hastily installing them, his Martins climbed easily to 10,000 feet and with new bomb sighting methods, sank the *New Jersey* with 2000 pounders.

Britain had pioneered the idea of an aircraft carrier in World War I and had several in service. Japan was converting two cruisers. But despite the *Ostfriesland*, Congress allowed only one, the old collier, *Langley*. The next session of Congress, however, reacting to Mitchell's victory, authorised the conversion of two cruisers under construction, which became the *Saratoga* and *Lexington*, which were still in service in World War II.

Mitchell obviously could not be disregarded, despite the enemies he had undoubtedly made. He had served as Assistant Chief of the Air Service under two consecutive chiefs, Major-General Charles T Menoher and Major-General Mason M Patrick. Neither enjoyed having him as a deputy because his refusal to stop crusading had become an embarrassment. When he was needling the navy to provide an obsolete battleship, Menoher, who had been given the job specifically to discipline the fliers, was begging him to 'speak softly' and, when he refused, Menoher had actually asked the Secretary of War to remove him only a few weeks before the *Ostfriesland* triumph. The Secretary of War, John W Weeks, persuaded Menoher to withdraw his request but finally, under General Patrick, who as it happened was in agreement with Mitchell's crusade for a separate air force, he was finally removed.

By this time, however, he was not a voice crying in the wilderness. Many other fliers, both army and navy, were thinking along similar lines and Mitchell was only the axis round whom their thinking revolved. They were already saying that air warfare was beyond the scope of armies, even though related to them, and must therefore be organised

146

separately. The law of concentration demanded such a measure but air warfare, by its very nature, needed to be organised by airmen rather than army men.

In the summer of 1919, the Secretary of War, Newton D Baker, had sent an eight-man aviation mission to Europe to gather ideas as to how America should meet the challenge of the air. It was headed by the Assistant Secretary of War, Benedict Crowell, and its members went their separate ways across Europe. Britain already had a separate air force and when the members of the mission reassembled, they had all reached very much the same conclusion. The dynamite in their report was one that Secretary Baker had not expected, because one of their recommendations was 'The concentration of the air activities of the United States, civilian, naval and military, within the direction of a single Governmental agency, created for the purpose, equal in importance and representation with the Departments of War, Navy and Commerce.' It was just what Mitchell and his supporters had always demanded.

Baker couldn't suppress the report but he considered the mission had gone too far in suggesting a centralised air force, and nothing was done about the recommendation. Congressional hearings became the platform for Mitchell, therefore, and at one of them, Benedict Crowell, the leader of Baker's mission, was asked with a trace of sarcasm 'if he believed that within a few years Congress would be discussing ... a United States aviation academy along the lines of West Point or Annapolis, the army and navy academies.' Risking the displeasure of Baker, Crowell replied briskly, 'I think we should be discussing that *now*.'

A Bill, proposing an independent Department of Aviation, became a hardy annual and was still around in 1925. Admiral Hilary Jones said indignantly that 'malcontents and agitators' – by whom he clearly meant Mitchell and his followers – 'should attend to business or get out of the service. This propaganda,' he continued 'has been going on ever since the Armistice. In its inception it was selfish. It has

147

become worse. It has long since passed the stage of legitimate agitation for reform and ... become a menace to the security of the country.'

Mitchell was quick to reply to the admiral and the first thing he did was charge the navy with doing its best to hinder the 1921 bombings. His term as Assistant Chief was due to expire and there were already rumours that he might not be reappointed. At another hearing, he claimed that any third-rate nation with air power could defeat the United States, and, with prophetic insight, claimed that Japan 'could take the Philippines and Hawaii and other Pacific islands within two weeks and we couldn't stop it.'

This seemed blasphemy and, as predicted, Mitchell was not reappointed, reverting to his permanent rank of Colonel and assigned as Air Service Officer of the VIII Corps Area at San Antonio, Texas. Although he had been pushed as far from Washington as possible, he refused to be silenced. 'I have not even begun to fight,' he said.

Soon afterwards, Major General Charles P Summerall, Commandant of the II Corps Area, in a speech in New York, said that the Air Service could never be anything more than an aid to infantry. He said that 'the most extravagant claims have been entertained for the aeroplane, none of which ever approached realisation.' He insisted that the public was being deceived by 'loose, fanciful and irresponsible talk by people whose experience of war was limited to the narrow field of aviation.' It was obvious whom he meant when he said, 'I cannot imagine a worse enemy ... than one who would destroy the unity of action of our forces by removing the Air Service as an integral part of the army or navy ...'

Meanwhile, irritated by the army's successes in flying, the navy attempted to reap the same sort of publicity with a flight from California to Hawaii, the longest uninterrupted over-water stretch remaining to be conquered – 2100 nautical miles. Two new twin-engined flying boats, PN-9s, and a Boeing PB-1 were to take off on 31 August 1925, each with a five-man crew, and the navy strung destroyers and the new carrier, *Langley*, at 200-mile intervals along the route.

PN-9-1 led off, but the PB-1 failed to start and PN-9-3 was forced down after 400 miles. Missing the final destroyer that marked its route, PN-9-1 radioed that it was low on petrol. Silence followed and for days the nation was in suspense until, just as hope was abandoned and after ten days adrift on the water, a submarine found the flying boat and towed it to port. While this drama was being enacted, another tragedy struck the navy when the dirigible, *Shenandoah*, broke into pieces over Ohio with the loss of fourteen lives.

Mitchell grabbed at the two incidents with both hands. On 5 September, he delivered a blistering statement to reporters. 'These accidents,' he said, 'are the direct results of incompetency, criminal negligence and almost treasonable administration of the National Defence by the Navy and War Departments.' He claimed that in their attempts to prevent a separate air service handled by aeronautical experts, they had gone to unreasonable lengths. 'All aviation policies, schemes and systems,' he insisted, 'are dictated by the non-flying officers of the army or navy ... who know practically nothing about it.'

This wasn't all. 'The lives of airmen,' he went on, 'are being used ... as pawns in their hands.' Congress, he asserted, was being used by the Navy and Army Departments 'as if it were an organisation created for their benefit ... We are utterly disgusted with the conduct of our military affairs applying to aviation. Our pilots know they are going to be killed if they stay in the service, on account of the methods employed, in the old floating coffins that we are still flying.'

This time Mitchell had gone too far, and the War Department, fully aware that it would make a martyr of him, had no choice but to court martial him. He had been well aware of this and, while waiting for official reaction, he went fishing. He was not arrested for several weeks but he was relieved of duty and ordered to Washington where he was met by a drum and bugle band of the American Legion and a barbecue was given in his honour.

In October, the War Department announced there would be a court martial based on conduct prejudicial to good order and military discipline, and eight charges were drawn up, one of them taxing Mitchell with making a statement 'highly contemptuous and disrespectful' to the War Department. He was finally placed under technical arrest.

The then President of the United States, Calvin Coolidge, who had to issue the order for the court martial, was aware of the uproar Mitchell had caused and he appointed a nine-man Aircraft Inquiry Board to study and make recommendations on the nation's air policy. Taking Mitchell's testimony at once, they heard him blame 'bumbling amateurs' for the recent accidents, and claim that the sending of the *Shenandoah* on an inland cruise was nonsense and a violation of the law defining army and navy jurisdictions.

The court martial started on 28 October 1925, going on until 17 December, the longest court martial in US military history, chiefly because Mitchell was allowed a surprising latitude in his evidence. Despite the number of courtrooms and auditoriums available, the court sat in a second floor room of a shabby brick warehouse used for the storage of records and office furniture. The room had to be cleaned of inch-thick dust and cobwebs, splinters protruded from the bare floor, the walls looked as if lined with cardboard and the windows commanded a view only of a narrow alley. Besides the court, the room could accommodate forty newspapermen and eighty spectators, and the only thing that could be surmised was that it was a deliberate attempt to deprive the trial of any sign of judicial pomp or dignity. Despite this, crowds gathered outside, among them women from the Social Register.

Mitchell's counsel was Colonel Herbert A White, a judge advocate from the VIII Corps Area. He also had a civilian attorney, Congressman Frank Reid, of Illinois. The officers appearing for the prosecution were Colonel Sherman

Moreland, Lieutenant-Colonel Joseph J McMullen and Major Allen W Gullion. The original panel of judges included eleven generals and a colonel – not one of them a flier – among them General Douglas MacArthur, who was to be the senior US General in the Pacific during World War II, but at the time commanding the III Corps Area and an old friend of Mitchell's. General Summerall – the man who had criticised advocates of a separate air force – was president.

Mitchell seemed in no way depressed, and arrived in a neat uniform with four rows of medals on his chest and accompanied by his wife, who sat with him throughout the trial. Smiling, he shook hands with all the judges, but within a short time the defence began to challenge them, chiefly General Summerall on the grounds of 'bias, prejudice and hostility'. Summerall left the room flushed and angry, and the number of judges was reduced to nine, with Major-General Robert L Howze as president.

Congressman Reid pleaded free speech and insisted Mitchell was being tried for things he had said and should therefore be permitted to prove the truth of his statements. The Government had no wish to make a martyr out of Mitchell and the court permitted a long string of defence witnesses in support of Mitchell's views on air power, the condition of the Air Service and the desirability of a separate air force. The charges against Mitchell didn't touch on these points at all and they had no bearing on his guilt or innocence, so that, in effect, the court became the best forum Mitchell could ever have wished for.

Among those who spoke for him were Rickenbacker, America's greatest ace in World War I, Major Carl ('Tooey') Spaatz, Representative Fiorello LaGuardia, once an airman and later Mayor of New York, and Rear-Admiral William S Sims (US Navy, retired). Prosecution witnesses were the pilot of PN-9-1, who contradicted Mitchell's assertions about inadequate preparations and poor equipment for the Hawaii Flight, and Lieutenant-Commander Richard E Byrd, later a polar flier, who similarly denied what Mitchell had said about the amphibians he had flown to Greenland that summer. Grover C Loening, who had built the machines, defended his work, and a string of government witnesses belittled Mitchell's descriptions of the DH-4s as 'flaming coffins'. A great deal of talk was allowed about whether or not anti-aircraft fire could forestall a bombing attack.

During the testimony of a witness for Mitchell, one of the panel of judges, Brigadier-General Edward L King, was heard to comment that the witness was talking 'damn rot'. It almost ended the trial there and then. Reid protested angrily and it took some days to decide that the remark did not constitute undue prejudice.

The surprise of the trial was the appearance for Mitchell of Mrs Zachary Lansdowne, widow of the Commander of the *Shenandoah*, who said a clumsy attempt had been made to influence her testimony. She insisted that the technical aide to the Secretary of the Navy had called on her and wanted her to twist facts. She also said that the Commandant of the Lakehurst Naval Air Station had presented her with a typed statement of a similar tone. He had wanted her to sign it but she had torn it up. Her testimony was offered as an indication of military incompetence.

Major Gullion summed up for the prosecution with a wild diatribe that accused Mitchell of being of the 'charlatan and demagogue type', claiming that he would make sure that the united Air Service of his dreams would have him as its head. Mitchell, he said, was 'a good flier, a fair rider, a good shot, flamboyant, self-advertising, widely imaginative, destructive, never constructive except in wild, non-feasible schemes, and never very careful about the ethics of his methods.' He demanded dismissal from the service.

After several hours of deliberation, on 17 December the court gave its verdict. The accused was found guilty and was to be suspended from rank, command and duty, with forfeiture of all pay and allowance for five years. They claimed to be showing leniency because of Mitchell's military record.

Mitchell took the verdict composedly and shook hands with the judges. A reporter, rummaging in the waste paper basket in the judge's room, claimed that he found proof that MacArthur had voted against the sentence. Mitchell talked him out of making his discovery public. In his memoirs, MacArthur said that his service on the court martial was one of the most distasteful orders he had ever received. He was, he wrote, thoroughly in accord with the concept of air power, and that, far from betraying his friend, he had without doubt saved him from dismissal from the service. Mitchell, he said, was clearly wrong in the violence of the language he had used but was absolutely right in his views.

Congress erupted in an uproar at the result and was very critical of the sentence. One representative called it 'unusual, cruel and shameless'. The decision not to dismiss Mitchell, he said, meant that he could not work yet he was retained without pay – a verdict, he thought, that insulted free America. A few Air Service officers resigned in protest.

In an attempt to soothe tempers, a month later President Coolidge restored Mitchell's allowance and half his basic pay, but Mitchell showed his contempt by promptly resigning his commission. In his letter of resignation, he denounced the 'military bureaucracy' who, he said, had 'coerced, bulldozed and attempted to ruin patriotic officers' who disagreed with their views. Finally, he said he felt he could better serve his country by bringing a realisation of the true condition of national defence to the people as a civilian rather than being muzzled in the army. Free now to say what he wished, he set out on a lecture tour, fighting on with a flow of speeches and writings. He lived like a gentleman and bred livestock on his Virginia estate.

Meanwhile the Aircraft Inquiry Board, instituted by Coolidge, gave a categorical 'No' to a separate department for air and denied that the United States was in any danger of attack by air. But it nevertheless recommended that the position of Assistant Secretary of War in Charge of Aviation should be created and that a flying officer should be placed on the general staff. To encourage civil aviation, it recommended a Bureau of Air Navigation in the Department of Commerce.

Without doubt, it was the uproar raised by Mitchell which had led to the appointment of the board, and its report led quickly to legislation which put American aviation on a sound footing. The days of the barnstormers were past. At the next session of Congress, the Air Service was upgraded to the Air Corps, its personnel increased, and the requirement laid down that its commanding officers should be fliers. It meant, in effect, that at last the United States got an air ministry. Five-year programmes were set up for both navy and army aviation but it was to take another twenty years before a separate air force was instituted.

Mitchell had started it on its way, however, though unfortunately he didn't live to see it. Ten years after his resignation the Senate passed a bill to put him on the retired officers' list with the rank of Major-General, but it was quashed by the House Military Affairs Committee. As it was, Mitchell entered hospital in New York for a rest and on 19 February 1936, died of a heart attack.

Ironically, as he was being taken to his native Wisconsin for burial, the Air Corps was placing its order for the first of the new B17 Flying Fortresses, which in World War II were to be the spearhead of the air power for which he had fought so long. And his prophesies about air attack were proved entirely accurate when, on 7 December 1941, the Japanese destroyed the US Pacific Fleet by their bombing attack on Pearl Harbor.

Mutiny In The East

About the time when Billy Mitchell was first beginning to conceive his ideas about air power, conditions in India gave rise to two separate incidents, both of which brought about the end of an honourable regiment of the British Army.

Despite the slaughter on the Western Front and the apparent indifference of the leaders, both civilian and military, to the sufferings of the soldiers throughout the 1914–1918 war, the only semblance of mutiny in the British Army in France was the outbreak in 1917 at Etaples, at a reception camp for drafts of men from the United Kingdom whose demonstrations against conditions were allowed to get out of control. The French Army had rebelled earlier in the year from sheer weariness, the influence of the Russian Revolution and a general disillusionment with their military leaders following one failed offensive after another. The British Army in France, however, somehow managed to avoid such extremes. But, though in France it avoided the disgrace, in the East it was not so fortunate. Both mutinies concerned Indians. In one case it was the Indians who mutinied. In the other case it was Irishmen protesting that what they were doing to Indians was being done also to the Irish in Ireland. Both incidents concerned proud regiments.

War is always an opportunity for men with nationalistic ambitions and the period when an oppressor nation or occupying power is heavily involved in a war is always a chance for the oppressed to make trouble to advance their

155

cause for freedom. 1914–1918, which produced the chance for self-determination to Poles, Czechs, Russians, and the small Baltic states, was also the opportunity for India and Ireland, both countries suffering from British oppression.

Mutiny had never been unknown in the British forces. In the eighteenth century, the Highland regiments of the British Army, who could be called Britain's earliest colonial levies, revolted against their conditions. Contrary to romantic belief, the Highlander was rarely a willing soldier and was often recruited by threat, sold by chiefs he trusted, or had his pride outraged by contempt for his dress, while the family he hoped to protect by enlistment were often evicted in his absence to make way for sheep.

The Black Watch were the first to rebel in 1743, and the mutinies continued until 1804. The Seaforths defied the Crown on Arthur's Seat for three days. Atholl Highlanders held Portsmouth for a week. The Argyll Fencibles threatened the security of Scotland. Strathspey men defied their officers at Linlithgow. And the Black Watch and Fraser's Regiment were prepared to fight a bloody battle in defence of their native dress.

In 1797, in protest against conditions, sailors of the Royal Navy mutinied at Spithead and the Nore, and in 1857, sepoys of the East India Company's army mutinied in an upheaval that was not put down until 1859 and left a trauma of fear among British families in India that lasted until World War II.

Mutinies start for a variety of reasons and in Singapore in February 1915, there was an outbreak among the 5th Light Infantry of the Indian Army, an entirely Muslim unit composed of Rajputs and Moghul Pathans and one of the oldest regiments in the British Indian Army. The regiment had been borne out of the disturbed relations with the Mahratta powers in Central India at the end of the eighteenth century. In expectation of war with them, the strength of the Indian Native Army in Bengal was increased and a new regiment of two battalions, the 2nd Bengal Infantry, was formed.

156

The first battalion was raised at Fategarh and the second at Cawnpore in 1903 by Captain Jeremiah Martin Johnson. First called the 2nd Battalion The 21st Regiment Bengal Native Infantry, it became the 42nd Native Infantry in 1824 and a light infantry regiment in 1843. After the Indian Mutiny, the surviving Bengal regiments were renumbered, and the 42nd became the 5th Bengal Native (Light) Infantry. In 1885 the word 'Native' was dropped and, after the army reforms of 1902, the regiment became known as the 5th Light Infantry, though to its men it was always known as Johnson's Regiment after the man who raised it. Its battle honours included the Arakan, Afghanistan and Kandahar, 1842; Ghunze, 1842; Kabul and Moodkee, Ferozeshah and Sobroan, 1857. It fought in the Second Afghan War of 1879–80 and in the Third Burmese War of 1885–7. From then on it was involved solely in garrison duties until 1914 when it received its first overseas posting to Singapore. Unfortunately, at that time, in Lieutenant-Colonel Edward Victor Martin, who assumed command in 1913, it possessed a leader in whom his British officers had no confidence and for whom his Indian officers had no respect. In addition, these two elements had their own factions which quarrelled unceasingly with each other. Thanks to Martin's over-lenient methods of dealing with troublemakers, the regiment had become undisciplined and was seething with discontent, and a number of the men – including non-commissioned and Indian officers – were a prey to the insidious and disruptive influences of anti-Raj Muslim extremists who were members of a world-wide movement known as Ghadr (in translation, Mutiny).

With war in the near future, Germany had taken full advantage of this movement through its embassy and consulates in America, and German agents throughout the world had acted as distributors of propaganda. The headquarters of the movement were in San Francisco and had the open friendship of officers in the local German consulate. In July 1914, it moved to Geneva and, after the outbreak of war in August, was invited to operate from Berlin, where its officials worked under the guidance of the German War and Foreign Offices, their object to ferment revolutionary activities among Indian troops in India and overseas. Emissaries travelled throughout the sub-continent and to Rangoon, Singapore, Hong Kong and Japan, asking for volunteers to start mutinies, offering them only death, martyrdom and freedom for India as a reward. The most emotive opportunity for gaining support came when Turkey entered the war in November 1914, as an ally of Germany, and German, Turkish and Indian propaganda on a pan-Islamic plane denounced Britain for using Muslim soldiers to fight Turkish Muslim troops.

Another cause of discontent in the regiment was that a vacancy had been caused in the ranks of jemadars (Indian subalterns) by the death of a Pathan officer. His clan naturally expected his successor would come from among them, but a contender was Havildar Imtiaz Ali, a long-serving Rajput to whom Colonel Martin had promised promotion. Unfortunately, he was obliged to withdraw his nomination when the Government of India disagreed and a Pathan was selected. This antagonised Imtiaz Ali and his friends and, though this cause was dismissed as unimportant by the court of enquiry that sat after the mutiny, there is no doubt that it helped to stir up the unhappiness in the regiment.

An additional abrasive element was the presence in Singapore of prisoners of war from the German cruiser, *Emden*, which had operated in Far Eastern waters until destroyed off the Cocos-Keeling Islands in late 1914, as well as sailors from captured merchant ships, and German aliens who had been resident in Singapore. There were around 300 of these men, the most enterprising among them a rollicking, portly Oberleutnant called Julius Lauterbach, the former master of a German merchant ship and a man with a great sense of humour. Perhaps unwittingly, Lauterbach fanned the discontent by convincing certain of the NCOs of the 5th, who had taken over guard duties at the prisoner of war camp, that the Germans were winning the war and that all the stories about British victories were false. Lauterbach's activities were only undertaken to further his own personal plan to escape but they had the effect of increasing the discord in the 5th.

Problems existed in every strata of the regiment. The British officers were divided about the quality of their commanding officer but united that their influence over the men had been eroded by his passion to be the 'soldiers' friend'. Pathan and Rajput officers were rent with antagonisms which filtered down to the men, and there were two cliques, one led by the Subedar-Major, Khan Mohammed Khan (the principal native officer in the battalion holding a rank equivalent to Lieutenant), and the other comprising Subedar (company commander) Dunde Khan and Jemadars (subalterns) Chisti Khan and Abdul Ali Khan, who were later identified as ringleaders of the mutiny. Their being at variance militated against the maintenance of discipline but fortunately there was no sympathy between the Indian officers and men of the Left (Pathan) Wing of the Regiment and those of the Right (Rajput) Wing.

The sepoys didn't like life in Singapore and had complained about their rations; and the whole situation was compounded by the anti-British propaganda spread in the Indian Muslim quarter of Singapore. The Indian officers were invited into Indian homes and the other ranks found their diversions in the Muslim quarter of the city, while their religious and social haven was in a mosque where they met and listened to the imam, Nur Alam Shah, a hypnotic speaker who was regarded almost as a prophet but was later revealed to be a member of a dissident Indian Muslim nationalist group. One final influence was that of Kassim Ali Mansoor, an elderly and wealthy Indian Muslim merchant, who was revealed as the tool of Indian Muslim activists working against the Raj.

The situation was ideal for an outbreak because, as a

result of the critical situation in France in early 1915, the King's own Yorkshire Light Infantry, who constituted the main defence of Singapore, together with a few other regular soldiers and officers, were withdrawn to Europe, and the defence of the island fell into the hands of the 5th Light Infantry, backed up by local territorial units such as the Singapore Volunteer Corps and the Malay Volunteer Rifles, consisting largely of over-age and under-trained civilians masquerading as soldiers, together with a few Sikhs and police, and a few men of the Royal Army Service Corps and the Royal Garrison Artillery.

On 27 January, Colonel Martin learned that the regiment was to be transferred to Hong Kong and, while the news was received with chagrin by the British officers who wished to move nearer to the war, it was received with mixed feelings by the soldiers who believed they were going to the Middle East to fight against the Turks, their Muslim brothers. It was a very potent factor.

On the morning of 15 February 1915, at the Alexandra Barracks, the regiment was inspected by Brigadier-General D H Ridout, before leaving the following day for Hong Kong. During the afternoon a single shot was fired from the gates of the barracks by Sepoy Ismail Khan, a young Rajput. It was thought at first that a soldier had run amok but, when more shooting was heard, it was assumed that sepoys were at rifle practice at the range.

Colonel Martin was asleep in his bungalow at the time but his second-in-command, Major William Cotton, who had also been resting in the humid heat, was alert at once. But in no time scores of men from the Right Wing of the battalion had taken over the magazine at the barracks, while loyal men tended to disappear for their own safety. Loaded down with ammunition, the mutineers began to spread out, looking for white officers or civilians to shoot.

Because it was the Chinese New Year, which was always celebrated with hundreds of fire crackers, at first no one was certain what was happening and there were cases of men and women playing cricket, golf, tennis or polo, returning home, still in their whites, to discover their lives were in danger. About 100 mutineers moved in extended order to the German prison camp where, within the space of half an hour, they killed four officers, nine men and – by accident – one German, and wounded several others. Weapons were thrust on the Germans who were asked to lead them, but they declined to take part, feeling that, while war was war, this was mutiny and they should have nothing to do with it. However, Lauterbach, who had decided to escape by building a tunnel, took advantage of the confusion to vanish and eventually found his way to Java from which he again escaped with the aid of disguises and faked passports, even passing through British-run Shanghai. Reaching New York, he signed on a ship as a stoker to cross the Atlantic, and, reaching Germany, finally made a new career in the German Navy.

Isolated in his bungalow by the outbreak, Martin managed to contact men of the Malay States Volunteer Rifles who, finding themselves being shot at as they moved off to find out what all the firing was about, were more than willing to join him inside. Soon afterwards, they were joined by Major Cotton who later brought in his wife and a few loyal sepoys, and they proceeded to fortify the house.

The Indian soldiers were now roaming round the outskirts of Singapore, and by midnight thirty-three British and Asians and an English woman had been killed by them. And there were more to come.

Brigadier-General Ridout found himself in the invidious position of being caught completely unprepared. The only regular battalion under his command had gone beserk, their commanding officer out of contact with his officers, while, to face 400 or so trained and well-armed men, he had a few British gunners and sappers, none of them trained for infantry operations; some men of the Sultan of Johore's Military Forces, who had been due to augment the garrison but were entirely without fighting experience; the Singapore

161

Volunteer Corps, who had just started parade ground drill and had had no firing practice; a few European infantry officers and men; and a number of Chinese and Malay infantry companies, the police, the Malay States Volunteer Rifles, sixty men of the 36th Sikhs and a solitary naval vessel in the harbour, the survey sloop, *Cadmus*.

However, he had one great asset. Colonel C W Brownlow, commanding the Royal Artillery, the next senior officer in Singapore, had a formidable service record. He had joined the army in 1880 and had taken part in operations in the Zhob Valley and on the North-West Frontier. He was a man of determination and initiative and, given command of the motley force expected to restore the situation, he immediately ordered everybody he could find to be prepared to mount a counter attack as soon as possible.

Martial law was declared and the decision to place the vulnerable women and children aboard ships in the inner roads for their own safety was taken that night. It was clear the sepoys were making British soldiers and civilians their targets, and the death of the Englishwoman, a young bride of only a few days, brought fears of an orgy of rape and murder. The steamers and coasters in the inner harbour were warned to be prepared to receive a flood of people and to have steam up in case of the need for instant departure. Fortunately the transport, *Nile*, which had been designated to take the 5th to Hong Kong, was available with supplies on board, and other vessels were the familiar coasters of the Straits Steamship Line, but these had not been stocked with extra food and drink or with mattresses and pillows for sleeping on deck. The conditions gave rise to a lot of bad temper and the thin veneer of breeding and good manners went overboard with the realisation that first come would be first served. Unused to looking after themselves, the women began to lose their tempers and those with influence found the best berths.

The relief force, the mixed bag organised by Brownlow, dressed in a variety of garbs and carrying a variety of

162

weapons, prepared early next morning to advance to the recapture of the barracks. As it moved off, with sailors in the van, the Volunteer Rifles were carrying weapons which were not loaded. They were so inexperienced, one of them had almost shot the man in front and the ricochet had wounded another man, so for safety all weapons had been unloaded. However, after a brisk fight, they cleared the barracks with only one man, a naval stoker, killed. As daylight increased, the men in Martin's bungalow, plagued by sniping, saw the relieving force come into sight but, although there were around eighty men with arms able to attack the rebels in the flank, they allowed 300 to 400 mutineers to stream away on either side to hide in thick country at the back. Brownlow had had visions of rounding them all up at one go and he was furious at the indecision. Two of Martin's officers had suggested it was time to join in but Martin did nothing. When they met, Brownlow didn't hesitate to tell him what he thought of him. According to a witness, Martin 'got the rough edge of Brownlow's tongue for about ten minutes'.

Other small garrisons were relieved and by nightfall the situation was well in hand. The following day white people living in isolated parts of Singapore Island were rescued by motor car and boat and news arrived that six companies of the Shropshire Light Infantry could shortly be expected from Rangoon, and that French, Russian and Japanese cruisers were on their way.

Because of the war, the mutiny was passed off as no more than a local disturbance, but forty Europeans had been killed and the Government of Singapore had received the shock of its life. It took until 8 March for normality to return and the colony was in a state of ferment for weeks. But, with the aid of sailors from the ships which had arrived, the mutineers were finally rounded up and a court of enquiry gathered enough evidence to enable a summary court martial to be convened. Colonel Brownlow acted as president, and the trials were held in public. This was an extraordinary departure from normal procedure in wartime, but it was deemed advisable to give full publicity to the proceedings so 'it would then be seen that the men were being tried for mutiny and shooting with intent to kill, and not, as alleged, for refusal to go to Turkey', a reference to a rumour that had begun to spread among Muslims when it was first known the trials were to be held in secret.

The ringleaders of the mutiny, Dunde Khan, Chisti Khan and Abdul Ali Khan, were soon pinpointed. Dunde Khan had been found 200 miles inside Johore and Chisti Khan had surrendered to a patrol in Keppel Harbour, after spending a night in the jungle. Abdul Ali Khan had been killed by volunteers during the mopping up operations, as was Ismail Khan, the man who had fired the first shot. Imtiaz Ali, 'that very discontented man', had gone to a mosque, shaved off his beard, donned Malay costume, and then wandered aimlessly until he had surrendered to a police patrol.

The trials went on day after day, sometimes of single individuals, sometimes of groups of two or more, once of forty-five men at once. Two men had already been executed by the Malay States Volunteer Rifles but the next executions were carried out inside the gaol, with members of the public admitted as witnesses. Finally twenty-two men were executed together. Word had spread of the very large number of stakes standing ready outside the gaol wall. Four feet apart, they extended for nearly 100 feet. An estimated 15,000 spectators got their fill of horror. The firing party alone numbered 110 men all drawn from the volunteer forces. It was a harrowing role for the part-time soldiers. Some of the prisoners could not stand the strain and when one man started to cry out it affected the others, until the whole line was swaying, shouting and praying. When the situation looked like getting out of hand, the officer in command shouted the order to fire, but there was so much noise the men at the far end of the line didn't hear it and there was only a scattered volley. Some prisoners fell and lay still. Some lay on the ground, writhing. Some seemed to stay upright at their posts. Members of the firing party then

164

began to reload and fire individually, one man stepping out of the ranks to fire a second shot.

The executions continued at intervals over the next few weeks and by the end two Indian officers, nine havildars, eleven naiks, and 180 sepoys had been tried and all, except one sepoy, had been convicted. Both the officers, six havildars and thirty-nine sepoys were executed. Two havildars and sixty-two sepoys were sentenced to transportation for life, and a havildar and seventy-two sepoys to transportation for terms ranging from seven years to twenty years. Twelve sepoys were given rigorous imprisonment from one to five years, and five sepoys simple imprisonment for terms of one month to two years. In addition, it was reckoned that around 150 sepoys had been killed in the operations against the mutineers. Nur Alam Shah, the imam, was deported, and the elderly civilian, Kassim Ali Mansoor, was hanged.

The sepoys, simple Indian peasant soldiers all of them, were the victims of cleverer men working for their own ends. They had been deluded again and again by Indian and German agents using religion and Indian nationalism to help their cause in the war that was taking place in Europe.

On 3 July 1915, the remnants of the 5th Light Infantry, seven British and Indian officers and 588 other ranks, sailed from Singapore to war. There were no friendly send-offs, no band or enthusiastic crowds. The men who had stayed loyal were all that remained of a once-proud regiment with a string of battle honours. They were not sorry to be leaving.

They sailed to West Africa and arrived in time to join the final Anglo-French offensive against the Germans. Under the command of Cotton, they engaged the enemy in the Bare area and the Germans in the Cameroons surrendered in February 1916. The 5th then crossed Africa to join in the campaign in German East Africa under General Smuts, and at the end of 1917 moved to Aden. At the end of the war the regiment left for India, where four years later it was disbanded during the reconstruction of the Indian Army.

*

In 1920, five years after the disgrace of the 5th Light Infantry, the second mutiny occurred, this time in a much more civilised manner but for all that no less a crime against the ordinances of the army. This time it concerned one of Britain's oldest and finest regiments, the Connaught Rangers, a unit comprised largely of Irishmen.

Probably no country in the world has raised such passion in its countrymen as Ireland. Forced to acknowledge the English as masters since the days of the Anglo-Normans, Ireland had been fought over by English armies since the Middle Ages. Suppression and bloodshed were always part of her history, so that the mutiny of the Connaught Rangers in India in 1920 was just one more episode in a long and tragic list of Irish attempts to find their place in the world.

In 1920 Ireland was a seething cauldron of trouble. There had been endless rebellions as the Irish, intensely religious and passionately patriotic, tried to resist their English overlords. The wars fought in Ireland were barbarous because the English persisted in regarding the Irish as savages and the Irish were struggling for all the things that England hated. There were atrocities, and confiscations of land were common, but when Charles I tried to restore the country to something approaching prosperity, his efforts came to a stop with the outbreak of the English Civil War. The execution of the King, whom the Irish had tried to help, released Parliamentary troops, and under Cromwell the Irish were crushed. The garrisons of Wexford and Drogheda were massacred and every priest who could be found was slaughtered. 'The curse of Crummell on ye' was a malediction that was used in Ireland for centuries.

There was more fighting when, in 1690, the deposed James II tried to recover his English kingdom, and, with Parliament in the hands of the great Protestant families and the Church under the control of absentee and often irreligious bishops, the Irish became downtrodden, so that thousands of them emigrated. Since England refused their services, the flower of the Irish nation began to serve the enemies of England.

In 1846 the potato crop failed, and with thousands of evictions, hordes of Irishmen emigrated to America. Political unrest increased and when Gladstone brought forward his Home Rule for Ireland Bills, they were rejected. A new Home Rule Bill in 1914 received royal assent but was suspended because of the outbreak of war and, contrarily, many Irishmen volunteered to serve in the British forces. But trouble was still brewing and in 1916 there was a rising in Dublin which was doomed to failure from the beginning and many Irish patriots were shot.

Irish representatives returned in the general election of 1918 met in an independent parliament in Dublin to affirm the independence of their country. Fighting started between the forces of the Crown and the supporters of Sinn Fein and, to support the police, the British began to raise irregular forces to suppress the wave of unrest. Lloyd George was bent on showing the Irish that he could be ruthless and he decided on a short, sharp shock. The Black and Tans were his answer.

Recruited by advertisement, they were, according to Winston Churchill, 'carefully selected from a great press of applicants.' 'Praise be to God,' wrote Calton Younger in his book on the Civil War in Ireland, 'that the British were kind enough not to send their larrikins.'

Determined that the Irish should appear as malcontents and murderers, and not as romantics fighting for freedom, the British Government set out to keep law and order and, for ten shillings per day all found, the 'carefully selected' men became temporary constables of the Royal Irish Constabulary. As there were not enough RIC uniforms to go round, they had to make do with an ensemble of khaki and dark green with black belts, which put some inspired wit in mind of a famous pack of hounds, the Black and Tans. Given perfunctory training, they appeared in Ireland late in March 1920.

The misdeeds of the Black and Tans have been recounted over and over again. When, using stealth and surprise, the Irish retaliated, the forces of the Crown struck back with ever less pity or scruple. Terror was met with terror. Atrocity was piled on atrocity in a ghastly game of tit for tat that seemed to have no end. In twelve months nearly eighty policemen and soldiers were killed, but curiously English visitors could still enjoy holidays in Ireland and at the races the bookies took the money of IRA men and Black and Tans with fine impartiality.

In August 1920, the Black and Tans were joined by the Auxiliaries, a force of about 1500 men under the command of Brigadier-General F P Crozier. They were distinguished from the Black and Tans by their tam o'shanters, but, ruthless as the 'Tans', they carried out some of the most notorious outrages of these outrageous days.

By the end of November, the 'Auxies' had rampaged through the countryside without check. 'Terror,' said Calton Younger, 'was their business' and they were practised exponents. Tough ex-officer adventurers, misleadingly called 'cadets', they were braver, more refined, than the ruffianly Black and Tans but just as cruel and just as treacherous, and they killed, bayoneted, burned homes and razed to the ground any village that happened to be in the vicinity of an ambush or a mined road.

The Black and Tans remained always apart and, universally hated, they left a record of looting, drinking, wrecking and burning. They dragged men behind lorries, cut out tongues and murdered even children. Even the Loyalists in Ireland were shocked at their behaviour. In Dublin, men hunted each other through the streets, spies and informers betrayed one another, households were roused in the night and even the beds searched. Innocent men were bundled off in lorries and babies cried as guns were hastily hidden in their cots. As the British became increasingly ruthless, feeling against them grew and even Irishmen who had had brilliant records in the British Army and had once been proud to admit to them, now made their way to the IRA. This feeling of betrayal and disgust found its way from Ireland abroad, to England, to America, and finally to India.

In India at the time there were several Irish regiments, among them the Connaught Rangers. The British Army had always had to recruit in Ireland and, at the time of the Crimea, the Welch Fusiliers were Irish almost to a man. Out of 1400 killed at the Alma, 750 proved to be Irish. This wasn't simply because the pay didn't, as Macaulay suggested, attract English youth, but was also due to the fact that the Irish, throughout their history, have always proved themselves ready for a fight – anybody's fight. As one historian has suggested, the horror at the casualties in World War I arose from the fact that for the first time in a hundred years, the majority of them were English.

Many British regiments were first raised in Ireland because there were always enough Irishmen who enjoyed soldiering and there were always regiments that had Irish names. Among them was the 88th Foot, raised in 1793 by Lord Clanrickarde in Connaught, where it did its recruiting and from which district it took its name. It was nicknamed The Devil's Own for the reputation it acquired not only against the enemy but also among the more sober units of the British Army. The 94th Foot was later linked to the 88th under the title of the Connaught Rangers.

The regiment served in the Egyptian campaign of 1801, won twelve honours for the Peninsular War, went through the Crimean campaign, and helped restore order in the Central Provinces during the Indian Mutiny. In 1877–9 they fought in South Africa and again in 1899–1902, and during World War I they raised six battalions which fought in France, Flanders, Macedonia, Gallipoli, Palestine and Mesopotamia.

They were a fine regiment, with a proud record, but in India in 1920 the duties of the First Battalion were as servants of an occupying power. As the trouble in Singapore had showed, India, like Ireland, was thinking in terms of independence and was using the same methods as the Irish to get it, and suddenly it occurred to men of the battalion that what they were doing in India was exactly the same as the Auxiliaries and the hated Black and Tans were doing among their own villages and towns in Ireland.

The First Battalion was quartered at the Wellington Barracks, Jullundur, in the Punjab, and they contained a large proportion of veterans of the recent war with medals, decorations and wound chevrons. The Second Battalion remained at home, training recruits, first in England and then on the Rhine. Not a single Irish regiment was stationed in Ireland, with good reason because at the time hundreds of Irishmen were carrying arms and the sending of Irish regiments to Ireland would in effect be sending a trained and armed regiment which could well change sides.

Since the rebellion of Easter Week in 1916, the determination in Ireland to be free of English rule had grown in intensity and the hatred of the Black and Tans grew. 'The curse of the Tans on ye' had replaced 'The curse of Crummell' as the bitterest maledictions. Even *The Times* and the *Manchester Guardian* were moved enough to protest at their activities, and the *Daily News* wrote, 'In all our annals there has been nothing to parallel this record of organised savagery.'

Although the Government kept Irish regiments clear of the distasteful activities in Ireland, it could not prevent the men of those regiments from learning what was going on. Letters arrived in India from victims of the outrages, stories appeared in Irish newspapers sent from home, and soldiers on their way to India who had taken their embarkation leave in Ireland brought the stories at first hand.

Some of the stories were rejected at once as exaggerations and in the Connaught Rangers many men had always believed that the patriotism of the 'Shinners' (the Sinn Fein) was merely a means of avoiding serving in the recent war.

They felt that the Shinners were afraid of being conscripted, and many Irishmen in France had considered the Easter Week Rebellion a stab in the back. Roger Casement came up against this feeling when he tried in Germany to recruit, for the Germans, an Irish Brigade from Irish prisoners of war.

The Wellington Barracks were spacious and well sited, but June and July in the Punjab were tremendously hot and at Jullundur the temperature rarely fell below 100 degrees, so that after duty the men lay gasping on their beds, just waiting for the wet canteen to open. Normally parades and exercises were completed before the sun had climbed to its height, but that June the Connaughts had had to take part in a series of vigorous training exercises that reduced their khaki drill to sweaty rags. Open-necked shirts were not worn in those days, but tight jackets done up to the neck, with heavy solar Topees, full packs, haversacks, ammunition pouches, side arms, entrenching tools and rifles. Some of the men began to suspect that the strenuous work was ordered deliberately to tire them sufficiently to make them indifferent to any news they might hear from home.

One man, Joseph Hawes, from County Clare, who had been one of the first to join up in 1914, was far from indifferent. On leave before embarking for India he had seen the Tans in action. Wearing his uniform, he had been one of a crowd, at a hurling match, hustled from the ground at bayonet point.

In the wet canteen stories went back and forth, letters from home were exchanged and tempers began to rise. On Sunday, 27 June, with the temperature well above 100 degrees, Hawes sat with his regular companions, Paddy Sweeney, Stephen Lally, Paddy Gogarty and William Daly. There were regular schools of boozers but these men were only moderate drinkers and all about them they could hear the anger of the other men about what was happening in Ireland, so that eventually Hawes began to think that something should be done.

General Dyer's action at Amritsar the previous year had

killed over 300 men, women and children and left hundreds wounded. The Connaught Rangers had played no part in the massacre but it was one of the points that Hawes made that what the Connaught Rangers were doing in India was being done by Englishmen in Ireland. He had made up his mind, he said, to go to the guardroom the following day and refuse to soldier. It appeared to be spontaneous but later events suggest that perhaps it wasn't. Nevertheless, Hawes and his friends agreed to act together.

Finishing their beer and feeling, with fine Irish quixotism, that they could no longer accept the sparse comforts provided by the British Army, they went to a disused room in one of the barrack bungalows and lay down on the bare boards. On the Monday morning, they set out for the guardroom, explaining on the way to a friend, Corporal Flannery, that they were not refusing to soldier because they had no guts but because of their love for Ireland.

Flannery agreed that, if the five were shot out of hand – and, with events in India as they were, it was a possibility – he would inform their relatives, but he also attempted to dissuade them. William Daly backed out, but the other four pre- sented themselves at the guardroom at 8 a.m. where Hawes addressed the corporal of the guard, the sergeant being away at breakfast. He protested against the British atrocities in Ireland and said they were refusing to soldier any longer in the service of the King. The bewildered corporal decided that Hawes and his friends had had a night on the booze and wanted to sleep it off in the guardroom, an old dodge among soldiers. He accordingly put the men inside as requested, but when the sergeant returned from his meal he decided he wasn't having the guardroom turned into a home of rest and ordered the four men off the premises. They stood fast. The sergeant could understand drunks, but he now began to think these men were 'Bolshies' and ordered them back inside, where they joined five others already in for minor offences.

What Hawes and his friends had done soon spread through

172

the barracks. A detachment of the battalion was at that time stationed in the Punjab Hills about twenty miles away at Solon, and a second detachment was at a hill station, Jutogh, also about twenty miles away. This was normal enough because, during the hot months in India, wives and children were quartered in the cooler hill stations with about half the strength of the battalion who were later replaced by the other half.

The detachment at Solon comprised most of C Company, with about 50 NCOs and men remaining at Jullundur. At 9 a.m., the cadre at Jullundur was mustered on parade according to normal routine. They were erect and smart and in this fashion, to the sergeant's surprise, a private from Athlone called Tommy Moran stepped the one pace forward prescribed for a soldier who wished to make a statement and asked to join the other four in the guardroom. Despite his surprise, the sergeant ordered up two corporals, Cox and Keenan, to escort him there. The two corporals took a pace forward and, rigidly at attention, refused, saying they supported the men in the guardroom. Realising that getting Moran to the guardroom was going to be harder than he'd thought, the sergeant ordered Moran to accompany him to see the Major.

Major Johnny Payne, from Cork, who had been decorated for bravery in France, was at that moment holding orderly room, the daily session when any man could see him or his deputy and when others were marched in hatless to answer charges. Hearing what had happened, Payne abused Moran and reminded him of the oath of allegiance he had taken and of the dire penalties attending the breaking of that oath.

When Moran insisted on going into the guardroom, Payne reminded him that they had fought together in France and begged him not to let the regiment down. Moran remained silent and Payne had no alternative but to order the sergeant to take him to the guardroom, not by the front door, but by the back door so they wouldn't be seen by the men still on parade. They were seen, nevertheless, and twenty-nine more broke ranks and demanded to be included. The rebellion was spreading and the prisoners had now reached the number of thirty-four; within moments it became thirty-five as one of the men of the guard threw down his rifle and, without uttering a word, joined the others in the guardroom. The five original inmates, in for genuine offences, added their voices to the rest as they sang *The Wearin' o' the Green* and other rebel choruses, and shouted 'Up the Republic of Ireland!'

At 10 a.m. when B Company returned from rifle practice on the range, the officers went to their quarters and the men were marched on to be dismissed. As they heard the songs coming from the guardroom, however, they halted without any word of command being given. At that moment, Colonel Deacon, the Commanding Officer, arrived with several officers and the Regimental Sergeant-Major, to be informed of B Company's irregular action in halting without being ordered to do so. He ordered B Company to sit on the steps of their bungalow and soon afterwards, led by Hawes, the thirty-five self-immured prisoners were brought out and stood in line before the Colonel.

Deacon didn't harp on their reasons but impressed on them the seriousness of their action. They all knew, he said, the proper course to take under army regulations if they wished to make a complaint; their action was mutiny. They were on active service and they knew of the explosive situation in India and what could happen to their wives and children if they were no longer in a position to defend them. He was summoning up the old bogey of the Indian mutiny and the massacres of English women and children at Lucknow, Delhi and Cawnpore. It was a potent argument.

He went on to mention the battle honours the regiment had won and their proud service in France and begged them to reconsider their action. When he had finished, Hawes stepped forward, and pointed out respectfully that all the honours the Colonel had mentioned were for England. 'Not one of them,' he insisted, 'was for poor old Ireland'.

174

'But there's going to be one added today,' he ended. 'And it's the greatest honour of them all.'

Feeling the Colonel's words had won the other men over, the Battalion Adjutant muttered to the RSM, 'When the men return to their bungalows see that Hawes is put under arrest.' Softly as he spoke, however, he was overheard by Private Coman, a Tipperary man, one of the thirty-five prisoners. 'Never mind putting Hawes in the guardroom!' he shouted. 'We're *all* going there!' And turning to his friends, he commanded, 'Left turn, lads! Back to the guardroom – quick march!' Regimental to the last and in perfect step, the volunteers wheeled into the guardroom and stepped back behind the bars.

As the thirty-five men disappeared, the men of B Company were still sitting on the bungalow steps listening to what was being said. There were over 100 of them, all armed and all with ammunition in their pouches, and when the officers ordered them to fall in they didn't move. The order was repeated and again ignored. Baffled, the CO, the officers and the RSM moved away, followed by most of B Company NCOs. Immediately the B Company men rose and pressed towards the guardroom to congratulate the men inside.

Then someone asked if they were just going to stand there, arms in their hands, and do nothing, and it was decided – somewhat illogically, since the prisoners were voluntary prisoners – to release the men inside. A dozen men entered the guardroom and, as the others crowded round the door, rifles in hand, the sergeant of the guard had little choice but to agree and the thirty-five men were escorted to their bungalows.

The whole of B Company, to which Hawes and Gogarty of the original four had belonged, were now in revolt, supported by the twenty-nine of C Company who had supported the original four. No parade of D Company was held that day for fear of another demonstration, and men from all companies offered Hawes their support and urged him to organise the movement. They were told to return to their bungalows and await the *Fall In* bugle which would summon them to a meeting. In the meantime, they were to take no orders from officers or NCOs. As it happened, no one was giving any, because Colonel Deacon, deciding there was little he could do, had reported the matter to his superior, the Garrison Commander at Jullundur, and was leaving it to him. In the meantime, he and his officers kept to their quarters so that the mutineers were virtually in control of the barracks.

The assembly was sounded just before noon and over 300 men, among them a few NCOs, flocked to the Royal Army Temperance Hut where Hawes and others were sitting on the platform normally used for concerts. Among them was the original corporal of the guard who had first put the volunteers under arrest. Sweating in the heat, they listened as Hawes asked for suggestions. There were a few who regarded the revolt as an opportunity for paying off grudges, one notorious drunk suggesting that the entire sergeants' mess should be rounded up and held for trial. Another wild suggestion was the capture of a troopship to take them home to Ireland. Everybody tried to talk at once but in the end seven committee men were elected – Sweeney, Gogarty, Hawes, Tommy Moran, two NCOs – Corporal Davis and Lance-Corporal McGowan – and Corporal Flannery, the man they had trusted to let their relatives know if the worst happened. Flannery, an educated and articulate man, was elected spokesman, and he told the men to return to their bungalows until the next step had been arranged.

After a discussion, the seven decided to protest against the policies of the British Government towards Ireland, coupled with a demand that their country should be given its freedom. It was naïve but no more naïve than the demands of the patriots who had seized the General Post office in Dublin on Easter Monday 1916. It was also decided that there should be no bad behaviour and that order and discipline should be maintained throughout. Guards were posted and duties were carried out immaculately, but the green, white and gold tricolour of Ireland replaced the Union Jack within the precincts of the barracks. Bugle calls were organised, as were proper mealtime parades, and the Indian workers carried on as normal. One other decision was that any man who didn't wish to be involved could opt out, and a few men with families or with pensions to lose accepted.

Meanwhile, the officers remained curiously lethargic. Some of them may have been sympathetic, but none could have agreed with mutiny. Yet they seemed to throw in the sponge after nothing more than a few perfunctory efforts to recall the men to duty. In addition to war weariness, however, defence cuts were in the air and few of them felt any security in their careers – least of all the Irish officers who could see the writing on the wall. After General Dyer's disgrace after Amritsar, too, there was a feeling that it didn't pay to take drastic action.

The men who had accepted the mutineers' offer to opt out shifted their bedding and equipment to a separate bungalow and a sentry was posted for their protection. A few unpopular NCOs were roughly handled by men with grievances, but on the whole the conduct of the mutineers was beyond reproach. They took over the guardroom where the five original occupants had been given their freedom, and sentries were regularly posted and regularly relieved, marching about their posts in a smart soldierlike manner at all times with their arms at the slope, as laid down in orders. To an outsider, nothing had changed save that the different flag flew from the flagstaff and that the men had started to wear green, white and gold rosettes, made from material bought in the local bazaar by two of the soldiers, Frank Geraghty and Paddy Kelly.

Nothing was heard from from the officers until about 4 p.m. when the OC Troops in Jullundur, Colonel Leeds, appeared and asked to see the ringleaders. It got him nowhere. After repeating all that Colonel Deacon had said and receiving the same reaction, he left. Soon afterwards two officers and the

177

RSM arrived at B Company's bungalow and ordered the men to fall in outside with rifles and bayonets, hoping that they could be disarmed and thus more easily dealt with. With none of the leaders around and lacking leadership, most of the men were obeying when Hawes appeared and called the men a lot of sheep and told them to get back to their quarters. His personality did the trick and, as the officers and the RSM looked on helplessly, the men returned to their bungalow.

Perhaps to offset the show of weakness by B Company, it was decided that the whole body of mutineers should march to the CO's quarters and repeat their protests and demands. Led by the committee, marching smartly in column-of-fours under the orders of Corporal Flannery, around 300 men advanced to the CO's bungalow.

Unimpressed by an assurance of their determination to preserve order, Deacon asked what would happen if they were attacked by the natives. A few like Hawes and Flannery were aware that the cause of the Indian people was not unlike that of the Irish people, but to most of the men, uneducated and illiterate as they were, there was no common cause. The spokesmen gave assurances that not a single weapon or round of ammunition would be allowed to fall into the wrong hands but Deacon was still unimpressed, and Hawes added one more humiliation. When the Colonel repeated his warning of an Indian attack, he said, 'Well, if I'm going to be shot, I'd just as soon be shot by an Indian as by an Englishman.'

That evening, arriving in a pony and trap to see the tricolour waving in the wind, came Mrs Carney, wife of Captain Carney of the Royal Army Medical Corps, the regiment's medical officer. She was probably the only European woman who had not fled to the hills. Both she and her husband were Irish and supporters of Home Rule and she had arrived simply because she wished to see the tricolour flying.

Carney had joined the ranks of the volunteers raised by

the Irish Nationalists before the war in response to the threat of armed resistance by Ulster Unionists to the modest measure of self-government desired by Ireland and approved by a majority in the Houses of Parliament. The war had caused the measure to be shelved and when the war broke out, Carney had decided that his place was in France. Serving with the RAMC, he won the MC for bravery and had remained in the army after the war. He appreciated the aims of the mutineers but, as an officer, he considered the action they had taken was wrong. He had returned home on the day of the mutiny to inform his wife what had happened, and had predicted that it would mean the end of the Connaught Rangers, perhaps of all Irish regiments. He was more immediately concerned, however, with the future of the mutineers, most of whom were mere boys who didn't realise what they were facing. Mrs Carney, a young romantic woman who loved Ireland, didn't see eye to eye with him, but Carney felt that every effort should be made to stop the mutiny in the hope of saving the men from the worst penalties. He knew most of the soldiers and their wives and children, some of whom he had brought into the world, and feeling the men might listen to him, he asked permission to speak to them. Colonel Deacon refused the request.

On the morning of 29 June, two men from Jullundur, Privates Kelly and Keenan, set out for Solon where the bulk of C Company were on detachment, to inform them what had happened. Among the men at Solon was Private James Joseph Daly, younger brother of William Daly, one of the original five who had decided in the wet canteen at Jullundur to take action but had later backed out. Jim Daly was a twenty-year-old who was probably the most politically conscious of all the men involved in the mutiny.

His grandfather, also James Joseph Daly, had enlisted in 1810 and was with the Rangers at the siege of Ciudad Rodrigo in the Peninsular War in 1812, when he so distinguished himself he was promoted on the field from private to colour sergeant. James Joseph, his grandson, enlisted in the regiment in 1915, at the age of 16 and took part in many of the savage battles of the Great War, fighting like his grandfather to preserve the British imperialism that was crushing his native Ireland. He was with them when the depleted Irish division rolled back the last German attempt to win the war in 1918. He was a member of the Irish Republican movement and a natural leader, and the object of Kelly and Keenan was to persuade him to organise a protest like that at Jullundur.

Solon lay on the lower edges of the Simla Hills, with Simla, the headquarters of the British Army in India, higher up, and Jullundur was linked to both places by road and rail routes which crossed an arid and almost treeless plain. Kelly and Keenan took a cross-country route to avoid detection, footslogging for the most part under the pitiless sun.

Shortly after they had left Jullundur, one of the loyal NCOs, Sergeant William Edwards, an Englishman who had married an Irish girl and, as often happened, had become more Irish than the Irish themselves, decided to try to beat the messengers. He believed in the scrupulous observance of his soldier's oath of allegiance and, when he learned of the mission of Kelly and Keenan, he tried to find an officer willing to take steps to defeat it. Incredible as it might seem, however, on this amazing day not a single officer was to be found in his quarters, so, on his own initiative Edwards took a train in the direction of Solon and reached the first stop in ample time for the authorities to head off the two messengers. But nobody would believe his story and he was even accused of being drunk. At two more stops en route, he begged officers and military policemen to take the necessary steps to prevent the mutiny spreading and, finally, at the last stop before Solon, Edwards himself was arrested and for three days remained in the guardroom. On his return to Jullundur, he was reprimanded for being absent without leave.

At Solon, Kelly and Keenan found Daly all right, but word of their arrival had reached the authorities and four

180

regimental policemen closed in on them and arrested them –
but not before Daly had heard their shouted message about
the events at Jullundur urging him to organise a similar
effort at Solon. Rumours had already reached Solon and the
commander there, in daily communication with battalion
headquarters, was ready for any possible repercussions in his
own area.

The first move organised by Daly was more dramatic than
the gesture of Hawes and his friends at Jullundur. The
officers at Solon were still surprisingly complacent considering the rumours and, at about 8.30 p.m., Captain
Badham was presiding at dinner in the officers' mess when,
as they drank the King's health in port, there was a sound of
marching feet on the gravel outside and a shout of 'Halt!
Right turn!' The officers were startled. Parades at that hour
were unknown.

The officers had risen when the mess waiter approached
Badham and told him that there were men outside who
wished to speak to him. In front of the mess, about seventy
men stood in impeccable double-rank formation. Ordering
them to stand at ease, Daly approached Badham and
repeated the same protests and demands that had been
made at Jullundur. He also insisted that Kelly and Keenan
should be released from the guardroom. He spoke respectfully, however, and his manner was courteous but firm, and
he stood at attention as he spoke.

Badham ordered a chair to be brought, and, climbing on
to it, addressed the men as Deacon had done at Jullundur,
urging them to return to their duties and make their repre-
sentations in the proper manner. His warnings were received
in stony silence. When he called them to attention not a man
moved, but when Daly gave the same order, seventy pairs of
highly polished boots thudded together as one, and they
right-turned and marched off in perfect order.

Returning to their huts, the mutineers hoisted the tricolour, which appears to have been in readiness, something
that suggests that the action may well have been planned

181

between the leaders at Solon and the leaders at Jullundur long before the detachment of C Company left for the hills and before the original protest at Jullundur. At Solon, the mutineers and loyalists were almost equally balanced, but under Daly, the mutineers held the initiative. No threats were used to persuade loyal men to vacate their huts, but they did so to make way for Daly's followers, many of them sympathising but for a variety of reasons preferring not to be involved.

Daly and his men were determined to stick to the policy of passive resistance adopted at Jullundur, but as at Jullundur, there were a few small acts of violence against loyalists. On the whole, however, they were not committed by men sincerely devoted to the cause of Ireland's freedom.

The following morning, Captain Badham appeared at Daly's bungalow to urge the danger of an attack by Indians encouraged by stories of the mutiny, which must by that time have been circulating in the bazaar. He suggested that to avoid weapons falling into the wrong hands, rifles should be handed in to the magazine where they would be stored under an armed guard. It seemed a strange way to resist an attack by natives, since rifles were normally kept handy in special racks in the barrackroom. Daly and his followers gave a blunt refusal but later in the day, Father Baker, a Franciscan monk who was the Rangers' regimental chaplain, appeared. Daly was a devout Catholic and he allowed himself to be swayed by Father Baker's plea that he should use the opportunity to show that his policy of non-violence was genuine. After much heartsearching he agreed that all rifles and ammunition held by the mutineers should be handed in, and he himself supervised the collection. The weapons were stored in the magazine under a guard composed of bandsmen, all of whom, like many bandsmen in the Irish regiments, were Englishmen. The only weapons retained by the mutineers were their bayonets, and Daly promised Father Baker that he would neither indulge nor encourage others to indulge in any kind of violence and would only wait for an answer to the demands they had made.

Meanwhile, at Jullundur, after the departure of Keenan and Kelly and Sergeant Edwards, a car drove up to the guard-room containing Colonel Jackson, an officer on the staff of the GOC, Northern Command, India, who said he wished to meet the committee. They appeared properly dressed for duty, with belt and sidearms, and Jackson was saluted, a compliment they had not paid their own officers since the beginning of the trouble.

Jackson pointed out that he, too, was an Irishman from Roscommon and had served with and commanded Irish soldiers in action and knew their fighting quality. He pointed out that the Connaught Rangers were second to none but warned that, no matter how brave, a few hundred men could never hold out against the whole British Army in India. At that very moment, he said, two battalions of infantry with machine guns and artillery were on their way, but if no resistance were offered there would be no bloodshed. If they gave up their arms, the Rangers would be conducted to a nearby camp to await an answer to their protests which, he promised, would be forwarded to the highest authority.

The discussion which followed Jackson's appeal lasted for hours. The mutineers insisted that they would not be dis-armed by troops from outside and it was suggested that they should disarm themselves and arrange for the rifles and ammunition to be collected and stored in one of the bunga-lows over which they would place their own guard until they could be handed over to the troops who were to relieve them. Following the hand-over, they would march – with a guide but not with an escort – to the camp chosen for them. It was a face-saving formula and Colonel Jackson, in effect, had achieved his objective.

As they awaited the arrival of the relieving troops, the mutineers maintained the usual guards and sentries and threw out patrols, who confirmed what Jackson had said.

Troops were appearing on all sides and Jullundur was surrounded.

On the day after Jackson's visit, the 300 men cleaned their weapons and handed them over to their leaders who checked them and saw them stored under guard. Only the guard and the sentries retained their weapons.

Late in the afternoon of 1 July, two battalions of infantry, a company of machine gunners and a battery of artillery, entered the barracks, which were not walled in, from four sides, watched by some of the Rangers from the tops of their bungalows. The troops that arrived were prepared for trouble and were taking no chances. They consisted of the Seaforth Highlanders and the South Wales Borderers and, despite the smart salutes they received from the sentries and the loud cheer raised by the mutineers, they advanced ready for action with fixed bayonets and rifles at the port. They were able to relax a little when they saw how scrupulously the Rangers had observed their side of the arrangement but there were enough of them, with their machine guns and artillery, to indicate to the Rangers that without their weapons they were now helpless.

By the time the mutineers had been completely disarmed and the relieving troops had taken over all guard and sentry duties, the committee had ordered their followers to pack their kit and parade for the move to a camp two miles away which had been prepared for them. Mrs Carney watched them as they left with their bullock carts, pet monkeys and cockatoos. They bore themselves well, determined that the relieving troops should see what real soldiers looked like.

The camp chosen for them consisted of an open space 200 yards square, enclosed by a barbed wire fence six feet high. Inside were rows of bell tents where, despite the tropical sun, the Rangers were expected to live, eat and sleep. The prisoners, which was what in effect they now were, filed through a gap in the wire under the eyes of a company of South Wales Borderers with rifles and fixed bayonets. A guard was mounted on the gap in the wire and a machine gunner, his weapon trained on the tents, was mounted on a platform at each corner of the compound. A shade of canvas had been erected over the guns but even then the gunners were relieved every half hour. Nothing was done for the Rangers. What they were in was nothing more than a prison camp.

In the crowded and sunbaked tents there was no relief to be had. After the prisoners had been given a meal of black tea, bread and margarine, Major Payne arrived with a subaltern and about thirty men of the South Wales Borderers armed with rifles and bayonets. The prisoners were marched under escort to a walled-off enclosure near the camp which had once been a sort of parade ground. The Rangers went willingly, expecting there to hear their awaited 'answer'.

As they formed into a square in the enclosure, Major Payne began to read a list of names of men who were to fall in apart from the others. It immediately aroused suspicions because all the names called out were those of men who had been prominent as ringleaders, and the named men returned to their places. More names were called, with the assurance that they were only for fatigue duties, but now nobody moved. Major Payne pointed at Moran who had defied him when he had insisted on joining the original four in the guardroom.

'Arrest that man,' Payne ordered. Several of the Borderers moved to obey the order, but Moran's friends crowded round him and, with nothing but their bare hands, wrenched the rifles from the Borderers. Hustling them away, they threw the rifles after them. The struggle had not been difficult because no British soldier enjoyed acting against another British soldier.

Payne had reached the limit of his patience. 'Five rounds, standing, load,' he roared. The Borderers loaded their weapons and he raised his handkerchief.

'When I drop this,' Payne shouted, 'shoot them down like dogs!'

At this point, a Belgian priest who had been assigned to

185

the camp hurried forward and stood in front of the line of muzzles. 'I will die with these men,' he told Payne and, as they argued, Colonel Jackson, who had organised the surrender, rode into the compound and, taking up a position between the mutineers and the men who stood ready to fire, told the Borderers to order arms. When Payne explained that the men had refused duty, Jackson brusquely ordered him to leave with the armed party.

Captain Carney, the medical officer, also visited the camp that morning and, seeing the conditions under which the men were living, ordered several who were suffering from the heat to be removed to hospital. He also sent word to Command Headquarters, protesting about the conditions. His first protest brought no action, so twenty-four hours later he sent another stronger protest, stating that the treatment the men were suffering was 'inhuman'. Summoned to headquarters, he was asked to withdraw the expression. He refused and demanded that his protest, exactly as he had worded it, be sent to the highest army authority in India. His subsequent career seems not to have been affected by his courageous stand and he rose in the Second World War to be a Brigadier.

On Sunday, 4 July, after Mass performed by the Belgian priest who had saved them from Payne's wrath, Captain Carney's protest began to bear fruit. The mutineers were marched back to the barracks at Jullundur where they were confined to one large bungalow, round which had been erected a barbed wire fence reinforced with sentries and machine guns. All bedding had been removed so they had to sleep on the floor. For three days their diet was black tea and dry bread, but they were free from the tremendous heat and had the advantage of the punkahs which stirred the air in the bungalow. No charge had been yet laid against anyone.

The following day they were visited by two priests who said they were Irish. They asked the committee to appeal to the others to return to duty, saying that if they did, no action would be taken. If they persisted in their stand, however, they claimed, it might lead to their deaths in circumstances which would shame their parents – a powerful appeal to a simple Irish countryman. Hawes protested that surely it was the priests' duty to tell their people *why* they died, and the priests left after again urging the mutineers to think well before refusing this last chance. They said they would return the following day for an answer.

When they came, the committee insisted on their stand and, studying the priests' sorrowful demeanour, the seven men of the committee began to fear the worst, and called on their followers to elect a duplicate committee to take over if they themselves were shot out of hand or separated from the rest. A second committee was duly elected from the ranks of the thirty-five men who had been the nucleus of the protest.

At 6 a.m. on the morning of 7 July, while the mutineers were still half-asleep, 200 Seaforths, armed with iron-tipped entrenching tools, entered the bungalow and, dragging forty-seven of them from their beds, hurried them outside before any resistance could be organised. The captives included both committees and all the original thirty-five who had volunteered for the guardroom. Among them also was Sergeant Woods, an Englishman who had won the DCM in France and was the only man of his rank – though not the only Englishman – to join them. When he lined up with the rebels, he was asked by an officer what Ireland had to do with him. His reply was that the men behind him had fought with him for England; he was now fighting with them for Ireland.

The forty-seven men were handcuffed and placed in leg irons and loaded onto two lorries to be driven back to the compound from which Captain Carney's protests had rescued them. There they were kept for two days without food or water and this time without even the shelter of the bell tents. Again Carney protested to headquarters, but it was evident that the ill treatment was designed to break their spirits. After two days without food, drink or shelter and with hardly a man able to stand upright, an officer arrived with an armed party and once more offered them a chance to return to duty.

The authorities were eager to end the mutiny without too many questions being asked, but once more their offer was refused and the principal leaders of the mutiny were again pushed into lorries and taken back to Jullundur, where they were confined to cells facing the bungalow where their followers were still held prisoner. As they watched from their cells, Colonel Deacon placed four officers in the positions of company markers on the parade ground outside the fenced-off bungalow. As the men from inside the bungalow waited on the verandah, Deacon called out, 'In the name of the King, I command you to fall in on your markers.'

The men in the cells raised a shout of protest but their followers were now without leaders and with one exception they fell in, by companies, on the four officers. Major Payne addressed to the one dissenter the appeal he had made to Moran, reminding him they had fought together in the trenches and warning him that the mutineers were going to their deaths. The man replied that he would rather die with the men in the cells than fall in under Payne and his gang of cowards. He was marched under escort to join the forty-seven who greeted him with a cheer.

The men from the bungalow were marched up and down in front of the cells as a means of reasserting discipline and then dismissed to their bungalows. The mutiny at Jullundur was over, and that evening, the forty-eight who remained were transported by lorry and train to Dagshai Prison nearby to await trial. There they were soon to be joined by Daly and twenty-seven others from Solon.

Following his protest at Solon, Daly, with the other occupants of his hut, had watched their rifles and ammunition being stored in the magazine, one of a group of headquarters and administrative buildings which stood on the summit of a small hill. They had retained only their sidearms.

The following day passed without incident and outside their bungalow the men who had refused to soldier mingled freely with those who had remained loyal, going to the dining hall for meals and using the canteen for refreshment. The loyalists were not restrained from being friendly and, as at Jullundur, the officers were again curiously conspicuous by their absence. The NCOs were guardedly non-aggressive and no attempt was made to persuade the mutineers to return to duty.

However, when the hand-over of arms had been arranged, a call for help had been sent by the company commander to an English battalion, the Royal Sussex Regiment, quartered nearby. Until the arrival of two companies of this battalion, the policy adopted by the officers was to lie low. Apart from Major Payne, who always went the wrong way about things, they all seem to have shown nothing but inertia, whereas at Jutogh nearby, where A Company was quartered, the company commander acted with energy and imagination so that those men remained unaffected.

At dinner in the officers' mess that night at Solon, a rumour reached the company commander that an attempt was to be made by the mutineers to break open the magazine and recover the arms. Knowing it to be guarded only by bandsmen, the company commander ordered the guard to be strengthened under the command of two junior officers armed with revolvers which they were to use if attacked. Actually, though the rumour probably went the rounds, Daly was fixed in his determination to avoid violence and, thanks to his qualities of leadership, he was firmly in control. When the rumours reached him about 10 p.m. as the canteen closed, stories also began to be whispered about Jullundur where, so the rumour went, there had been another massacre like that at Amritsar and hundreds of men had been mowed down with machine guns. Surely, Daly was asked, they weren't going to sit there helpless and allow the same thing to happen at Solon? They should break into the magazine and recover their arms so they could die like

189

soldiers. Without doubt, the beer drunk in the canteen was talking but Daly, a total abstainer, insisted he was going to keep his promise to Father Baker.

He was sneered at and accused of being afraid and, still little more than a boy, he reacted in a very normal way by deciding after all to lead his men to the magazine. Twenty-seven men agreed to follow him but Daly insisted the operation should be properly planned and went to the foot of the slope on which the magazine was situated to reconnoitre the position. By the light of the moon they could see the guard had been strengthened and in place of the lone sentry there were now several men with rifles at the ready, while others could be seen lying on the flat roof, also armed.

Daly had now committed himself but, with the two scouts, he returned to the mutineers' bungalow and stressed the strength of the guard, trying to put them off. The volunteers insisted it was nothing but bluff and at midnight, holding bayonets, the only weapons they possessed, the party deployed at the foot of the slope and, led by Daly, began to advance in line up the hill, moving in review order, unhurried and in step – clearly visible to the men on the roof of the magazine.

'Halt! Who goes there?'

Guile, both in the method of attack and in the answer to the question, might have been more sensible but Daly was an open honest young man.

'I am,' he said, 'Jim Daly of Tyrrellspass, Westmeath. Hand over your rifles and there'll be no trouble.'

'If you advance another step,' the officer on the roof of the magazine called, 'we'll fire.'

As he spoke, the cassocked figure of Father Baker came running from the direction of the men's quarters, but before he could remind Daly of his promise of no violence, Daly set off.

'Come on, boys,' he yelled. 'Charge for Ireland!'

Clearly marked by the white shirt he was wearing instead of the army greybacks worn by the others, he ran up the slope, waving on the men behind. A volley rang out and two of the attackers fell. Father Baker managed to reach them and, with outspread arms, managed to restrain the rest from going any further.

'Cease fire,' he shouted to the men on the magazine and, turning to Daly, angrily told him the bloodshed would be on his head. The men on the magazine held their fire and Daly, a strange mixture of fighter and pacifist, agreed to withdraw. Two men were lying on the ground, one of them, Private Smith, already dead. The second, John Egan, from County Mayo, a man who had been wounded at Mons and Ypres, had been shot through the lung. A third man by the name of Sears was killed by a stray bullet while walking to his quarters some distance away.

Shocked by what had happened, the attackers withdrew, carrying the dead and wounded; and now, after the attack, many of the mutineers who had happily followed Daly began to have second thoughts and returned quietly to duty. When, forty-eight hours later, two companies of the Royal Sussex Regiment marched into the camp, all but the faithful twenty-eight had deserted the hut where the tricolour flew. The English soldiers forced an entrance and overpowered its small unarmed garrison, who were manacled and placed in leg irons like the men at Jullundur and, with Egan, almost dead of his wound, travelling by ambulance, they were removed to Dagshai prison to await trial with the men from Jullundur.

The conditions imposed on the seventy-six men who were the moving spirits in the mutiny were appalling. Their diet continued to be black tea and dry bread, the tea drunk out of old food tins as they were provided with no utensils whatsoever. They were locked in separate cells for twenty-three hours out of twenty-four and received no pay so that they were unable to buy cigarettes or other small luxuries. Twice daily, they were taken to the prison yard for half an hour of exercise, walking round in single file in a circle under the eyes of sentries, one posted at each corner of the yard. These men, though they couldn't hand over cigarettes, were not unsympathetic and kept lighting one, taking a couple of puffs and throwing it down where it could be picked up by one of the prisoners. But several of the Rangers were struck by dysentery and one, an Englishman called Miranda, died.

Desperate, seven of the prisoners planned to break out and raid the Solon canteen five or six miles away for supplies. The break-out was a masterpiece of ingenuity. Men wishing to visit the lavatory were taken there under guard and one evening all seven men asked to be conducted to the lavatory together, indicating that if they were compelled to go as usual in rotation it would be too late. With most of them suffering from dysentery, it was a good excuse. It had been arranged through the Indian prison barber, who was a zealous disciple of Indian independence, that one of the apertures through which the lavatory buckets were extracted from behind should be left unlocked and, with the prisoners thinned down by dysentery and starvation, it was possible to climb through. While one of the seven, Sweeney, engaged the guard in a discussion about the stars, on which subject he was something of an expert, the other six pushed aside the lavatory bucket and escaped. By the time Sweeney emerged from his cubicle and it was discovered that six were missing, the escapers were well on their way to Solon.

Hurrying to their objective, they made their way to the canteen and, breaking a window, filled empty palliasse cases with cigarettes, matches and food. By the time they returned, the prison had been ringed with troops so, while the others lay low, one of them, Alfred Delaney, blundered forward and, as he was stopped by a sentry, he yelled out 'Look out, lads,' to give the impression that his companions were close by. As the sentries fanned out round Delaney, the rest broke back *into* the prison and stored their booty in a safe place.

Why did the Irishmen not make a dash for safety while they were free? Why, in fact, did they not right at the beginning of the mutiny simply march out of camp and disperse? With the whole of India available to them, certainly some of them would have remained free, especially with the aid of Indian sympathisers who were suffering from the same sort of oppression. But they were thousands of miles away from home in a strange land whose inhabitants spoke a strange tongue and who, on the whole, the ordinary British soldier made little attempt to understand. Most of them, of course, were uneducated men and many were simple country lads from the west of Ireland who would have been lost in the tumultuous chaos of India. They suspected there was nowhere they could go and that every man's hand would be against them and a lot of them were married and fearful for their wives and families who, from the beginning of the protest, apart from the help organised by the wives of Colonel Deacon and Captain Carney, were being given nothing but a bare subsistence. Nevertheless, the fact that not one of them tried to escape his fate today seems unbelievable.

The first of three courts martial met on 23 August. The trials were spread over three weeks, the men from Jullundur being tried first in two groups, the first group consisting of over thirty men who were considered to have played a minor part in the mutiny. Sixteen, who were considered to be the leaders and were tried separately, included Hawes, Gogarty, Moran, Sweeney, and Delaney. The third trial was of the twenty-eight men involved in the wild attack on the magazine at Solon.

Each trial was a general court martial, presided over by Major-General Sir Sidney Lawson, commander of the Presidency Brigade, the brigade stationed in the Presidency of Madras. With him sat six officers, all of the rank of major or captain, and a major of the Judge Advocate General's department was present to advise on legal points. Most of the accused, suspicious of the impartiality of any officer, elected to defend themselves, while Dawes, Daley and a few others refused outright to acknowledge the court's jurisdiction.

During the second court martial, Corporal Flannery is alleged to have tried to 'rat' on his comrades by handing in a written statement pleading he had only joined the outbreak with the intention of controlling the wilder element and persuading the mutineers to return to duty. As the statement was read, several of the accused broke free and tried to attack him.

When the courts martial ended, the findings and sentences were made known to the accused. A few were acquitted and sent back to the battalion. The rest from the first batch were given sentences ranging from a year's hard labour to three years penal servitude. Most of the second batch received harsher sentences – 10-15 years penal servitude. Five were even more harshly punished – Hawes, Gogarty, Delaney, Moran, and, despite his efforts, Corporal Flannery. Each man was visited by the prison governor who handed him a buff OHMS envelope, saying as he did so, 'I'm sorry to have to give you this.' Inside was a notification that the court had sentenced them to death, subject to confirmation by the Commander-in-Chief, India.

The court martial trying the men from Solon received a special plea from the prosecuting officer. Daly, he asserted, and those who had followed him in the attack on the magazine were not only guilty of mutiny but were also responsible for the deaths of Smith and Sear. Daly pleaded not guilty and gave evidence on his own behalf, denying that he had taken part in a mutiny and claiming that during the attack on the magazine he had only been trying to persuade the others to desist. In the evening, the governor visited the cells with his envelopes. Those men who had been recognised by the defenders of the magazine were all sentenced to death – among them Daly, Egan, despite his wound, and others. Also sentenced to death were the messengers from Jullundur – Keenan and Kelly. The remainder received various terms of imprisonment.

The fourteen under sentence of death were segregated in a separate wing of the prison. By mid October, the

194

Commander-in-Chief's decision was made known and the men were paraded in the exercise yard to hear the promulgation of the sentences. All had been commuted to imprisonment, except Daly, who was not present and whose death sentence was to stand.

In his cell, as the governor appeared, Daly rose and, a soldier to the last, stood to attention. 'I have to tell you, Daly,' the governor said, 'that in your case the sentence . . . has been confirmed. . . . It will be executed twenty-one days from today.'

Daly smiled. 'Ah, well,' he said. 'It's all for Ireland.'

That night Daly wrote to his mother. 'I take this opportunity,' he wrote, 'in writing to you to let you know the dreadful news, that I am to be shot on Tuesday morning, the 1st of November. What harm? It is all for Ireland. I am not afraid to die . . . If you will be happy on earth, I will be happy in Heaven . . .'

During the following three weeks, the only cheerful face was Daly's and he was the only man who managed to sleep the night before he was to die. Father Baker visited him constantly and heard his penitence for breaking his promise to avoid violence. His comrades in the cells recited the Rosary as he walked out to his death, wearing an improvised collar of Ireland's green made from the lining of his topee.

He stepped outside, thin, his uniform in tatters, his complexion showing a prison pallor. He shook the hands of his escort and when the provost sergeant tried to put a black bag over his head, he tossed it to the ground. 'Let me see the boys who are going to do for me,' he said. 'Let me die like an Irishman!' A dispute started and he only agreed to wear the bag on the pleading of Father Baker, who said it would spare the feelings of the men of the firing squad. He also finally agreed to be bound to a chair but asked for the hood to be raised one last time so that he could see the sun. The request was refused but he wouldn't allow his arms to be bound and he was shot as he sat with his hooded face turned towards the rising sun. He was just twenty-one.

195

The firing party had been drawn from an English regiment, the Royal Fusiliers, but an anonymous correspondent to Sam Pollock, an Ulsterman who wrote an account of the affair, pointed out bitterly that 'they were all Irishmen – and not one of them missed!'

Daly was buried in the Simla Hills in the Dagshai military cemetery. Like Byng and many others, he was a victim of the prevailing circumstances. He was a brave man who seems also to have been honourable if naïve. He couldn't withstand the sweep of history or the pull of nationalism and was a scapegoat for the times he lived in, even, it might be said, for the politicians who refused to give Ireland her due and grant her the freedom she so earnestly desired.

Since Private Miranda had died in the prison hospital, there were now only sixty of the mutineers at Dagshai. The tolerant soldiers who had acted as sentries were withdrawn and they were replaced by Military Provost men, the British Army's official gaolers, a set of men who in those days carried a reputation for brutality. The five chief leaders, Hawes, Gogarty, Sweeney, Delaney and Moran, were worked over with truncheons and then charged with attacking their goalers. Without being allowed to speak in their defence, they were placed on a diet of bread and water and their hands were handcuffed behind their backs, and, according to Hawes, the handcuffs were not removed even to allow them to eat.

About the middle of December, still handcuffed and in leg irons, they were taken by train to Bombay to embark for England. 'See what you get for fighting for England,' they shouted to the curious onlookers. On board ship they were offered exercise, but under conditions which they refused, and once more they were manacled and their legs put in irons. In the end, the OC Troops changed his mind and they were given some relaxation and a better diet. From Southampton, they were distributed among a variety of English prisons where they found themselves with long term prisoners and Irish detainees. They kicked against every prison regulation and after a while were moved from Portland to Maidstone in Kent, where the governor, Captain Cavendish, by a quirk of history, was a kinsman of that Cavendish who had been Gladstone's Chief Secretary for Ireland and had been assassinated in Phoenix Park. In 1923 one of the men, called Oliver, died in prison, but Ireland's struggle was now moving towards a climax and rumours began to reach the men at Maidstone. When the word of truce with Ireland arrived, they expected to be released at once but the British Government insisted that their offence had been military not political. Another protest was arranged but before anything could be done they were released. They all travelled on the same ship across the Irish sea and on their arrival were fêted by their fellow countrymen. A memorial in Glasnevin Cemetery commemorates their story today.

What came of it all? Their action had been one of a series of untidy, irrational and seemingly hopeless gestures of protest staged by Irishmen over nearly 800 years, but it was one of many small things which, in the end, forced Lloyd George to do justice to Ireland. The account of the mutiny, written by Sam Pollock, who was also serving in an Irish regiment at the time, indicates that the mutineers acted only out of an honourable intention to help Ireland but, despite its sincerity, it seems heavily biased towards the Irishmen, and Colonel Jourdain, the last Commander of the Rangers, felt that there was also an unmentioned discontent behind the mutiny. The fact that the men in Solon had their flag ready even before the outbreak there certainly seems to indicate that the mutiny was not, as Pollock suggests, entirely a spontaneous protest. Probably there was also bitterness of a different sort because after the war, when Lloyd George, with a politician's easy conscience, had promised a land fit for heroes to live in, many had been forced back into uniform by unemployment.

Nevertheless, they had made their stand but, though they

were dead right in their beliefs, they were totally wrong in their methods. They behaved with incredible naïvety throughout, not only in handing over their weapons but also in believing that the authorities could ever regard their protest as anything but mutiny. If their beliefs were genuine, however, what else could they have done? As regular soldiers they had to serve their time, so they protested in the only way they knew. But for Daly's wild attack on the magazine, they might even have suffered shorter terms of imprisonment, but never would the army authorities of the day have taken any other view than the one they did. In the army there is never any grey, only black and white, and the men, whatever their reasons, were guilty of the one crime the army can never accept.

There is another possible view. Were the Irishmen, like the mutineers of the 5th, the victims of a concerted nationalist movement started hundreds of miles away from where the mutiny occurred? There are things about the affair that seem to suggest it might well have been stirred up by civilian Irishmen in India who saw an opportunity to make a point. Without doubt, most of the mutineers were innocent of guile and were moved only by their feelings for Ireland, but were there also men among the leaders who had been approached by Irish agents? The accounts of the affair are inevitably pro-Irish and, while they make no mention of such a possibility, it can't be overlooked, and the men might well have been the scapegoats for more devious characters.

The Rangers came to an end two years later. Many Irish regiments were disbanded and the Connaught Rangers' turn came in 1922. Irishmen still take the Queen's shilling, however, slipping across the border to enlist or offer themselves for service in the Irish Guards, and it is a fact that in the home of at least one of the mutineers, Pollock saw a photograph of the mutineer's son, who was serving in Pollock's own old regiment, the British Army's Royal Inniskilling Fusiliers. In World War II, the percentage of Irishmen killed or wounded in action against Germany or

Japan was higher than that of many 'official' belligerents, and there is a wonderful story of a boy from Cork, part of an RAF bomber crew, who got into an argument about Eamonn de Valera, the Irish leader, with his fellow crew-members as they were bombing Berlin. 'I'll tell you one thing "Dev" did for us,' he yelled furiously into the inter-com. 'He kept us out of this fucking war!'

A final Irishness comes to the story. After a long struggle, the survivors of the mutineers who had suffered imprison-ment, were awarded small pensions by a vote in the Dail, the Irish Parliament. The amount awarded was based on the length of service in the *British* Army.

Private Slovik

During World War I, from 4 August 1914 to 31 March 1920, many British soldiers were condemned to death. Of these, 346 were shot by their own comrades, to set an example to other soldiers. In most cases the sentences were for desertion or cowardice and, because of the conditions of trench fighting, were imposed all too often by relatively junior officers with no knowledge of court martial procedures. Many of the condemned men were poor soldiers determined to avoid the front line, but there were others who were suffering from shell shock or exhaustion and among them, too, were men who had been excellent soldiers but had seen just too much of battle and been pushed too far. It made no difference. The sentences were confirmed by senior officers who spent most of the war miles behind the line and had no conception of the horror or the squalor of the front line or of the demands the cold, the damp and the constant shelling made on a man's resources.

The RFC and the RAF were inclined to take a more sympathetic view and were among the first to realise the cost of drawing too heavily on a man's moral resources. The demanding experience of aerial combat accelerated the wearing out process and they knew it was unwise to drive a man beyond the limit.

During World War II, there were only four executions in the British Army. Three of these were in a Colonial regiment and were for mutiny, while the fourth, a private in

200

the RASC, was executed for wartime treachery. All were hanged.

The American Army was different and, up to 1945, no member of its forces had ever been executed for desertion in the face of the enemy since 1864 during the American Civil War. On 31 January 1945, that was changed with the execution of Private Eddie D Slovik, who without doubt was made to pay for the failure of thousands of other American soldiers to stand up to the demands of war; the scapegoat chosen to stop the rot of desertion in the American Army in the last months of 1944. Eddie Slovik was an American of Polish descent, a Catholic who grew up around Hamtramck, Michigan, and served in the 109th Infantry, of the 28th Division, a National Guard unit from Pennsylvania.

During World War II when America mobilised against the totalitarian challenge, many young Americans were called up but one out of every eight was excused from military service 'for reasons other than physical'. They were not young men with physical defects but men who were considered temperamentally unstable, maladjusted, perverted or more than normally nervous. Of the 10,110,103 who were put into uniform, only 2,670,000 were actually trained for combat, and of these probably as high as 1,000,000 managed to escape combat with bad conduct discharges, self-inflicted wounds or some form of mental insufficiency described by a psychiatrist. Among those who evaded combat were around 40,000 who deserted in the face of the enemy – not the minor offences of overstaying leave, drunkenness or absence without leave, but those who actually disappeared when about to face the Germans. Most of these men were tried by courts martial and confined in disciplinary centres or dishonourably discharged. Of them, 2,864 were tried by general courts martial and received sentences of from twenty years to death. Of the death sentences decreed, forty-nine were approved by the convening authority.

However, death sentences had never been actually executed since the Civil War, neither in the wars against the Indians, in

201

the Spanish-American War or World Wars I and II. Despite the sentences, no man was put to death and, in fact, not many ever believed they would be, because it was widely accepted that the people of the United States would no longer accept the extreme penalty for a man who refused to fight. The practice was therefore followed of commuting the death sentences or reducing the prison sentences and quietly releasing the prisoners after the war was over.

This was so in every case except that of Private Slovik, whose sentence, given by a divisional court martial on 11 November 1944, was executed at a time when the 28th Division was heavily engaged in the Hürtgen Forest in Germany. It had been confirmed on 27 November by Major-General Norman D Cota, one of the great American forward leaders of the war. What had happened was that General Eisenhower had decided that the American Army was suffering too much from desertion. There were increasing numbers of American deserters in prisons near or inside Paris or even roaming free in the city, and on 23 December, he decided enough was enough. The last American to assume such a responsibility had been Abraham Lincoln.

Slovik, his full name Edward Donald Slovik, was born of Polish parents in a poor district of Detroit. His father had been born in Poland, his mother in the US. It was the second marriage for his father who was a punch-press operator employed on motor car bodies at a time when money was scarce because there was a depression and not many cars were being sold. Eddie Slovik had one brother and three sisters and attended Dickerson and Kosciusko High Schools in Hamtramck, and the Davidson and Pulaski Schools in Detroit.

Leaving school when he was fifteen, he became involved with a group of bad lots, drinking, staying out all night and stealing. He started with petty thefts when he was ten or eleven and his first entry into police records came when he was twelve, in 1932, when he and his friends broke into the basement of a brass foundry. They intended to steal brass

202

but the smoke from a fire they started attracted a policeman. Slovik was put on probation. From 1932 to 1937 he was involved in more petty theft, breaking and entering and disturbing the peace, and was finally sent to prison. At the age of almost eighteen he was transferred to the Michigan Reformatory at Ionia, having been sentenced in October for a term of six months to ten years for embezzlement, after confessing to pocketing change while working for a drug store and taking home candy, chewing gum and cigarettes without paying. The total amount mentioned in the charge was $59.60 over a period of six months.

Slovik had blue eyes, sandy hair and, by no means ill-looking, was considered to be alert, mentally clear, and showing no unusual behaviour. He was, however, regarded as a lone wolf, though friendly and with a weak character. No one ever visited him in the Reformatory and in March 1938, he became eligible for parole. Twice refused parole because of his juvenile record and a poor home environment, his parole finally came in September the same year.

On leaving prison he found work in a chain grocery store, reported regularly to the parole officer and avoided trouble for four months. Then, one night, full of beer, he and two friends stole a car and smashed it up. Slovik ran away from the wreck but turned himself in to the police later the same night. The following day he pleaded guilty to driving away a car and violation of parole, was sentenced to two and a half to seven and a half years, and sent to prison, but again transferred to the Reformatory at Ionia in March. There he was set to work in the furniture factory but was reported for stealing a bottle of denatured alcohol which, in fact, he had stolen not to drink but to rub on his legs. He had had bowed legs as a child and the bones had been broken in several places, which left scars and recurring pain and forced him to wear the lightest shoes he could find.

Transferred to another department, he met Harry Dimmick, the supervisor, who took an unexpected liking to him because he was a good worker whom Dimmick thought had the makings of a good citizen. He was trusted and from then on never gave a minute's trouble. In 1940 he merited a favourable report and when, in 1942, he left Ionia he was twenty-two years old, in good health and with a friendly smile. He had a job waiting for him and all he had to do was stay out of trouble.

By this time, the depression that had blighted his child-hood had vanished in the prosperity brought by the war. While he had been in prison the Battle of Britain had been fought, as had Bataan and Corregidor. By now, however, the tide of defeat had turned and American Marines were approaching Guadalcanal and the Desert Rats were on the way to Alamein which was to be their springboard to victory in North Africa.

Slovik's elder sister, Margaret, worked as housekeeper for a plumber, James Montella, who owned the Montella Plumbing Company in Dearborn, Michigan. Montella's bookkeeper was a 27-year-old Polish girl, Antoinette Wisniewski and, between them, the two women persuaded Montella to give Slovik a job. For Montella, Slovik worked hard and he was happy in Dearborn which was free from the vast slum areas of Detroit and Hamtramck. He was invited to the Wisniewski home and soon fell in love with Antoinette who was lame as a result of infantile paralysis. She watched his behaviour carefully and when he was called up went with him to the draft board, both of them satisfied when he was classified 4F. Believing army service unlikely, they were married on 7 November 1942, and for the next twelve months Slovik's life was happier than he could ever re-member. He began to earn more money and even managed to buy a second-hand car.

Neither he nor his wife, safe as they were thousands of miles from either the European or the Pacific War, gave the fighting much thought, despite the climactic battles being fought in North Africa, in the Pacific and at Stalingrad, then, on the anniversary of their wedding, Slovik received a letter changing his classification from 4F to 1A and he was directed to appear for a medical examination. With an all-out war being waged, the United States had suddenly found itself in need of soldiers.

Men who were specialists had been commissioned from civil life, and the navy and the air force had taken their share of the best men. Other technicians had been snapped up and the best of the unskilled were snatched up for the Marine Corps and other specialist groups. The infantry in the last years of the war, then, were what was left and recruits were used as replacements, trained with one group and sent overseas with another, before finally being sent to yet another. By 1944, the United States were employing for replacement infantry the very young, the older or married men and the marginal men who had originally not been wanted but were now being called up. The United States had been getting a bad deal from its infantry. A soldier was expensive to train and keep happy but then he was killed, wounded, became sick, cracked up or simply bolted. The barrel was being scraped and, at that time before the atom bomb, it was believed that the attack on the Japanese home islands and for the second front in Europe would result in thousands upon thousands of casualties.

On 24 January 1944, Slovik left New York Central Station for his basic training in Texas. He had come to lean heavily on his stronger-minded wife and, with his weak character, was lost without her. His letters home were loving but there were few references to the war or to Hitler or even to the invasion of Europe. Most of them were full only of complaints. He didn't like the army, having to carry a pack or a rifle, and he complained about his quarters and the food, and began to consider breaking loose because, since he still had six months of probationary time hanging over him for his difficulties with the police, a simple offence would have sent him back to Ionia and out of the army.

Antoinette tried to cheer him up with her letters and even tried to get him a discharge on the grounds that she was dependent on him. The reaction, inevitably was, 'There's a war on. We all have to make sacrifices.'

Slovik himself tried to work his discharge but he also tried hard as a soldier, though in one of his letters there is a plaintive cry, 'I hate guns!' Always he refers to 'they' as being his persecutors. He never defined who 'they' were, and what he meant was simply the United States. However, he began to respond to treatment. He was being well fed and even began to feel a pride in the fact that on marches he didn't have to fall out. Nevertheless, he never stopped trying to work his discharge on compassionate grounds. His company won a cup for the best company but suddenly he found himself alone as his friends went on leave before going overseas. Because Slovik was trying to get his discharge and his future was uncertain, he was held back, idle, doing guard duty and trivial jobs about the camp.

Then on 7 July 1944, he wrote to his wife saying that by 1 August he would be overseas. He arrived in Detroit on leave on 12 July for eleven days and when he left for Fort Meade, Maryland, the money he carried in his pocket came from the rings his wife had pawned to give him pocket money. Once again he started to complain, wishing this time he was back in Texas, which in fact he had hated when he was there.

By 1 August, as he had predicted, he was on his way overseas and was writing home from New Jersey. Just after dawn on 7 August 1944, he was aboard the old *Aquitania* as she left the New Jersey pier carrying 7,000 replacement soldiers heading for Britain and eventually Normandy. Slovik was destined for the 109th Infantry in the 28th Division.

The 28th's first elements were organised by Benjamin Franklin before the American War of Independence, three companies serving in the Continental Army as Washington's bodyguard. They also fought in the War of 1812, the Mexican War, the Philippine Insurrection and along the Mexican border. At Gettysburg during the Civil War, the Philadelphia Brigade of the 28th Division were among the stubborn defenders of Cemetery Ridge, the high water mark of the Confederacy. In France in 1918, once again it was the 28th Division who held their ground during Germany's last desperate attacks and, at one point in the Meuse-Argonne offensive, a battalion of the 109th Regiment was commanded by a sergeant because all the officers were out of action. G Company came out of the fight with only sixty of its 240 men still on their feet. In four and a half months of combat, the 28th lost 14,139 men, of whom 2,874 died in battle.

Even as Slovik left New York, his division was fighting one of the bloody battles of the Northern France campaign and taking heavy losses. From August 1944 to August 1945 the 28th suffered 26,286 casualties, of which 3,266 were battle deaths. The divisional strength was 14,243. The 28th were a National Guard division and it had a proud record, and one of the things that all men were required to know was the divisional history, something which somehow always managed to strengthen a man's will in combat. Slovik never had the chance to learn it because of the replacement system or perhaps because of his concern for himself.

Slovik might have acted differently if he had, but his thoughts as he crossed the Atlantic were not with the unit he was about to join but with his own woes. Private John P Tankey, of Detroit, who had made a friend of him, noticed that during the crossing Slovik lay on his bunk, staring at the deckhead in a preoccupied manner. Once, as he cleaned his weapon, he said, 'You know, Johnny, I don't know why the hell I'm cleaning this rifle. I never intend to fire it.'

On 14 August Slovik arrived in Edinburgh, was transported by train to Plymouth, given two days instruction in hedgerow fighting then shipped to Omaha Beach, where he set foot on French soil on 20 August.

Bloody Omaha, where the Americans had taken their heaviest casualties of the D-Day landings, was no place for a man like Slovik. With its scattered wreckage, the points where men had died and its ominous history, it was more than enough to worry him. With the other men he spent five nights near the beach, then, issued with ammunition and told they were assigned to G Company, 109th Infantry, the group set off, twelve men in a truck, towards Elbeuf on the bank of the Seine eighty miles north-west of Paris. The route chosen could hardly have been worse for the newcomers. As the German 7th Army had been compressed into the Falaise Pocket, they had been forced onto the open roads in daylight and had been massacred by rocket-firing planes. Short of petrol and forced to use horse-drawn transport and artillery, the Germans had been trapped and the Pocket had been reduced to a ghastly killing ground. With shocked eyes, Slovik and the others found themselves passing mile after mile of charred, gutted, torn wreckage, with men, horses, guns, wagons, trucks, tanks, all jammed together in hopeless bloody confusion, with here and there a charred corpse still sitting at the steering wheel of a burned-out truck.

As they neared Elbeuf, German SS men, bombarded by the artillery of the 28th Division, were trying to hold open a river crossing for remnants of the fleeing army and Slovik's group could hear the firing. As it grew dark, they debussed and began making their way into the town. Shells were going over and they were fired on two or three times. They had no officer and were commanded by an NCO, and around midnight they were told to dig in. As they dug their foxholes, shells were still going over and the inexperienced newcomers were scared.

What seems to have happened then is that, following the order to dig in, another order was given to move deeper into the city in search of G Company. Several men did join the company in Elbeuf but two of them, John Tankey and Slovik, did not. Tankey claimed that they didn't hear the order and were still in their holes when tanks appeared. They thought they were lost but the tanks turned out to be Canadian and they were invited to tag on. For six weeks Slovik and Tankey lay low.

The Canadian unit, the 13th Provost Corps, was commanded by a sergeant-major and equipped with motor cycles, jeeps and trucks. They found Slovik and Tankey useful, resourceful foragers more than willing to work, and they were even given transport. With the Canadians they went to Calais and Boulogne and during this time Slovik gave up carrying ammunition and instead filled his pouches with stationery collected from the Red Cross. When a German pilot was turned over to them it was Slovik who treated him with kindness, offering him food and cigarettes. They remained with the Canadians about forty-five days, making no attempt to find their unit. Slovik talked constantly about going home. He still felt that he had never had a break until he was married, and then the army had snatched him up.

The 109th took part in a huge parade of victory through liberated Paris on 29 August but Slovik was quite happy to remain with the Canadians, cooking and foraging, doing every job necessary except the one for which he had been trained. When the two men finally reported to 28th Division HQ at Elsenborn, Belgium, on 5 October, they were not placed under arrest. Their cases were not unusual because, following the action at Falaise, many soldiers had lost contact with their units because of the replacement system being used by the United States under which junior NCOs led around a dozen men forward from a depot to join their companies. It wasn't a good system because there was not time for the men to become battle-wise or adapt themselves to the conditions, and the cry, heard everywhere, was 'Don't send us any more replacements. We haven't time to bury them.'

Tankey and Slovik reached the 109th Regimental HQ near Rocherath, Belgium, on 7 October, but again nothing was done about their absence. They were sent to G Company and in the subsequent fighting, on 5 November near Hürtgen, Tankey was hit by a piece of shrapnel. Slovik had made no attempt to go forward, however. His first disappearance, known as the first desertion, had been ignored in the confusion and Tankey felt that, despite his insistence that he would never fire his rifle, Slovik would now buckle to. Instead, however, Slovik told Captain Ralph O Grotte, Commander of G Company, that he was too scared and nervous to serve in a rifle company and that, unless he could be kept in a rear area, he would run away. The Captain told him there was nothing he could do about it and assigned him to the 4th Platoon and, for safety, forbade him to leave the company area without his permission. Slovik came back a second time and asked Grotte if he could be tried for being absent without leave. Grotte put him under arrest and returned him to his platoon, where he was ordered to stay. An hour later, Slovik returned once more. 'If I leave now,' he asked, 'will it be desertion?' Grotte replied that it would.

According to Tankey, Slovik reappeared without his rifle, walking fast, then Grotte arrived and told Tankey, 'You'd better stop your buddy. He's getting himself into serious trouble.' Tankey ran after Slovik, stopped him and pleaded with him to return. Slovik said, 'I know what I'm doing,' wrenched himself free and kept walking. Tankey never saw him again. This was what became known as the second desertion.

Slovik probably spent the night of 8 October in a barn, but about 8.30 a.m. on the 9th he reached the Military Government Detachment of the 112th Infantry in Rocherath and handed one of the cooks a slip of paper containing handwriting and said he had made a confession. The cook informed Lieutenant Thomas F Griffin, who telephoned the 109th to send someone to collect him. A military policeman took Slovik to the orderly room of the 109th and handed the sheet of paper to Lieutenant W L Hurd, the provost officer, who delivered it to Lieutenant-Colonel Ross C Henbest. It was green, an army post exchange flower-order form, and had been written on both sides. It was Slovik's confession. It contained the words, 'I told my commanding officer my story. I said that if I had to go out their (sic) again I'd run away. He said there was nothing he could do for me so I ran away again and I'll run away again if I have to go out their.'

Henbest warned him that the confession could be very damaging and suggested he take it back and destroy it. He refused and was confined to the divisional stockade.

Why had Slovik acted so recklessly? His company was not under fire, so why didn't he simply pretend to soldier and then 'get lost' again when the regiment moved forward? Why did he confess without being asked? Why didn't he claim simply that he had failed to hear an order, a common enough excuse? Why, finally, did he put it all down in writing?

Without doubt, he intended to desert so he could be tried by court martial and imprisoned, thus avoiding dangerous duty against the enemy. Many American soldiers took this course. Many actually sought court martial and it was assumed that Slovik had thought carefully about himself. He had called his CO's attention to his desertion, even written out a confession, all of it part of a calculated effort to make certain he would be jailed and remain in jail until the end of the war, by then – late 1944 – clearly not far off.

He wasn't afraid of jail. He had been there before and the idea had probably been in his mind from the moment he had been called up; he had doubtless been working on the idea whenever his friend, Tankey, had noticed his preoccupation. He was well aware that never since 1864 had an American deserter risked more than confinement in a safe jail, far more comfortable than active service conditions, with the chance of being quietly released after the war was over. That way he would avoid all danger and, in fact, while he was held in the 109th Prisoner of War Enclosure, the US Army went through one of the most difficult periods in its history and Slovik avoided all of it.

The Americans who had paraded in Paris had thought the war was over but suddenly in December, in the Hürtgen Forest, Hitler unleashed the Ardennes counter-offensive. Casualties were heavy and reinforcements rushed forward with such speed organisation became impossible, while wounded sometimes had to be carried miles through the tangles of pine forests shattered by artillery fire.

Modern man is not trained to exist in spartan conditions and the Americans, in particular, with their sophisticated home life, found it particularly trying. They were hungry, half-frozen and, like most soldiers in action, frightened. It was twice as difficult for the replacements. They had not had the time to acquire any loyalty to their units, no time to absorb their traditions, no time even to make any friends among the old hands, by whom they were often regarded as 'rookies'. The army had swept up all kinds in its effort to keep up its numbers and among them were some splendid men who, despite the difficulties, more than proved their worth. But there were others who had not even been good citizens at home, and it didn't take them long to make up their minds that safety was a better bet than staying where they were in the cold and wet, with the chance of dying just round the corner.

During this period of snow, casualties, cold rations and the endless stream of replacements, the desertion rate boomed. A commander could go forward at night expecting to find 200 men in the line and be lucky to find seventy. There was an epidemic of 'combat fatigue', always supported by psychiatrists, and the divisional commanders began to grow angry at the ease with which men were avoiding duty. Thousands of men were even deliberately seeking courts martial to evade combat and Slovik was one of them.

On 26 October, Slovik had been transferred to the divisional stockade at Rott in Germany. One day two youngsters, who had also bolted, had their courts martial and as they returned to the stockade, which was a barn, he yelled 'How much did you get?'

'Twenty years,' they shouted back.

'I'll settle for twenty right now,' Slovik said. 'How long do you think you'll have to stay after the war's over?'

'Maybe six months.'

The army was still trying to be fair and the highest legal representative in the 28th Division, Lieutenant-Colonel Henry J Sommer, had Slovik brought to his office.

'Slovik,' Sommer said. 'You're in trouble, and I'd like to help you get out of it. We don't like to court martial anybody. We do that as a last resort. If you'll go back to your outfit and soldier I'll ask the General if he'll suspend action on your court martial. I'll even try to get you a transfer to another regiment where nobody will know what you've done and you can make a clean start.'

Slovik refused but said he'd be willing to take a job away from the line with a quartermaster company or something like that. Failing that, he preferred to take the court martial.

Sommer continued to try and Slovik continued to insist on his demands. In the end, Sommer sent him back to the stockade. He had heard too many men like Slovik say, 'I want my general court martial.'

Two other officers, Captain Edward P Woods, his defence counsel, and the divisional neuro-psychiatrist also saw Slovik. Woods found there was nothing he could do. Slovik had made up his mind. The psychiatrist could find no evidence to show that he was not responsible for his actions and pointed out that Slovik had never sought medical attention for physical or nervous complaints.

There was considerable conflict between the ever-sympathetic psychiatrists and the West Point mind of the generals. The generals insisted on simplicity and their responsibility was enormous. The psychiatrists could only advise and had no responsibility for the major issue, the war. Moreover, they were often in disagreement with each other. General Norman Cota was the general concerned with Slovik's case, and as Slovik represented weakness, so Cota represented strength.

Cota was a powerful 51-year-old who came from a poor family from Chelsea, Massachusetts, that was a mixture of English and French Huguenot. He managed to get to West Point, with classmates like Generals Collins, Ridgway and

Mark Clark, all of whom distinguished themselves during the war. He fought in North Africa with the 1st Division, and at Omaha Beach on D-Day was Assistant Commander of the 29th Virginia and Maryland Division, who had the job of blasting with hand-carried charges through the iron and concrete beach obstacles. He won the Distinguished Service Cross that day and most of the men who were there agreed that he earned it. He had stamped up and down watched by men who were pinned down and found it hard to believe that a man could stand upright and live. Finally, he had set off inland without looking back – 'Let's get off the beach,' he said – and behind him men began to stir and follow him. As the movement began, Cota personally directed the opening of two access roads.

At St Lô, he won the Silver Star for gallantry and received the Purple Heart for a wound. His personal example was tremendous as he walked about in the open, defying the enemy fire to encourage the young Americans. He took command of the 28th Division in August 1944, and led them the rest of the way to the end of the war. He had none of Patton's belligerent swagger and was a modest, quiet man with a sense of humour, to whom duty was everything.

However, he was aware that fatigue was an enemy every army commander had to consider, but he thought it unwise to talk too much about fatigue as a 'disease', as the psychiatrists tended to do. He had visited treatment centres for combat fatigue and found that the psychiatrists were actually asking the men who appeared, 'Have you had enough?' and 'Do you want to go back up the line?' To Cota such questions were nonsense and offered an obvious answer. He was well aware that men grew tired and in need of rest, but they weren't suffering from a disease and there was nothing wrong with most of them that a good rest wouldn't cure.

The usual treatment was a dose of seconal to knock a man out for twenty-four hours, hot food and a chance to relax, after which many were able to return to the front. There were never many combat exhaustion cases when the army was on the move forward but when the advance came to a grinding halt before the stubborn resistance of the Germans in the cold and wet, the cases increased at once and Cota was concerned that too many men were being sent back.

As Billy Mitchell's was the longest court martial in American history, so Slovik's must have been among the shortest. The court was convened at 10 a.m. on 11 November 1944. By 11.40 a.m. a verdict had been returned. It was inevitable. Slovik had not only asked for a court martial, he had also condemned himself.

The trial was held on the second floor of a public building in Rotgen, twenty miles south of Aachen in the Hürtgen Forest, while below German civilians queued up for ration cards. The court comprised nine officers, the presiding officer Colonel Guy M Williams. All of them were non-combatant officers inevitably, because the combatant officers were involved in the fighting, and these circumstances seemed to favour Slovik, who was charged with desertion at Elbeuf and Rocherath and on the general charge of desertion. He pleaded not guilty.

Private George F Thompson, who had been with Slovik at the time of Elbeuf desertion, Lieutenant Hurd, to whom Slovik had handed his confession written on the green slip of paper, Captain Grotte, who had interviewed Slovik, the cook to whom Slovik had first handed his confession, and the officer to whom the cook had passed it, all gave evidence. Of necessity, because there was little to say, their evidence didn't last long. Slovik's rights were explained to him and he was advised to confer with his counsel and decide what to do. After doing so, Slovik announced, 'I'll remain silent.' He was found guilty on all charges.

At this stage, no one knew of Slovik's convictions as a civilian and he was sentenced to be dishonourably discharged and to be shot. But Slovik's civilian record did not influence the court. All they knew of him was that he appeared to be a good-looking, healthy soldier openly defying the authority of the United States. He had confessed to running away and to be willing to run away again. Colonel Williams, the presiding judge, felt he didn't have the right to let him get away with it when other men were suffering and dying. However, he insisted on three ballots and every one returned the same unanimous verdict – death. Nevertheless, though the members of the court thought that Slovik deserved to be shot, in all honesty not one of them thought he ever would be shot. All thought the sentence would be cut down, and so did Slovik. When he walked from the courtroom he was firmly of the belief that his calculations had been correct, and while his Division was deeply involved in the Hürtgen Forest, Slovik was heading for Paris and safety, firmly of the opinion that before long he would be home again with his wife.

Once Slovik had received the death sentence, it was up to General Cota to review the decision, approving it or disapproving of it. He could not wash his hands of it and he called on Colonel Sommer to prepare a review of the case. In it Slovik's civilian record, which had been received from the Federal Bureau of Investigation, was mentioned for the first time. It was one of the reasons why Sommer did not recommend clemency. 'I never expected Slovik to be shot,' he said later. 'Given the common practice up to that time, there was no reason . . . to think that the Theatre Commander would ever actually execute a deserter. But I thought that if ever they wanted a horrible example, this was one. From Slovik's record, the world wasn't going to lose much.' For the first time, Slovik's record was militating against him, and it was on this point that his calculations had gone wrong. He had felt that his record was good because he had put behind him all his bad companions and the criminal behaviour of his youth and, after all, when he had emerged from prison in 1942, the army had at first wanted nothing to do with him.
Nevertheless, it was true that many officers who knew of the case gained the impression that Slovik had been a

hardened criminal, and were unable to grasp that his most serious crime was the embezzlement of $59.60 worth of candy, cigarettes and chewing gum over a six month period.

General Cota himself was probably not influenced by the record. Nevertheless, he had had enough of going forward in the dark to find so many empty foxholes. He felt, he said, that it was his duty to approve the sentence. 'If I hadn't,' he said, 'if I had let Slovik accomplish his purpose, then I don't see how I could have gone up to the line and looked a good soldier in the face.' However, he removed the sentence of being dishonourably discharged from the service, probably trying to help Slovik's next of kin and make it possible for them to receive their insurances and accumulated pay and allowances. He was not surprised when the Theatre Commander confirmed the sentence, but he was irritated to learn that Slovik was not to be dealt with in Paris, but was to be sent back to him for the sentence to be carried out. He realised, though, what was in the Theatre Commander's mind: a deserter had to be shot by his own unit.

Perhaps the man most surprised by the confirmation of the sentence was Slovik himself and on 9 December he wrote to General Eisenhower. He claimed he had had no intention of deserting and quoted the fact that he had voluntarily given himself up. But he didn't back away from reiterating that he had wanted a transfer from the line because of his 'nerves'. He explained about his earlier criminal record and showed how, since his marriage, he had stayed out of trouble. He also thought he had had a good record as a soldier until he first ran away.

In fact, the letter was never read by Eisenhower, but by other officers who in turn briefed him, and in any case, Eisenhower's thoughts at the time were engaged with the Battle of the Bulge, launched on 16 December, and occupying a large part of the American Army. Slovik's timing had been unfortunate. Nevertheless, following the usual procedure in the office of the Judge Advocate General, the record of the trial had to be examined and found legally correct and the case was studied by seven distinguished lawyers.

But there were no protracted discussions and the details were clear. Eisenhower was unhappy because he had hoped that, as in the First World War, the record of executions for desertion would remain clear. The review of the case pointed out the common practice of automatic clemency for deserters under death sentence but suggested that it was not something to be granted as a matter of course, and that its exercise should depend on the facts and the considerations of military discipline. The reviewing officers were aware that not only Slovik – like other deserters – but the members of the court which had found him guilty, had assumed that he would not be shot, and they probably saw this as an opportunity to end that dangerous assumption.

They were in possession of Slovik's civilian record and this time they felt it showed him to be merely a bad boy rather than a confirmed criminal, and they knew that many 'dead end kids' had become brave soldiers.

The last reviewing authority, the office of the Judge Advocate General with the European Theatre, made the final check. The man in charge, Brigadier General E C McNeil, was known as a merciful man. The Board of Review felt the case was one of aggravated desertion, with the accused deliberately seeking safe incarceration in preference to soldiering, and the view was expressed that if serious and aggravated desertions had been punished with death early in the war there would have been far fewer. Their view was that a soldier who, with calculating deliberation, chose to shirk combat – thereby increasing the burden on his comrades – should be punished so severely that others would be dissuaded from following his example. Slovik had performed no front line duty whatsoever and obviously did not intend to, and his conduct showed a deliberate plan to secure trial and imprisonment in a safe place. The imposition of a less severe sentence would have accomplished his purpose entirely.

218

The sentence having been reviewed, Slovik was ordered to be shot on 31 January 1945, in the area of the 109th Infantry, the unit he had deserted. It took place at Ste Marie-aux-Mines in eastern France and, after a very severe winter, the snow was deep. A house on the northern outskirts was selected because behind it was a garden enclosed by a high stone wall, and on two sides of the garden were snow-covered hills. Carpenters built a barrier of boards several inches thick and placed an upright post in front of it. Assuming that the condemned coward would probably not be able to walk to the post a 'collapse board' with straps was made, with a hood of black cloth.

There was a snowstorm throughout most of eastern France during the evening and night of 30 January. The twelve men and the sergeant of the firing squad had been selected. They didn't relish the duty and one at least tried to get out of it. They had all been chosen as expert riflemen. During the evening Slovik was brought by weapons carrier from Paris, handcuffed and with his ankles bound. He had asked his guards to release him and let him run for it.

The morning of the 31st was bitterly cold. Slovik was confessed and given the Absolution and said the Act of Contrition to Father Carl Patrick Cummings. He was also helped to say a Rosary and was given a bundle of letters from his wife. 'The only break I ever had in my life,' he said, 'was this girl. But I've lost her now ... They wouldn't let us be happy.'

He also told Father Cummings that he wanted his comrades in the regiment to know that he wasn't a coward – at least, not that day – and brooded on the fact that, while he was able to sit quietly with a priest before he died, the men in the line never knew when death was going to strike them down. 'I guess that's what I couldn't take,' he admitted. 'That uncertainty.' He asked Cummings to tell the men of the firing squad that he didn't hold against them what they were going to do, and begged that they should shoot straight so that he wouldn't suffer.

The request was passed to the firing squad and as Slovik's hands were being tied, he calmly observed to Sergeant Frank J McKendrick, 'They're not shooting me for deserting the United States Army. Thousands of guys have done that. They just need to make an example out of somebody and I'm it because I'm an ex-con. I used to steal things when I was a kid, and that's what they're shooting me for. They're shooting me for bread and chewing gum I stole when I was twelve years old.'

As they waited, Major William Fellman apologised for the fact that he would have to read the order for the execution again while Slovik was standing at the post before the firing squad, and it was cold outside. 'That's all right, Major,' Slovik said. 'I've heard it so many times, one more time won't do any harm. But read fast, will you?'

Meanwhile the twelve rifles that were to be used had been loaded, one with the ritual blank, and the witnesses were formed up in rows, officers and other ranks, together with a further group of officers, including General Cota. The execution procession moved into the garden and once again Slovik was allowed the Act of Contrition. He made no final statement. The crash of the volley echoed among the hills behind the house. The shooting reflected the nervousness of the firing squad. Not one of the bullets had struck Slovik's heart, but all eleven bullets were in the body. When Doctor Robert E Rougelot applied his stethoscope to the body, Slovik was breathing shallowly. Lieutenant S E Koziak passed behind the firing squad and, as they pushed their rifles backwards, still facing front, he began reloading them. As he did so the chaplain spoke curtly to him. 'Give him another volley if you like it so much,' he snapped.

As Koziak reloaded, it was noticed that in his haste he was pointing the rifles directly at the witnesses. Colonel L R Elson said, 'Be careful, Lieutenant. Let's not kill one of our own accidentally here this morning.'

The reloading was pointless. 'The second volley won't be

necessary,' the doctor said. 'Private Slovik is dead.' It was only three hours since Slovik had arrived in Ste Marie.

'That,' General Cota observed, 'was the roughest fifteen minutes of my life.'

The collapse board had not been needed and it puzzled the witnesses that Slovik, who had claimed to be a coward, had conducted himself with such dignity and courage.

'Slovik,' Father Cummings said, 'was the bravest man in the garden that morning.' As one of the firing squad said, 'I can't understand why a man who had the guts to face a firing squad like that wouldn't stay in the line with the rest of us.'

Father Cummings, giving what he called 'the commercial', said that Slovik had finally found his courage. 'For two thousand years,' he observed, 'the Catholic Church has been supplying what Eddie Slovik needs on the day he meets his death. From where else can a little man find strength?'

It has been asked since why the President of the United States, the constitutional commander-in-chief of the forces of the USA, was not informed and why he did not exercise the final authority. But by an act of Congress in 1920 the confirming power was delegated to theatre commanders. If the President had known, perhaps Slovik would have escaped. The scum of the American Army was confined in the 10th Replacement Depot at Lichfield, in England, and they included murderers, rapists and flagrant deserters, who after the war complained they had been badly treated. The commanding officer, although totally exonerated, was never again promoted. The pressure on President Truman was too great. One other man in the 28th Division left the line, bought forged papers which enabled him to reach his home in Chicago, and he turned himself in, in the last days of the war, confident, as Slovik had been, that he would be free. He was sentenced to death but the President insisted he wanted no more death sentences and that deserter ended up a free man.

Large numbers of men who had never been in trouble with the law in civilian life served time in military jails, and returned home with records that showed court martial convictions or dishonourable discharges. Senators and Congressmen were flooded with complaints and Rear Admiral Robert J White summed up the groundswell of criticism by saying, 'The emotions suppressed during the long ... period of global warfare were released by peace, and erupted into a tornado-like explosion of violent feelings, abusive criticism of the military, and aggressive pressures on Congress for fundamental reforms of the court martial system.'

But Slovik's was a flagrant case and, though there were many others, some involving officers, perhaps the truth was that, although many Americans felt that deserters should be shot, nobody wanted the responsibility. Desertion was never a major problem in the Pacific Theatre because it was essentially an air and naval war and there were no long periods of static warfare so that the conditions for desertion did not exist. In the long bitter winter in Italy, France and Germany the desertion problem became acute.

Perhaps the last word remained with General Cota who said later that Slovik was a product of the replacement system. 'It was a cruel system,' he said, 'probably necessitated by the nature of the war, but it was cruel nevertheless, and I never liked it. Men had a right to go into battle as members of a trained unit, flanked by friends and associates and if possible led by leaders ... they have come to trust.'

Slovik, the chosen scapegoat for thousands of American soldiers all as guilty as he was, was buried in an unmarked grave in the Oise-Aisne American Cemetery at Fère-en-Tardenois, close to Château Thierry where Americans had distinguished themselves by their fighting qualities in World War I. He was buried separately from the graves of the men who had died in battle. Perhaps General George S Patton, himself disgraced for berating a soldier he felt was not giving as much as he should, summed it all up.

In 1940, before the United States had entered the war, he said he was worried because he felt the country could not field a fighting force. 'We've pampered and confused our youth,' he said. 'We've talked too much about rights and not enough about duties. Now we've got to try to make them attack and kill ... We're going to have to dig down deep to find our hard core of scrappers.'

In making application to see the documents in the affair, William Bradford Huie, who wrote about Slovik's case, recalled what his great-grandmother had said to one of his cousins who was trying to collect his First World War bonus. 'Son,' she said, 'the United States of America don't owe you a damn cent for fighting its wars.'

That position was already out of date in 1942 but, as Huie remarked, the US is reluctant to expect patriotism, loyalty and sacrifice, and seems afraid to ask its citizens to fight for it. There were men who deserted in World War II and during the Korean and Vietnam wars because they were confused about what the United States had a right to demand of them, and the response to Vietnam showed that the reaction had not changed.

There is an ironic footnote to Slovik's fate. Many years afterwards, arrangements were made by Bernard Calka, a Polish-American army veteran, to obtain a pardon for Slovik from President Reagan and to have his remains returned to American soil to be buried next to his wife, Antoinette, who had spent the rest of her life trying to clear her husband's name. The body was exhumed on 8 July 1987, under American army supervision for return to the United States by air. On 10 July, however, it was found that the casket containing the body had not arrived in Detroit as expected, but had been sent by accident to San Francisco.

The mistake was eventually rectified and the remains were finally buried on 11 July.

Doubtless, if he'd been able, Slovik would have complained that 'they' had been at him again.

Captain McVay

Even as Eddie Slovik was being buried in Northern France events were in train, unknown to the world, that were to lead to the court martial of yet another American serviceman, this time the captain of a huge ship, who was to be made the scapegoat for the failings of the American Navy.

The court martial of Captain Charles Butler McVay, Commanding Officer of the heavy cruiser, *Indianapolis*, flagship of the US Pacific Fifth Fleet, at the end of 1945, is strange in a number of ways. In the first place, the ship had carried the components of the first atom bomb, dropped on Hiroshima on 6 August 1945, and it must be one of the few cases where the officer of an enemy nation was produced to give evidence against an accused man. The captain of the submarine that sank the great *Indianapolis* was brought from Japan to testify against the man whose ship he had destroyed.

When, in the summer of 1945, the United States were hoping to end the war with Japan by dropping the first atom bomb, the problem was how were they to deliver the bomb from the middle of an American desert to the Pacific island of Tinian where it was to be assembled. By this time, Tinian had become the largest air base in the world and, isolated from the rest of the airfield was one silver B-29, *Enola Gay*, which was to be the instrument allocated to deliver the brand new weapon which it was hoped would end hostilities at a stroke.

Long before the bomb fell on Hiroshima and even before the first test in New Mexico, thoughts were already being directed to the problem of delivering it, and special air force crews were completing training in modified B-29s at a secret base at Wendover, Utah, near the Nevada border. With seventy-five picked pilots and nearly 2000 officers and men to back them up, they had practiced steadily to perfect their technique. None of them knew what they were training for and, in the end, all but three of the B-29s flew to Tinian for the final act. The final three were to leave later with the last remaining parts of the bomb. The heart of the bomb – the sub-critical mass of Uranium 235 – was to be transported by sea.

The ship that was to carry it was chosen by sheer chance. Something larger than a cruiser was ruled out because of vulnerability, something small was ruled out for lack of room. From the point of view of speed and space a heavy cruiser was just right and the available ship happened to be the *Indianapolis*, which had the extra advantage of being a flagship and therefore possessed staff space that could be used to advantage.

The *Indianapolis* was a venerable vessel of pre-war vintage, the flagship of Admiral Raymond Spruance, Commander, Fifth Fleet, who had chosen her because she had adequate quarters for his staff, was fast enough to keep up with the carriers, and, being old, was not too valuable to be risked in an amphibious operation. She was known to be a tender ship, in other words she had a small metacentric height or, in plain language, it wouldn't take too much water inside her to capsize her. But this, and the fact that she had no sound-detection gear, was of small concern because, as flagship, she would always be in the company of other ships.

Since, however, Spruance was in Guam planning further moves in the island-hopping campaign towards Japan and had no need of the vessel for some time and, with the war in Europe already over, she was free to carry out the task. She was a good-looking ship known to the crews of newer ships as the *Swayback Maru* because of the cutaway hull which had been constructed to allow for catapults and hangars. She was ageing but still dignified and had been commissioned in November 1932 as the first of her class, of which only one other, the *Portland* was built. In 1933 she had taken President Franklin D Roosevelt and a party of friends cruising in the Atlantic, and in 1935 the President had reviewed the fleet off New York from her bridge. He was aboard again in 1936 for a tour of South America, and when war came the *Indianapolis* served in every corner of the Pacific. She had destroyed a Japanese ammunition ship in the Aleutians, three planes in separate actions at Tarawa, Woleai and Iwo Jima, and six more off Okinawa. At one time or another she had helped bombard nearly every Japanese stronghold in the Pacific but had suffered no damage until a kamikaze had struck her at Okinawa.

She had arrived in the San Francisco Navy Yard in April 1945, badly mauled on the port quarter. The kamikaze had fallen into the sea to do little damage, but the bomb released by the pilot had pierced the main deck, passed through a mess hall, a berthing compartment and the fuel tanks, and exploded under the hull, killing nine men and blowing two gaping holes in the hull. The damage had been controlled and the ship saved. Despite the damage, she had crawled back 8000 miles to California and by late June she was in shape again, with a new port quarter, the latest in radio equipment, radar and fire control mechanisms.

Her Commanding Officer, Captain Charles Butler McVay, had been in the navy for twenty-six years. He was now forty-six and his father had commanded several famous ships during World War I, ending up as Commander-in-Chief, US Asiatic Fleet. Though the son's service had been less spectacular, at least it had been solid and he was confident he would eventually reach the top of the naval ladder. Appointed to Annapolis by President Woodrow Wilson, he had graduated in 1919, and, after serving on various types of ship and in various posts ashore, he had become executive officer of the cruiser, *USS Cleveland*, and in 1943 off the Solomons, had won the Silver Star for conspicuous gallantry.

It was decided that McVay's ship should be the means of carrying the bomb because nobody was sure how the bomb would react. They believed everything would work but if it was transported by air and the plane carrying it should crash on take-off, it was conceivable that the city of San Francisco might well be removed from the map. McVay was ordered to make the ship ready for sea.

All men away on courses were ordered back to the ship, their courses abruptly terminated, liberty was cancelled and all hands turned to preparing the *Indianapolis* for sea. Among them were over thirty new officers and 250 enlisted men as replacements, most of them newly out of training schools. Extra life jackets came aboard, together with passengers due for Pearl Harbor, making the ship very crowded. She had her sea trials on 14 July, still crowded with men and unstowed gear, and arrived back at base on the following day, Sunday the 15th, when McVay was called to the office of Rear Admiral William Purnell and given a set of simple orders. He was to take his ship to Hunters Point Navy Yard where a small but vital cargo would be loaded. He would sail the following morning at high speed, dropping his passengers at Pearl Harbor, before continuing to Tinian, where the cargo would be removed. The cargo was not specified but he was told in no uncertain terms that it was more important than the ship itself and that if they were sunk en route and there was only one lifeboat left, the cargo was to be put in it. There was, however, no need for either himself or his crew to know what the cargo was.

About noon on 15 July, the internal components of the bomb were brought aboard. A metal cylinder, weighing about 200 lbs and containing the uranium core, was secured to the deck in the flag lieutenant's cabin, empty because all the flag staff were still with Spruance on Guam. It was guarded at all times by army officers from Los Alamos in New Mexico, where the bomb had been built. At the same

227

time, a fifteen-foot heavy wooden crate, containing the bomb's detonating mechanism was lashed to the deck in one of the ship's hangars, where it was guarded by Marines. Apart from the sentries, no one was allowed near either of the components.

At 5.30 a.m. the following day, the 16th, the first atom bomb was exploded at Almogordo, and at 8 a.m., two and a half hours later, almost as if she had been set off by a starter's pistol, the *Indianapolis* slipped her moorings and headed for the open sea.

On her first day at sea, the cruiser ran into rough weather and could make only 28 knots, but during the following days she reached 29 knots. On the fourth day, the ship reached Hawaii, setting a world record from the Farallon Light outside San Francisco to Diamond Head at Pearl with a crossing of 74.5 hours. Six hours after reaching Pearl, the *Indianapolis* moved on with a full supply of fuel and stores. One week later, on 26 July, she reached Tinian and dropped anchor half a mile off shore.

Senior officers swarmed over the ship and the two items of cargo were hoisted into a waiting barge. Moving on to Guam, McVay dropped the remainder of his passengers, mostly members of Admiral Spruance's staff, and reported to the port director of the Guam Naval Base, who routed him westward across the Philippine Sea to the island of Leyte. In Leyte Gulf he was to send a message to the Commander of Task Force 95, Vice Admiral Jesse B Oldendorf, who was steaming off the coast of Japan, reporting for duty. Before sailing northward, however, the *Indianapolis* was to spend ten days in the Gulf undergoing training because of the inexperience of over twenty-five per cent of her crew. Once in the Gulf, McVay was to report personally to Rear Admiral Lynde D McCormick, Commander of Task Group 95.7, at that time anchored in Leyte, with McCormick flying his flag in the battleship *Idaho*. McCormick would be informed by means of a copy of the order of *Indianapolis's* impending arrival.

Copies of the order were sent to seven diverse commands: the Tinian Port Director; the Port Director on Guam; Vice Admiral George Murray, Commander on the Marianas, from whose area of responsibility she would be sailing; Fleet Admiral Chester Nimitz, Commander-in-Chief, Pacific Fleet; Admiral Spruance; Vice Admiral Oldendorf; and Rear Admiral McCormick. It was no secret what the *Indianapolis* was up to, and the message was received and understood by everybody – except McCormick. As the *Indianapolis* left Tinian for Guam, McCormick's staff received a coded message containing the *Indianapolis*'s orders, but unfortunately the address was carelessly decoded by one of his staff not as 95.7 but as 75.8, so that it was assumed the message was not meant for them and the body of the message was not deciphered. The message was classified as 'restricted'. With a higher classification such as 'Secret' or 'Top Secret' a repeat would have been requested but, since it did not appear to be of sufficient significance, a repeat was not demanded, so that the unit to which the cruiser was heading had no idea she was on her way.

At 9.10 a.m. on Saturday 28 July, the *Indianapolis* left her mooring at Guam and headed for Leyte in the Philippines. This time there was no mystery or tension about a mysterious cargo and the old ship began to make a steady 15.7 knots, 16 knots being the limit placed on all ships to conserve fuel, which was having to be carried thousands of miles for the ships in the Pacific. Under rigid routing instructions, she was on a direct east-west line known as Convoy Route Peddie and at the very moment the instructions for her captain were being drawn up, sitting right in the middle of Peddie, waiting for a target, was the Japanese submarine, I-58, a 2600-ton boat with a crew of 105, under the command of 36-year-old Lieutenant Commander Mochitsura Hashimoto.

It was Hashimoto's fourth war patrol and the group with which he was operating had instructions to sink ships. During the war, the Japanese submarines had been used basically for reconnaissance and for supplying their distant garrisons but, with the war drawing to a close, the Japanese were growing desperate and their orders were to sink. American Intelligence was aware of this. Captain William R Smedburg, Assistant Combat Intelligence Officer for Fleet Admiral Ernest J King, Chief of Naval Operations in Washington, knew of Hashimoto's group and even roughly where they were, information which he passed on to Admiral Nimitz's staff at Pearl Harbor, who, in fact, often obtained the information before Washington and knew exactly where the four submarines of Hashimoto's group were situated.

Captain Clay Anderson, Pacific Fleet Operations Officer for Admiral King, also knew about Hashimoto's group and, following a sinking, had asked that a suggestion be made to Nimitz that it was a mistake to continue to route ships over the existing lanes. For some reason of his own, Admiral King did not give his authorisation for the message to be sent to Pearl Harbor, with the result that the *Indianapolis*'s route remained unchanged. No routing officer or ship's captain could, on his own authority, ever change a route but, to be fair, it required only the signature of a senior officer to do so in the event of an emergency. By a touch of irony, the Guam-Leyte route was actually on the point of being changed.

Before leaving Guam, McVay had seen Nimitz's Assistant Chief of Staff and Operations Officer, Commodore James B Carter who, although he must have known of the presence of Hashimoto's group, was only concerned with the planned training course for McVay's crew so that Admiral Spruance could move back on board his flagship, and he gave McVay nothing in the way of information on submarines.

McVay had then visited Lieutenant Joseph Waldron, Convoy and Routing officer for the Guam base, and, after a few questions, a route and speed were settled on. Because the *Indianapolis* did not carry underwater detection gear, McVay had then asked Waldron about an escort and was informed that, on the advice of Admiral Murray, the Commander, Marianas, no escort was needed. The last subject to be discussed had been the enemy and McVay agreed that this could be attended to by his navigator.

The *Indianapolis*'s navigating officer, Commander John Janney, had picked up his instructions the same evening. They indicated the speed of 15.7 knots, and that the cruiser was to zig-zag at the discretion of the commanding officer. The intelligence brief listed three possible submarine sightings but the information was clearly out of date or doubtful and, in fact, Janney had known of them already and had plotted them on his chart. More important than what was in the brief was what was not in it. There was no mention of I-58 on Route Peddie, or that another ship, the USS *Underhill*, an escort vessel, had recently been sunk along the route.

Much of this information had come from Ultra, the decoding sytem which gave the Allies information of what their enemies intended; but because of its highly secret nature, it was not allowed to be passed on except in a general manner, so that, while this would give the reader the information he required, it would not give away the source of the information. This was fine, so long as too much reliance was not placed on subordinates in the chain of command. In the case of the *Indianapolis*, though Commodore Carter, Nimitz's Chief of Staff and Operations Officer, knew of the submarines along *Indianapolis*'s route, he didn't pass it on to McVay. He *had* passed it on to Captain Oliver Naquin, Surface Operations Officer for the Commander, Marianas, who should have funnelled the knowledge to the naval base at Guam, which depended on him entirely for information on enemy activity in their area. But, in fact, they knew nothing of the sinking of the *Underhill*, of the dangerous group to which Hashimoto belonged, or of I-58. The intelligence reports being issued by the routing officer of the Guam Naval base were, in effect, worthless.

As the *Indianapolis* had left Apra Harbor, Waldron's

routing office prepared a message describing the anticipated movements of the cruiser. It pointed out the time and date of her departure, her average speed, her route and her time of arrival, and indicated that she would sail from one command area to another and the date of her passing what was called the 'chop' line, or the imaginary line along 130 degrees longitude east, separating the two command areas, the Marianas and the Philippine Sea Frontier. The message was sent to the operations office of the Marianas; the port director at Leyte; Rear Admiral McCormick, of Task Group 95.7, aboard the *Idaho*; Admiral Spruance; Vice Admiral James Kauffman, Commander of the Philippine Sea Frontier; Commodore Carter; Fleet Admiral Nimitz; Admiral Murray, Commander, Marianas; the commander of the Western Carolinas, a subordinate area under the Commander, Marianas; and finally Admiral Oldendorf, who was still off Japan, so that the message went in fact to Commodore Norman C Gillette who, with Kauffman on leave at the time, was acting Commander of the Philippine Sea Frontier.

This time McCormick's staff did decode the message but the staff of his superior, Admiral Oldendorf, did not. Reading the message, McCormick was confused. He assumed that either in San Francisco or Guam, the *Indianapolis* had been put through her refresher programme and wondered why she was reporting to Leyte. If his staff had decoded the previous message, he might have known. However, only recently two heavy cruisers had been detached from the Okinawa task force so he assumed that the *Indianapolis* would be diverted north as a replacement. If she did reach the Gulf of Leyte, however, he knew she would report to him and ordered his staff to mark her on the plotting board for an estimated time of arrival of 11 a.m. on the 31st.

Admiral Oldendorf remained totally in the dark, however, because he had not received Waldron's message. The system was that the routing office's message did not go directly to the task force but to the joint communications centre at Okinawa which, Oldendorf felt, was inefficient

232

in forwarding messages, and certainly somewhere there Waldron's message disappeared. All Oldendorf knew was that at some time the *Indianapolis* would arrive in Leyte but he didn't know when, because he had no idea of her departure date from Guam. Of the two commanders who should have known about her movements, McCormick knew she was on her way and when she was due, but couldn't understand why, Oldendorf knew why, but not when.

Within a few hours of the *Indianapolis* sailing, periscopes were reported along her route but no one thought it necessary to divert her.

On the evening of Sunday, the day after sailing, the officer of the deck, Lieutenant (Jg) Charles B McKissick, saw the reports of a periscope sighting about seventy-five miles south of *Indianapolis*'s track but he felt no alarm at the report, deciding it was too far away to be a danger.

The sea was choppy to rough, with poor visibility, the moon flitting between clouds, but the weather was warm and the water-tight doors on the second deck were open. On a ship so old and so crowded it was impossible to close everything and everybody was aware of it, right up to the top brass, and hundreds of men lugged mattresses and blankets on deck rather than sleep in the inferno below. If water got inside the hull, it could flow readily into the engineering spaces and she could fill and sink quickly, but there was nothing that could be done about it.

With the conditions that prevailed, McVay decided to use his discretionary powers to stop zigzagging, feeling a straight course at an increased speed was better than a slow speed with zigzagging, especially with alternate conditions of darkness and occasional moonlight. Somewhere between 7.30 and 8 p.m., as it grew fully dark the order was given to stop the zigzag and resume the basic course of 262 degrees. Just before 8 p.m. the cruiser increased speed to 17 knots to maintain her average speed of 15.7 knots and at 10.45 p.m. McVay went to his cabin and fell asleep – at just about the time when Lieutenant-Commander Hashimoto, of the I-58, was being roused.

Ordering the boat to be raised to 60 feet, Hashimoto swept the horizon and, seeing nothing, ordered the boat to surface. Suddenly the navigator called out that there was a possible enemy ship on a bearing of red ninety degrees. Hashimoto scrambled up the ladder, saw an indistinct blur and ordered a dive. The boat was carrying kaitens, or suicide torpedoes guided to their target by a man, but, seeing the ship coming straight at him, Hashimoto was less concerned with launching them than with getting out of the way. The kaiten pilots begged to be sent off but Hashimoto decided that the approaching ship, which he assumed to be either a battleship or a large cruiser, was such an easy target there was no need to waste a life and he would try the normal torpedoes.

The target's course and speed were estimated and, with the six bow tubes loaded, the range was set at 1,640 yards. Twenty-seven minutes after first sighting the *Indianapolis*, Hashimoto gave the order for the six torpedoes, set for a speed of 48 knots at a depth of 12 feet, to be fired. The torpedoes, five of which had magnetic warheads, had a spread of three degrees, except for the middle two, which were two degrees apart, and they left at intervals of three seconds. As the last one left, Hashimoto brought the submarine on a parallel course to the *Indianapolis* and waited.

At five minutes past midnight on 30 July 1945, the first torpedo smashed into the starboard bow of the *Indianapolis*. Three seconds later the second struck directly under the bridge, killing many of the officers who were berthed in this area. Water was sent soaring into the sky, and flame, steam and smoke roared out of the ship's forward stack. An enormous fireball swept through the forward half of the ship, and though the fire died away, the *Indianapolis*'s bow was gone and there were two gaping holes in her starboard side. From midships forward, there was no light, no power, no communication, no pressure and, since the rear half of the vessel was untouched, thousands of tons of water were being scooped into her as she continued her forward movement.

Half naked, McVay made his way to the bridge, thinking at first that the ship had been hit by a kamikaze. The bridge was dark and it was impossible to distinguish anybody. Because of the lost communications, it was impossible to have the engines stopped and the forward movement was only hastening the ship's end. From the moment she was hit the *Indianapolis* never lost headway. Within five minutes she had a twelve degree list to starboard and McVay was informed that she was going down rapidly. He found it hard to believe and felt it would be wrong to order Abandon Ship too soon. Two minutes later, however, the list was eighteen degrees, an increase of six degrees in two minutes. Sadly, McVay gave the order to abandon ship. It was clear that everybody who could get out from below must already have done so. Because of the lost communications, the order had to be given by mouth, but many men hadn't waited for it and had already jumped. Because the cruiser never lost headway, there was a line of bobbing heads for miles behind her.

McVay had just put his foot on top of the ladder that led down to the signal bridge when *Indianapolis* took a sharp twenty-five degree tilt to starboard and at 12.17 a.m., only twelve minutes after being struck, she was listing sixty degrees. Everyone and everything was thrown to starboard. The noise was deafening with material breaking loose and men yelling orders or screaming for help. McVay managed, with difficulty, to reach the deck where he tried to bring some order to the confusion, but then the ship took another heavy list and at 12.18 a.m. the former flagship of the Pacific Fleet was on her side, where she remained for another two minutes. McVay managed to reach the side of the ship as water rushed through open hatches and stacks and the ship began to settle.

Although a radio message had been sent from Radio Room I, the red pilot light, which was supposed to blink as

235

the key was pressed, did not show and it was impossible to tell whether it had gone out. The radio operator, Joseph Moran, was certain it had, on a frequency of 4235 Kc. Radio I was primarily a message receiving room, however, and normal transmissions were handled by Radio II (the transmitter room) and there Chief Radio Electrician L T Woods was sending out a plain language SOS on 500 Kc. The pilot lights were working and Woods had power because the power source of Radio II was the after engine room. Woods continued for about five minutes before ordering everybody to save themselves.

There was no response to the messages and the only explanation was that the antennas were down so that, though there was evidence of a transmission, nothing was going out. Although the *Indianapolis* was transmitting to the end, she was not heard. About five months after the sinking, it was reported that the Coast Guard cutter, *Bibb*, had picked up a fragmentary distress message, but *Bibb* denied this was true. The rumours continued to fly around, and the sea-going tug, *Pawnee*, was also reported to have picked up the tail-end of a message, as were the cruiser, *Salt Lake City* and the USS *Hyperion*. None of them were ever definite, however, and the messages were probably those requesting the whereabouts of the *Indianapolis*, from Leyte or Samar in the Philippines.

Standing on the ship's side, McVay began walking, unable to realise he had lost his ship in no more that fifteen minutes, then suddenly he was sucked off the side by the wave caused by the bow going down. Swimming desperately, he heard a swishing noise, felt hot oil on his neck, and looked round to see that the *Indianapolis* was gone.

It was impossible to tell how many men had survived but it was worked out later that between 800 and 900 had managed to and that 400 had gone down with her. As the watches had just been changing, many men were awake and had managed to escape. All that was needed was to get them out of the water.

*

At 1 a.m., with his torpedo tubes reloaded, Hashimoto gave the order to surface. He was keeping a sharp look-out for debris that would establish proof of the sinking but, because of the darkness, he couldn't see a thing. He was certain, however, that the ship had gone down because she could never have made off at high speed with the damage he knew she had sustained. Nervous of destroyers and aircraft, he moved north-east and an hour later dived, instructing his radio room to inform Tokyo that he had sunk a battleship of the *Idaho* class.

With the Japanese code broken, the US Navy was reading I-58's message at the same time as Tokyo, but were unable to determine the nature of the ship. Nevertheless, early that Monday morning, the Navy knew that an American ship had been sunk and knew roughly where. While the communications centre in Washington was translating the message, a check translation of the message was received from Pearl Harbor. They were basically identical so Washington took no further action because they knew Pearl had the message and any action necessary would be directed by the Pacific Fleet. In fact, no action was taken.

Had Fleet Admiral Nimitz and his staff taken steps to have the matter investigated, it was possible that the survivors of the *Indianapolis* might have been located within twenty-four hours, but Pearl Harbor ignored I-58's message because it was believed that it was intended to deceive. The Japanese often exaggerated their claims and had been known to claim to have sunk vessels that were 3000 miles away from what they said was the point of contact. Many Japanese combat reports were also put out as 'feelers', and contained a lot of false information, and having investigated all these reports with no results, a policy was developed of ignoring them. Neither the submarine's position nor that of any ships in the area were plotted. Had they been, it would soon have been noticed that Hashimoto and the *Indianapolis* were in roughly the same spot.

*

The men in the sea scrambled where they could on to rafts or clung to crates. There was a big swell running and it was possible while on a crest to see for a great distance. On the first day a monstrous shark investigated the raft McVay was on and nothing could drive it away.

At 1 p.m. a high-flying twin-engined bomber flew overhead towards Leyte – McVay's watch kept excellent time throughout the whole ordeal – and at 3 p.m. another aeroplane passed to the south, also heading for the Philippines. Vain attempts were made to contact them by flashing with a mirror. Two hours before the end of the first day, another plane flew overhead, its red and green lights plainly visible. McVay fired a Very Light but it went unnoticed, though spirits remained high because everyone was confident they would be picked up the following day. The ship was due in Leyte Gulf in the morning and when it didn't show up, a search would surely be made.

But things didn't work out like that. At some time on that Monday, the marker for the *Indianapolis* on the plotting board in the Marianas was removed on the assumption that the ship had passed into a new area. In fact, she had never crossed the 'chop' line and had sunk in the territory of the Commander of the Marianas, Admiral Murray.

Of the thirty-five rafts carried by the *Indianapolis*, only about twelve were freed, because the men waited for the order to abandon ship, which however, didn't come until the ship was well over on its side. As the ship tilted further, the strain on the straps grew greater so they couldn't be easily unhooked, and the lack of experience among many of the young sailors meant that instead of pulling a toggle pin to break them loose as they should have, they tried to cut the thick straps with knives.

The men in the water remained calm and quiet during the first hours. Most were unrecognisable because they were black from the heavy fuel oil which burned their eyes, clogged their nostrils and choked their throats. Quite a few of them were critically wounded, many with severe flash burns to the face, arms or body, some with compound fractures of one sort or another. There were few medical supplies available and many men died of shock during the first few hours. Before the sun rose, around fifty of the original number who were in the sea had gone. Bravery and self sacrifice came to the surface. Many of the wounded or men without life jackets had to be supported but there was always some man who was willing to help, and on the whole they remained co-operative and good natured.

By daybreak, the mass of floating humanity had split into three main groups, one of them of 400 men, which was separated from the other groups by miles of ocean. They hadn't a life raft or a drop of water or a scrap of food and were entirely dependent on their life jackets. Eventually, this group broke into three separate groups, one of about 200 men, one of about 100, and one of about fifty together with odd smaller groups, which were separated from each other by a distance of several hundred yards. The main object was to stay together and the leader of the group of 200, Marine Captain Edward Parke, managed to string his party together. Fortunately, there were enough of the kapok life jackets to go round because an order for the ship had been duplicated and though they were supposed to last only forty-eight hours before eventually becoming water-logged, in fact they worked well for the whole of the ordeal. The other type of life preserver, a rubber pneumatic type worn always round the waist, was too easily punctured and the wearer couldn't sleep for fear of flipping over on to his face and drowning.

Shortly after dawn on this Monday, a Ventura bomber on anti-submarine patrol flew over the men in the sea at a height of between 1500 and 2000 feet. The men in the water waved, splashed the water with their hands and one of them spread a green marker dye he possessed. They were all convinced they had been seen and estimated that within five hours they would be rescued.

But the pilot, Lieutenant-Commander Moss W Flannery,

couldn't see a thing because of the glassy sea which was dazzling to stare at. By 10 a.m. the reflection of the sun was so sharp that the men began to suffer from the glare which caused intense pain. Closing the eyelids didn't help. Ripping off clothing, some of the men made blindfolds. Fortunately their bodies, covered with fuel oil, didn't burn.

There was constant change among the three groups. A few men died and the bodies were allowed to drift away, some of the men reciting the Lord's Prayer as they did so. By this time, in the choppy sea, everyone had swallowed oil-soaked water and they were vomiting and beginning to suffer from thirst. In addition, although there were no major attacks, they were beginning to see sharks, and occasionally there would be a scream and the water would be churned red.

Tolosa, on Leyte, the headquarters of Vice Admiral Kauffman, Commander, Philippine Sea Frontier, to which *Indianapolis* was heading, was one of the world's busiest harbours at the time, over 1500 vessels arriving and departing monthly. But the despatch from Guam giving the itinerary of the *Indianapolis* was read and the ship's estimated position was marked on the plotting board. Everyone expected her to appear the following morning.

At 10 p.m. that evening, the Leyte Gulf naval base prepared a list of all ships expected to arrive or depart the next day, Tuesday 31 July. A footnote to the list stated that its value lay in its accuracy, completeness and prompt dissemination. The largest of the thirty-six ships due to arrive was the *Indianapolis*.

Forty-nine copies of the list were made and distributed to every officer who needed to know. Unfortunately, as the Pacific War had intensified, communications networks had become heavily overcrowded and, to alleviate the situation and provide security, Nimitz's Chief of Staff, Vice Admiral Charles McMorris, had signed a signal stating that 'Arrival reports shall not be made for combatant ships.' From this the assumption arose that if an arrival was not to be reported, neither was a non-arrival. Admiral King later admitted that the wording of McMorris's letter was faulty, but it had never occurred to McMorris or his advisers that the phraseology might result in the omission of reports on non-arrivals or a sense of complacency on the part of those men it was intended to affect.

When the message about the *Indianapolis*'s departure was received at Tacloban, the Acting Port Director, Lieutenant-Commander Jules Sancho, had only just arrived and hadn't even unpacked. His Operations Officer was Lieutenant Stuart B Gibson and the message passed from them to Commodore Jacobson, but none of the three paid any further attention. It was not the function of the Port Director or a Naval Operating Base to plot the movements of combatant ships, and they didn't even possess plotting boards. Nevertheless, by sundown on this last day of July, Gibson knew the *Indianapolis* had not appeared. But he did not report it. Having been ordered not to report arrivals he assumed he was also not to report non-arrivals. In fact, the burden did not rest entirely with him. The communications structure was wrong, and at 8 p.m. that evening, nine hours after the *Indianapolis* should have appeared, the Expected Arrivals and Departures List was prepared for the next day, and since she hadn't appeared, she was automatically put on the sheet for the next day, Wednesday 1 August.

By this day, the second in the water, the *Indianapolis*'s men were beginning to suffer from blisters and salt water ulcers. During the day two planes were seen and Very Lights were fired but without effect. Meanwhile at the Philippine Sea Frontier headquarters it was assumed that the *Indianapolis* had arrived, but since it had not been confirmed, the pin remained on the map, which indicated that the ship was presumably in. Only Lieutenant Edward B Henslee, the plot supervisor, knew she wasn't because the harbour entrance post had not indicated her passing. He was not disturbed, however, because ships were often 11 or 12 hours late, and he therefore marked her in on the Expected Arrival Report for the next day as an overdue vessel. It would not have taken him long to telephone the office of the Port Director to check, or for the Port Director to check with the Philippine Sea Frontier headquarters but, even if they had, probably nothing would have been done. Both the headquarters and the Port Director's office each had an officer who knew that the *Indianapolis* had not arrived but both had passed it off as unimportant.

Just as the Sea Frontier had plotted the ship, so had the Marianas, and on this day her marker was removed from the board on the assumption that she had arrived. No check was made. Plotting boards, in fact, were being kept everywhere on the movements of the *Indianapolis*, and even at the headquarters of the Commander-in-Chief, Pacific, Commodore Carter also assumed she had arrived and removed her from his plot. It was Carter who had passed on the order prohibiting the reporting of arrivals, but he made no attempt to check, assuming that she was safely at anchor in Leyte Gulf.

At 10 a.m. on this day, Admiral McCormick's group, 95.7, which the *Indianapolis* should have joined, left Leyte Gulf for a training exercise. McCormick had no knowledge of the *Indianapolis*'s movements because his staff had not decoded the Commander-in-Chief's message. But, knowing that the ship left Guam bound for Leyte, he expected to see her when he returned. He did not mention to Rear Admiral I C Sowell, his deputy in the Gulf, that the *Indianapolis* was due in and, as a result, Sowell also didn't check on the ship. McCormick had reasonably not considered the *Indianapolis* his responsibility until she arrived.

McCormick's superior, Vice Admiral Oldendorf, had received the Commander-inChief's message but nothing from the office of Waldron, the Routing and Convoy Officer at Guam. He should have received a message from McVay saying the *Indianapolis* had arrived safely but he was not perturbed because he was able to assume she had been diverted to some other task while at sea. The *Indianapolis* was unusual in this respect because, as flagship of the Fifth Fleet, her orders were constantly being changed by Spruance to suit his needs and senior officers were always doubtful of her movement reports. Also, as flagship of the Pacific Fifth Fleet, she had been fitted with a new type of radio teletype communication and early on the morning of Tuesday 31 July, this was due to be tested by a message from the Commander, Amphibious Forces, Pacific. When no answer was received, Radio Guam was contacted and asked to raise the ship. When Guam was unsuccessful, for the first time someone grew worried and a message was sent from the Commander, Amphibious Forces, Pacific, to the Commander-in-Chief, Pacific Fleet, asking when the *Indianapolis* would be ready for a further attempt. The message went out thirty-three hours after she had found her grave at the bottom of the Philippine Sea. Pacific Fleet headquarters told Amphibious Forces to forget about it and nothing more was done. Nimitz's Assistant Communications Officer, Captain Paul Anderson, was not at all concerned at the *Indianapolis's* failure to reply to the test message because the new equipment was very technical and he expected the *Indianapolis* to experience some difficulty on the first test, and nothing further was done to contact the ship. In fact, the new system had been tried on the trip from San Francisco to Pearl Harbor and found to be in excellent working order. McVay had been informed of this but, if the Commander-in-Chief's headquarters had been informed the information had not been passed to Captain Anderson.

On this day, Wednesday 1 August, the Expected Arrivals and Departures List was made up for Thursday 2 August, and, since she hadn't arrived, the *Indianapolis* was posted as an expected arrival for that day. By this time the ship was thirty-six hours overdue. At least one officer, Lieutenant James D Brown, an officer on the staff of the base commandant, who was responsible for preparing the Ships Present List, knew the *Indianapolis* should have arrived but he felt it was no concern of his because ships were constantly being diverted. Lieutenant Edward Henslee, of the Headquarters Plotting Section, Philippine Sea Frontier, had been aware the previous day that the *Indianapolis* had not arrived but throughout Wednesday he failed to inform his superiors. Yet another officer, Lieutenant William A Green, also became aware on Wednesday that the *Indianapolis* had not arrived but he took the same view as Brown: the *Indianapolis* must have been diverted.

By Thursday 2 August, most of the men in the water had passed beyond rationality and barely knew what was happening. At 9 a.m. on this day, Lieutenant (Jg) Wilbur C Gwinn, of the Pelelieu Search & Reconnaissance Command of Vice Admiral Murray, flew off from Pelelieu in a twin-engined Ventura. His navigational antenna had become useless but, since the weather was good, he decided to continue his anti-submarine patrol. Because the radio-man was busy, Gwinn decided to try to repair the antenna himself and, while working on it, happened to glance down. The plane was at 3000 feet and suddenly, quite clearly, he saw a thin snake-like slick of oil. Assuming it could only have come from a damaged submarine, he rushed back to his seat and brought the bomber down to 900 feet. The slick seemed never-ending and, as he followed it, five miles later, he saw about thirty men in the water, some of them clinging to a raft and trying to wave.

While shore-based officers had ignored the possibilities of a disaster, for the men in the water the ordeal had become a horror. By the second morning after the sinking, more men had died. Because they had been damaged during the launching of the rafts, some of the water beakers on them contained dirty water. They were also large, heavy and difficult to handle and inevitably became salty as soon as they were opened because they couldn't be resealed. Since also there was nothing in the way of a cup, much of the water was wasted as it was rationed out. The first aid equipment

244

had also been found to be generally useless because the containers were not watertight, and while the food remained in good condition, the staple diet was Spam, a wartime ham concoction which increased thirst because it was salty. What was more, the sharks which had appeared seemed to like it and as soon as a can was opened they arrived from all directions.

On this day, too, there was trouble from food stealing and by this time some of the men in their desperation were quietly committing suicide by slipping out of their life jackets. Fights also started and there were even murders for the possession of a life jacket. During the latter part of the day the sea grew calmer but thirst had by now become overpowering. Men started to drink sea water and some went mad. Several brave men wearing the rubber life belts tried to calm them and in the struggles the life belts were punctured and both victim and helper drowned. The sharks could clearly be seen in the clear water, though they were still going for the dead men rather than the living, and from this time on, what happened was nothing but a nightmare.

Aircraft flew over or near but all failed to see them – partly because the glassy sea made it impossible, and partly because they weren't looking for them. They were chiefly on anti-submarine patrol and they had no knowledge of the loss of the *Indianapolis*.

The suffering grew worse. Men became hysterical and began to suffer from hallucinations. Thinking Japanese were among them, more fights broke out. The sea was mirror-calm but the condition of the men was becoming critical. They were beginning by now to worry about their kapok life jackets which they knew were supposed to support them for only forty-eight hours and they were now well into their third day. Men continued to die and it was now becoming a question not of who would die but when, and they could not understand where the rescue ships had got to.

Knowing nothing of the suffering below him or anything of the sinking of the *Indianapolis*, Lieutenant Gwinn, in the

Ventura passing above them, couldn't understand where they had come from. He had no report of a large ship being sunk but he descended to 30 feet and skimmed the water, his radioman sending off a message at once. Extending his search, as he followed the slick he found more groups of men in the water and finally estimated he had seen around 150 of them. With his antenna out of action, the position he had given might not be correct, so he returned to the dark tunnel at the end of the bomber and managed to make a botched-up repair on it.

An hour and twenty minutes after his first message, which had reported only thirty survivors, he sent a second message, indicating there were now 150 and giving a better position. Receiving orders to remain in position and by this time certain he was looking at American sailors in distress, he began to drop everything he could that floated, such as life rafts and cans of fresh water. Though the water cans burst on landing, at least the men in the water knew they had finally been seen. Gwinn also released dye markers and smoke bombs and finally a sonabuoy, which could transmit a signal.

Because of the damaged aerial, Gwinn's first message about thirty survivors was garbled and still nobody jumped to the conclusion that the men in the water were from the *Indianapolis*. The men ashore assumed they were Japanese because a convoy escort had reported attacking a Japanese submarine, and there was no rush to mount a rescue. After the second report mentioning 150 survivors, however, it was realised it could not be a submarine because no submarine carried that many men, and it finally dawned on the headquarters of the Commander-in-Chief that it might be an American ship. Immediately ships were ordered to break radio silence and report their positions.

Gwinn's superior officer, Lieutenant-Commander George Atteberry, realising that Gwinn would shortly have to leave the men in the water, asked for flying boats and ordered out his own machine. During his flight out, he learned

246

the Catalinas were airborne. The pilot of the first one, Lieutenant R Adrian Marks, found the number of men reported in the water hard to accept and assumed he was merely to pick up a downed pilot, so that when he found them, the numbers startled him. He dropped everything he could, concentrating on the men who had nothing more than life jackets, then, realising the men were in very poor shape and that they were being harassed by sharks, he made up his mind to do something more positive.

He chose the spot where he thought the Catalina would do most good and put her down. Though the hull remained intact, rivets sprang loose in the landing and seams were burst open, but Marks took the Catalina to the survivors, trying to pick up the men who were floating alone. Survivors were pulled aboard one after another until, before night fell, Marks had picked up thirty men and crammed them into the leaking aeroplane. Only then was it learned that they were from the *Indianapolis*. He could not pass on the message, however, because he couldn't send it in clear and he just didn't have time to code a message, so it was that the navy did not learn of the loss of the heavy cruiser until just after midnight the following day, 3 August.

By now other planes were arriving, with Atteberry directing them where to drop their gear to the best effect. He was also in contact with ships racing to the scene but, as darkness settled, there was nothing more he could do but return home. With survivors packed like sardines into his Catalina, Marks taxied to another large group of men who were laid on the wings and covered with parachutes. The damage they did made it look as if the Catalina would never fly again, and it was impossible to move in case the machine ran down men in the water, so they settled down to wait. Just before midnight, a searchlight appeared and a ship began to head towards the Catalina. Another Catalina had also landed by this time and the crew saw bodies everywhere in the sea, but were able to pick up only one man before it became too dark.

*

At Frontier HQ on this Thursday morning, Lieutenant Green, Surface Control Officer, noticed that the *Indianapolis* had still not come in and, assuming that by now she had probably been diverted elsewhere, he requested permission to remove the ship from his board. Five hours later, he first heard of men in the water.

The Operations Officer of the Philippines Sea Frontier, Captain Alfred Granum, made a check and realised at once that they were in the spot where the *Indianapolis* should have been three and a half days before. His superior, Commodore Gillette, also checked and discovered that the *Indianapolis* had not arrived. He signalled Guam and copies were sent to Admirals McCormick, Oldendorf, Murray and Nimitz, Commodore Carter and to the *Indianapolis* herself. Messages flew backwards and forwards saying the *Indianapolis* had left Guam but where was she now?

Admiral McCormick, steaming into Leyte Gulf where he expected to see the *Indianapolis*, was also asked if she had reported but, when he replied that she had not, he was not worried because, like so many others, he assumed she had been diverted. Oldendorf couldn't understand why her non-arrival had not been recorded. In fact it had been and the officers at Leyte knew of it but had done nothing about it.

By this time ships were moving to the scene of the disaster, and stunned officers at Philippine Sea Frontier, Western Carolinas, Marianas, Pearl Harbor and at a dozen headquarters in the Pacific, waited for information on where the survivors had come from. The last thing that occurred to them was that a ship could disappear without anyone picking up a message and that the survivors could remain in the water for so long without being sighted.

By now, the men in the water were in slightly better shape. Rafts had been dropped, together with water, rations, and first aid kits. In the first minutes of Friday 3 August, the fifth day, the sea began to get up. One of the rescuing ships began to take survivors from Marks's Catalina and for the first time a message was transmitted indicating who they were. It was obvious by now that Marks's plane would never fly again and at first light the USS *Doyle* sank it with 40 mm gunfire.

The men who had been brought aboard *Doyle* were cleaned up and given water, soup, coffee and fruit, but their medical condition was very poor. As the last survivors were picked up and planes and ships made a final search of the area for any men who had drifted away from the main groups, the last man to be plucked from the sea was Captain McVay. That afternoon Philippine Sea Frontier headquarters issued instructions that all overdue ships were to be reported, and later in the day Nimitz ordered his commands to check their radio log books to ascertain whether distress messages had been picked up. He also instructed that until further orders all ships with more than 500 men on board should be provided with an escort. The *Indianapolis* had sailed with 1196 men on board, and of these 800 had escaped the sinking. But of these 800 only 320, two of whom died later, were rescued. Five hundred men had died through complacency and carelessness.

Even as the shark-ravaged bodies were lifted from the sea, questions began to be asked. The sinking had shaken the navy. It was the largest loss of life in a sinking in its history. There had been other severe blows – The *Franklin* (772 lost), the *Juneau* (676), the *Liscombe Bay* (644), but they couldn't be compared with the *Indianapolis* because they had been lost in battle and only one-third of the *Indianapolis*'s losses could be attributed to the Japanese. Instead of being killed in action, they had been killed by inaction.

As soon as the initial shock had passed, Nimitz issued orders which made it clear once and for all that a ship failing to arrive within eight hours of her estimated time of arrival was to be considered overdue, that she was to be reported at once and a new ETA was to be requested and, if necessary, air and surface searches were to be organised. Because the navy was occupied with the preparations for the invasion of the Japanese home islands, he also ordered that a court of enquiry should sit as soon as possible. Among those ordered to attend were Commodore Gillette and his operations officer, Captain Granum, Lieutenant-Commander Sancho and Lieutenant Gibson, but oddly enough, one of the members of the court was Admiral Murray, within whose jurisdiction the ship had been sunk and whose Operations Officer, Captain Naquin, had so signally failed to pass on the information of the presence of Hashimoto's group along *Indianapolis*'s intended course.

The court could not convene immediately. With the war rushing to its end at a tremendous pace, there were other things to do. The atom bomb had been dropped, Russia had entered the war against Japan and the following day the second atom bomb was dropped on Nagasaki.

The proceedings started on 13 August, and were held in secret. The first witness was McVay and, despite the fact that his orders stated quite clearly that he had discretionary powers to cease zigzagging when conditions permitted, the enquiry laid great stress on this point. Not a single question was asked of Waldron about the worthless intelligence report he had issued, while Captain Naquin's estimate of the 'negligible' submarine danger along Route Peddie was accepted. The loss of the *Indianapolis* had shown it was anything but negligible, but nothing was said about his knowledge that there were submarines across the *Indianapolis*'s path. Lieutenant Gibson admitted that he knew of the missing ship on the day she was overdue but had not reported it.

The ship's loss was announced the following day, 14 August, but it had clearly been carefully timed because this was the day when President Truman announced Japan's surrender and it was barely noticed in the excitement.

Various officers and men were called to relate their experiences in the water, and shore-based officers were asked about their actions when the ship had not appeared. Many of them claimed that reporting an overdue ship was not their business or that they had assumed the *Indianapolis* had arrived. Blame was shifted and seven days later the enquiry ended. Captain McVay did not make a closing statement, but Lieutenant Gibson, who had been involved in the delay in reporting the *Indianapolis* overdue, continued to argue that he had no directive calling for the reporting of non-arrivals.

The Judge Advocate closed the enquiry by saying that the apparent cause for the delay in reporting the missing cruiser was the failure to take notice of her non-arrival at Leyte. The report on the proceedings seemed to get things wrong, and stated categorically that the ship had been informed of submarine contacts along her assigned route, something which was quite incorrect. The court also assumed that Captain Naquin's estimate of negligible submarine activity was correct. If that were the case, however, why did the court harp on the question of zigzagging? The court also claimed that visibility was good, that McVay should have zigzagged and that there had been a delay in sending a distress message. All these assumptions were wrong. It finally recommended that letters of reprimand should be sent to McVay, Sancho and Gibson. Sancho shrugged his off. Gibson protested that he couldn't be blamed for not doing duties which didn't exist.

The court also recommended that Lieutenant Gibson be admonished, that Admiral McCormick should discipline his communications staff, that ships without escort should zigzag at all times, and finally that Captain McVay should be court martialled for inefficiency and negligently endangering lives. McVay had been chosen as the scapegoat to be shown to the nation.

Admiral Nimitz promptly disagreed with the findings and said so. Nine cruisers had been lost in battle, some in questionable circumstances, but nobody had been court martialled. McVay was unfortunate that his tragedy occurred so late in the war, and Nimitz was overruled by Admiral King, who felt the court of enquiry had not done the job for which it was assembled. He asked that an investigating officer should look into the sinking, and the Naval Inspector General, Admiral C P Snyder, was given the job. While he was at work, Admiral Louis Denfield, Chief of Naval Personnel, recommended more than once that the trial should be withheld and King himself agreed, but within a few hours he had changed his mind and, making a 180-degree turn, he asked for a trial to start at once.

The court martial of Captain McVay was to begin on 3 December 1945. It had been decided that of all the charges that could be levelled at him the only one that could be proved was his failure to zigzag. But that didn't seem enough and the charge of failing to order Abandon Ship was added, chiefly, it seems, to placate the American public who, by this time, had been appraised by the Press of the details of the disaster and could not understand the reason for the number of casualties and wanted to know the answer. If the navy wished to obscure the fact that its procedures had been wrong, McVay had to be to blame.

While this was going on, Hashimoto was discovered in Japan and transport for him was arranged to the United States. He was even given money to buy gifts for his wife and children while there. On 3 December 1945, the court assembled in an ordnance classroom of the Washington Navy Yard. McVay claimed he hadn't had time to prepare his defence and requested an adjournment until the next day. Since the Press had learned the navy was to produce an enemy officer as a witness against one of their own kind, the Navy Department issued a statement to let the public know what was to happen and on 13 December Hashimoto, wearing a ill-fitting suit, walked into the court room and bowed to the American interpreters and to the president of the court.

McVay's counsel, Captain John P Cady, immediately sprang to his feet. How could anyone, he demanded, come up with the idea of bringing to court to testify against a

United States officer an officer of a nation which had been judged guilty of despicable treachery, infamous cruelty and barbarous practices? The American people, he said, were disgusted. The Judge Advocate, Captain Thomas J Ryan, replied that Hashimoto was there simply to explain the explosions that had led to the sinking of the *Indianapolis* and pointed out that Hashimoto would not dare perjure himself.

Hashimoto took the stand but out of all of his evidence nothing appeared to be of any great value because none of it related to the charges. The navy's firework turned out to be a damp squib, and the only real point he made was that even if McVay had been zigzagging the ship would have been hit, anyway. By sheer chance, he had surfaced at the perfect time and place for an attack. Half an hour later he might never have seen *Indianapolis*, and if *Indianapolis* had been escorted by vessels with sounding gear the tables might have been turned. The only thing his presence achieved was the prompting of angry questions in the House of Representatives about the evidence and the fact that one of the hated Japanese had been called. One member touched on the tender spot and suggested that instead of McVay being brought to trial those responsible for failing to pick up the men in the water should have been court martialled instead. Nothing was done, however, and the evidence remained.

The trial lasted thirteen days with thirty-nine witnesses for the prosecution and eighteen for the defence. A key witness was Captain Glyn Donaho, whose submarine exploits during the war had become legendary. He pointed out that zigzagging made no difference to an attack, but then McVay unwisely asked, at the last moment, if zigzagging was disconcerting to a submarine commander and Donaho had to admit that it could be, thus destroying the valuable evidence he had given on McVay's behalf.

After a retirement of only two and a half hours the court found McVay guilty on the charge of failing to zigzag and acquitted him on the second charge of failing to abandon ship in time. He was sentenced to lose 100 numbers in his temporary grade of captain and 100 numbers in his permanent grade of commander. McVay's naval career was ruined. As the court closed, the members, who would doubtless have preferred not to be involved in the case at all, recommended clemency.

The verdict didn't please the public or the Press. The *Chicago Sun* pointed out that no evidence had been introduced with respect to possible blame ashore for the lack of a search for the overdue cruiser. In the public mind it seemed that officers had been sitting ashore twiddling their thumbs while 500 men had died in the water. Certainly the court martial had concentrated only on the zigzagging and the failure to abandon ship so, since the court martial had to deal only with these matters, the entire picture could not be offered to the public. The court of enquiry and the investigation of the naval Inspector General were considered to be 'secret', so that the general public learned only what the navy wanted them to know. It was never brought out at the court martial that McVay had sailed a straight line because no one had informed him of Japanese submarines along his route. Naquin had still insisted that the risk of danger was slight, yet when questioned by the Inspector General, he had admitted that he knew there were four submarines operating in the area of the sinking. Captain Granum, Operations Officer at the Philippine Sea Frontier, had also admitted to the Inspector General to being aware of sinkings along the route, yet at the court martial he said there was no more than the normal hazard to be expected in wartime.

It is obvious that these officers were holding back information but Captain Cady, the defending officer, was inexperienced in trials and other officers who could have testified to the dangers were never called. In February 1946, the navy issued to the Press a report on the loss of the *Indianapolis* which was the navy's final word but, while everything in it is true, the document's importance lies really not in what it says but in what it does not say. One paragraph that was cut from it indicated that it *was* known that four

Japanese submarines were operating in the area of the sinking but that the information did not reach the routing officer at Guam, and for this Captain Naquin was considered responsible.

In January 1946, Vice Admiral Denfield asked that McVay's sentence be remitted and that he should be restored to duty on the grounds of his excellent record. Admiral King concurred and finally the Secretary of the Navy, James Forrestal, agreed. After six months of misery, McVay, it seemed, was being asked to put the whole affair behind him. The public was not deluded, however, and appeared to blame not McVay, but the navy for its inefficiency. At a news conference in February 1946, once again the question of the knowledge of Japanese submarines across the *Indianapolis*'s route was ignored.

Admiral Nimitz produced a statement which indicated that four officers, Gillette, Granum, Sancho and Gibson, had been disciplined with letters of reprimand. The first the four men had heard of it had been when they had been telephoned. Three of them didn't fight the decision but Gillette did, so much so that in December 1946, another letter went out to each of the four men saying that the disciplinary letters they had received had been withdrawn. Since McVay's sentence had also been remitted, it seemed that, though the *Indianapolis* had been sunk, nobody was guilty.

After the trial, McVay served in New Orleans as Chief of Staff and Aide to the Commandant, Eighth Naval District and Commander of the Gulf Sea Frontier in New Orleans. In 1949, he retired to Connecticut with the graveyard promotion to Rear Admiral. He appeared to be content but friends said he was bottling things up inside himself. He never forgot the men under his command who had died in the water of the Philippine Sea and often said he wished he had gone down with his ship. On 6 November 1968, his gardener found him dead on his front lawn. He had shot himself.

As in the case of Byng, it was the system, the organisation, the plans that were wrong. Men in high rank, busy with the war, had worked out in good faith an arrangement they had thought was foolproof, but had failed to spot the points in it that could go amiss and this had resulted in the sinking of McVay's ship. The thing had come full circle. Like Byng's 'Fighting Instructions', the instructions at headquarters were faulty but, because they were there, they were never questioned. Everyone followed them rigidly and the deaths of the men in the water had arisen from the fact that they had been treated with indifference by complacent shore-based officers who were in no peril themselves. They must have become aware of the dangers inherent in the system; and, because of this, the lack of concern they showed – to the point of ignoring them – was disastrous. They went by the book and just didn't bother when a little effort might well have saved lives.

The speed with which the system was changed showed how quickly its faults could have been corrected and, considering that other ships had been sunk with large loss of life, the charges against McVay were barely supportable and might well have been framed because they allowed no questions on the system. But, like Byng before him, McVay was made the scapegoat for the mistakes of shore-based officers who didn't hesitate to protect their own rear, and he was unlucky in the fact that the war was hurrying to its end and people had become careless.

Bibliography

Babington, Anthony; *For the sake of Example*, Leo Cooper 1983

Brédin, Jean-Denis; *The Affair*, Sidgwick and Jackson 1987

Chapman, Guy; *Dreyfus*, Hart-Davis 1963

Delderfield, R F ; *The March of the Twenty-Six*, Hodder and Stoughton 1962

Dugan, James; *The Great Mutiny*, Deutsch 1966

Featherstone, Donald; *Captain Carey's Blunder*, Leo Cooper 1973

Flexner, James T; *Traitor and Spy*, Harcourt Brace 1953

Gardiner, Leslie; *The Royal Oak Court Martial*, Blackwood 1965

Glines, Carroll V; *Compact History of the US Air Force*, Hawthorne 1963

Guedella, Philip; *The Two Marshals*, Hodder and Stoughton 1943

Harper, R W E, and Miller, Harry; *Singapore Mutiny*, Oxford University Press 1984

Hatch, Robert McC; *John André, A Gallant In Spy's Clothing*, Houghton Mifflin, Boston 1986

Hough, Richard; *The Fleet That Had to Die*, Hamish Hamilton 1958

Huie, William Bradford; *The Execution of Private Slovik*, Jarrolds 1954

Kelly, Christopher; *The Battle of Waterloo*, Thomas Kelly 1817

257

Lech, Raymond B; *All the Drowned Sailors*, Severn House 1984Lewis, David L; *Prisoners of Honour*, Cassell 1973
Morris, Donald R; *The Washing of the Spears*, Cape 1966
Morton, H B; *Marshal Ney*, Barker 1958
Nathan A; *Gentleman Spy*, Sidgwick and Jackson 1970
Newcombe, Richard F; *Abandon Ship*, Constable 1960
Noonan, Miles; *Tales from the Mess*, Hutchinson, 1983
Palmer, Roy (Ed); *The Rambling Soldier*, Penguin 1977
Pollock, Sam; *Mutiny For The Cause*, Leo Cooper 1969
Pope, Dudley; *At 12 Mr. Byng Was Shot*, Weidenfeld 1962
Prebble, John; *Mutiny*, Secker and Warburg 1975
Walder, David; *The Short Victorious War*, Hutchinson 1973
White, T H; *The Age Of Scandal*, Cape 1950
Young, Calton; *Ireland's Civil War*, Muller 1968

Newspaper cuttings from the bi-centenary celebrations of Major André's death at Tappan in 1980

The Army Lawyer: A History of the Judge Advocate General's Corps, 1775-1975, US Govt Printing Office